How to Simplify Self-Publishing and Save Your Hair

Wolf O'Rourc

Published by RoRo, 2020.

HOW TO SIMPLIFY SELF-PUBLISHING AND SAVE YOUR HAIR

First edition. August 27, 2020.

ISBN: 978-1393985259

Written by Wolf O'Rourc.

Table of Contents

Dedicated to Draft2Digital

For Saving Author's Hair

Introduction

How to Simplify Self-Publishing and Save Your Hair has three parts that cater to different needs.

1. To publish a narrative without complex formatting, the **Quickie Guides** in Part I will get you going right away.

2. Part II presents the concept behind the guide and the **Self-Publishing Checklist** organized by task with links to further resources.

3. The **Reference** section in Part III goes into details for tasks grouped in the order they appear on the Draft2Digital or Kindle Direct Publishing platform.

The complexity of this guide makes any presentation wanting. Different formats serve various needs.

• To demonstrate the concepts in this guide, **low-priced black-and-white versions** exercise all the features of the Draft2Digital platform. The complex formatting exceeds the capabilities of its tools focused on narrative, however. Blank lines and borders disappear. Tables spill across pages. Color-highlights fades away. Using a theme with graphics and phrase caps adds more clutter. View the e-book horizontally in landscape mode, if you can. The large amount of screenshots blows up the file size, thus raising the minimum price required by online retailers.

• The **full-color e-book** gives a better reading experience, taking advantage of highlights to convey information better. The e-reader still controls most of the text formatting. Effects such as highlighting sections with different fonts or colors may disappear. Its production required a second, labor-intensive pass through Kindle Create, and pricing reflects that.

- The **full-color paperback** in an oversized format best reflects the source document and allows studying the screenshots in greatest detail. Of course, hyperlinks don't work in paperbacks. It required a third pass through KDP and expensive four-color printing.

- Finally, the **audiobook** allows listening to the narrative repeatedly during other activities, but comes from a fourth time-consuming production that had to compensate for lack of visuals.

The web changes constantly. If you come across a broken link, try again the next day to make sure it's not a temporary Internet hiccup. If the link continues to fail, please let us know at Links@WolfORourc.com.

All screenshots by the author.

Part I

1. Quickie Guides

1.1. A 15-Minute Recipe to Create a Book Cover

FIFTEEN MINUTES CAN make the difference between a bestseller and a shelf warmer. When you self-publish, the right free tools and a recipe can determine your author fate.

For we do judge a book by its cover. More precisely, in the digital age, we judge a book by its cover thumbnail. Marketing people believe that this little picture in the search results and Books you may like section contributes to 50% of sales.

The one-five minutes to go from a heap of pictures and text to professionally looking print and e-book covers can lift you into the Parthenon of best-selling authors—or wherever they hide out in your country. Developing an eye-catching and attractive design takes a bit longer, including properly researching U.S. Department of Writers prime grade titles and a seasoned book description and author biography.

Given its importance, you may want to turn to professional designers and artists to develop and execute concepts. **A good cover design follows psychological principles to attract and guide the eye**. The overall look **balances the various graphic elements, colors, and fonts with optimum placement of book titles and author names. Every genre also has conventions that readers recognize**, even if only subconsciously.

Long on time and short on cash? Do your own research. Study covers of bestseller in that subgenre and emulate their practices. Free tools like the Amazon **Kindle Direct Publishing (KDP) Cover Creator** and **Draft2Digital** will help you create your masterpiece for print and e-book in no time following this recipe.

Ingredients

1 BAG OF CASHEW GOURMET mix with premium chocolate chips (optional)

1 JPG, PNG, or TIFF image

1 book title, USDW prime grade

1 book subtitle (optional)

1-4 author names

1 book description, pre-seasoned

1 author bio

1 author picture, funny or serious (optional)

1 free Amazon Kindle Direct Publishing account

1 free Draft2Digital account

1-4 glasses of 1981 Chateau Lafite Rothschild, Macallan Lalique 62-year-old Whisky, or Bud Lite (totally optional, but so worth it, or not)

Directions/Steps

1. Wet your throat with your chosen beverage. so you don't suffer a thirst attack. Otherwise, fifteen minutes can feel like an eternity.

2. Fortify yourself with a generous helping of cashew gourmet mix to have the energy to power through this arduous journey.

3. Throw your garment into the laundry so the chocolate stains don't set before you finish.

4. Log in to your favorite KDP account, create a new e-book project, and enter the required metadata, including title and optional subtitle.

5. On the Kindle eBook Content tab, launch Cover Creator.

6. Upload your picture.

———————

COVER CREATOR COMES with premade elements, including an **Image Gallery** with categories from Animals to Concepts and Ideas to Technology. A field at the top lets you search by keywords and pick an image to grace the front cover.

You may not use covers made using stock images from the gallery outside KDP, however. Rather than risking a lawsuit that will cost Amazon a fraction of a single share of stock, I'll turn to my favorite free photo sites so I can show the results online.

A number of these offer free images under various terms.

- Pexels[1]

- Unsplash[2]

---

1. https://www.pexels.com/

2. http://unsplash.com

- Wikimedia Commons[3]

- Pixabay[4]

- Free Images[5]

- Free Digital Photos[6]

- morgueFile[7]

- Death to the Stock Photo[8]

Finding quality cover art takes time. Like with Cover Creator, **read the license agreement to ensure that it allows your chosen pictures on book covers.** Pexels[9], for instance, requires you to add value to images that you use on a physical product.

You may also want a free graphics editor like Paint.NET[10], The GIMP[11], or Canva[12] to create composite images or make color adjustments. Say if I were to (completely coincidentally) want a cover for a book titled *How to Simplify Self-Publishing and Save Your Hair*, combining pictures of books and hair comes to mind.

Fortunately, Mahrael Boutros at Pexels saved me the 207.16 seconds I would have to spend in the editor to combine pictures in layers by providing a free one touching on both themes.

---

3. http://commons.wikimedia.org/wiki/Main_Page

4. https://pixabay.com

5. http://freeimages.com

6. http://www.freedigitalphotos.net

7. http://www.morguefile.com

8. https://deathtothestockphoto.com/join

9. https://www.pexels.com/

10. https://www.getpaint.net/

11. https://www.gimp.org/

12. https://www.canva.com/

Cover Creator accepts JPG, PNG, or TIF files that meet the Amazon Publishing Guidelines[13] and have a minimum resolution of 300 dots per inch (DPI) for print. Any text already on it should be legible.

Amazon considers a **height/width ratio of 1.6:1** ideal, with a minimum of 1,000 x 625 pixels (px), and a **recommended 2,560 x 1,600 px**. The large size ensures you meet the DPI requirements. Upscaling small images results in blurriness and pixilation. If you download pictures from stock sites, go for a size that fits the cover. I hence downloaded the large version with 2,880 px height.

You do not need to resize your photo in one of the above-mentioned programs. Simply upload it, and the specialized tool takes care of Amazon's self-publishing requirements.

Thanks to integration with KDP, Cover Creator **combines your image with information from the Details tab** to create ten starting designs. The help comes at the price of flexibility. You have no choice beyond these, although you can change to one of eight layouts in the next step. Of course, you can download the finished cover as starting point for further manipulation in a graphics editor.

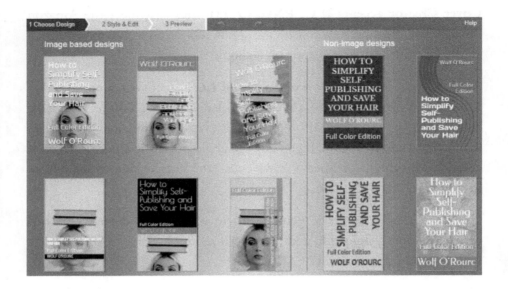

KDP Front Cover Creator Designs

THE **thumbnail view shows which designs work** on that scale on sales pages like the Kindle store. With some, the long title and subtitle become impossible to read, particularly with image-based designs, and thus the cover loses a lot of value in an ad. Since many readers will only see the small version to entice them to click the Buy button, make sure it gets the critical information across.

---

7. Have another gulp of your drink while you rack your confused brain to decide on the best design.

8. Nothing wrong with one more swig. Picking a design is so hard.

9. Wipe the chocolate stains off the keyboard (okay, maybe the gourmet cashew mix was not the best of ideas, but doesn't the wonderful bouquet of the Chateau Lafite make up for it?)

10. Adjust your design in the Cover Creator editor. This step may require additional drinks.

ONCE YOU FIND A GOOD starting design, **Style & Edit** lets you customize most elements of the cover.

The **three buttons** at the lower left apply **quick styles**.

- Select a pre-styled **color scheme** or create your own by picking primary, secondary, and text colors,

- Choose one of eight **layouts** to reposition the existing design elements,

- Choose **typeface sets**, pre-matched combinations of **fonts**.

Once you've refined the design, you can change individual items. Clicking the photograph brings up a dialogue box with options to **resize and rotate the image**. Dragging the square handles also resizes, whereas the round handles rotates. Dragging the entire picture will **reposition** it. **Click to reset image position** will restore the original one, which may be larger than the design. Similarly, **Undo** may not return to the state you want. To go back to picking a design, click [**Start Over**].

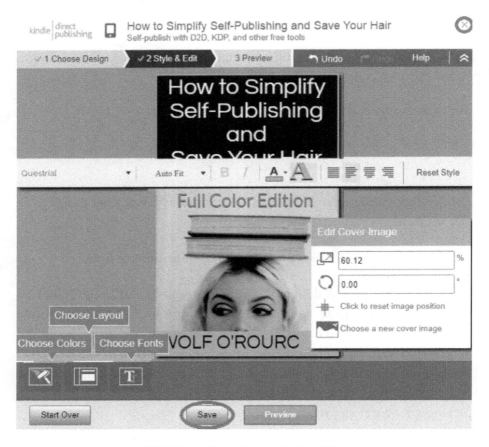

KDP Front Cover Creator Style & Edit

TO FORMAT TEXT ELEMENTS individually, clicking within their dashed box brings up the formatting bar with the following style choices.

- a good 40 typefaces,

- Autofit or one of 14 font sizes,

- **Bold** or *italics* (only available for certain fonts after selecting text),

- font color,

- drop shadow,

- alignment.

To pick a color, Cover Creator brings up a color palette. It has no means to specify number codes for a shade. **Note the exact scheme or positions of the colors you picked** to match them in the print version.

You **can insert or delete text.** Keep in mind, however, that **Cover Creator checks if writing on the cover matches the entries on the Details tab in KDP. Adding returns with [Enter] lets you wrap long titles or subtitles in a logical way without running afoul of this Amazon requirement.**

Preview lets you check the design in color mode, grayscale, and as a thumbnail. You can zoom in one level to focus on details. To see the cover with different device configurations, use the KDP Online Previewer once you exited Cover Creator.

––––––––––––

11. Celebrate your efficiency and productivity with another sip.

12. Make sure that the design follows good layout principles and all elements work together.

13. Ignore the blurry lines in the design and the voices in your head claiming you're drunk. You earned it.

14. Click [**Save & Submit**] to upload the cover and return to KDP.

––––––––––––

COVER CREATOR DOESN't have a button to download the cover for use with other publishing platforms. **Right-clicking the Preview image lets you save a high-resolution version.** Note that the KDP Online Previewer saves a low-resolution image, but includes the high-res one when you download the HTML book.

––––––––––––

15. Take a four-minute nap to sober up.

16. Wake up in a panic when you realize that you only have one minute and thirteen seconds left to finish the wrap-around print cover.

17. Continue setup of paperback.

18. On the Paperback Content tab, launch Cover Creator.

19. Upload the e-book cover you downloaded as starting point.

20. Down a drink in celebration, because the tool tells you the design to use with a front cover image.

21. Curse at Amazon because Cover Creator cannot automatically match the color scheme or pull the description and author bio.

———————

FOR A PRINT BOOK, YOU need to **extend the front cover across the spine and back**. Customarily, **the color scheme wraps around all three sides**.

You **can't finish a wraparound cover until you have converted your interior file** and know the exact number of pages. The platforms calculate the spine width based on the following.

- paper type (white/cream),

- print type (color/black and white),

- interior page count.

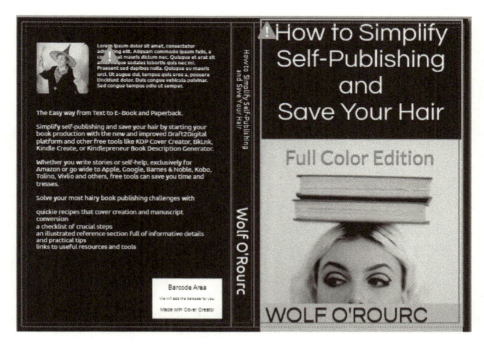

KDP Wraparound Cover Creator Style & Edit

THE PAPERBACK COVER Creator's **first design adds spine and back to an uploaded front cover** following industry practices. Its **spine shows the primary author name and book title in a contrasting text color**. Not much help other than making a template unnecessary. You have to pick a matching back cover color yourself. Fortunately, you do remember the color schemes you used above, right?

Customarily, the **back contains blurbs**, information printed on the back cover to describe the book and make it attractive to buy, **such as the book description and your author bio, plus your headshot**. Cover Creator doesn't fetch the text for the back cover from KDP's **Details** page or **Author Central**. If you have tight deadlines, you may want to switch to whisky at this point.

Amazon will add the **ISBN barcode** in the white rectangle in the lower right corner.

22. Down the rest of the bottle in despair.

23. With 23 seconds to go, breathe a sigh of relief because you remember that you planned to distribute wide.

24. Log in to Draft2Digital.

25. Upload the front cover you focus-grouped for weeks.

26. Click the Cover button.

27. Countdown the remaining seconds while D2D auto-magically creates a wraparound cover.

―――――――――――

DRAFT2DIGITAL AUTOMATICALLY generates a wraparound cover from the front one in the paper size specified. The **background color from the top extends all around**. Cover Creator frames the preview image in a neutral color. Remove that border before uploading to Draft2Digital.

Its tool pulls the **book description from the Details tab** onto the top of the back cover. The lower half splits into the **bio of the primary author from the Contributor Profiles** on the left, the matching profile picture on the right, and the **automatically generated ISBN barcode** below them.

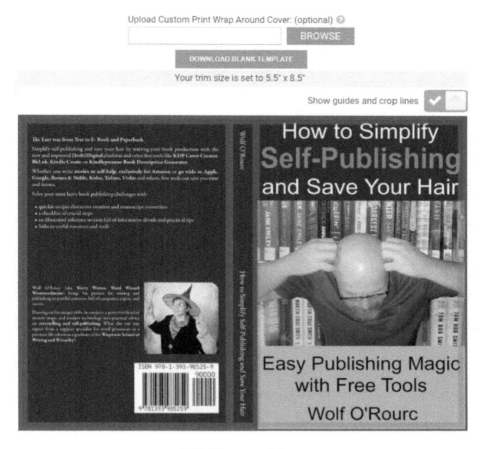

D2D Wraparound Cover

UNFORTUNATELY, **D2D only makes a** low-resolution image *unsuitable for printing* available for download. Nevertheless, your e-book and paperback now share finished covers, and the actual production only took fifteen minutes thanks to free tools.

---

28. Stop your 15-minute timer. **You've finished your covers**.

29. Take another sip to celebrate your accomplishment.

30. Go to bed and nurse your hangover.

1.2. A 15-Minute Recipe to Self-Publish Your Story

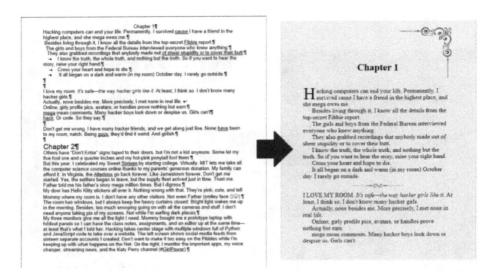

TIRED OF WIPING THE virtual dust off your manuscript? Scared of formatting your content according to a hundred-page style guide? Frustrated at missing out on the self-publishing revolution. Fear not. Fifteen minutes can change your life, literarily, with the right free tools and a recipe.

That's **one-five minutes to go from text to professionally looking e- and print book files**. But they don't sell themselves. **Marketing takes a bit longer**, including properly researching keywords, subgenre categories, and a seasoned book description. But if you're dying to see a finished book within the hour, because you promised your mother a copy for her birthday next week, start with something simple and improve the metadata later.

Oh, and you do **need front cover art**, a JPG or PNG **image with the book title and author name** on it. You can create your own with free tools like Paint.Net or Canva. Technomagic will convert it into a wrap-around print cover.

Ingredients

1 STANDARD BOX OF COOKIE mix (optional)

1 DOC, DOCX, ODT, or RTF manuscript

7 keywords

1-5 subgenre categories

1 book description, pre-seasoned

1 author bio

1 author picture, funny or serious (optional)

1 JPG or PNG front cover image, well done

1 free Draft2Digital account

1 cuppa joe or tea, or 1 glass of milk (optional)

1 spoonful of sugar, helps the medicine go down (totally optional)*

*Mary Poppins not required

Directions/Steps

1. Preheat the oven to the temperature on the cookie mix box.

2. Grab a cup or glass of your favorite working beverage so you don't suffer a thirst attack. Otherwise, fifteen minutes can feel like an eternity.

3. Open your manuscript in your word processor and check for consistency.

———

WHAT, YOU THOUGHT YOU were done with the manuscript? **You need to make sure you have no formatting issues that the Draft2Digital**

converter can't resolve. The aggregator, known among best friends as D2D, has embarked on a quest to save authors from traction alopecia amazonia, also known as ripping your hair out while using Amazon's Kindle Direct Publishing, or KDP.

D2D's author-friendly self-publishing tools anticipate common problems and clean them up. Best of all, they're free. No strings attached. **You can take the output and publish elsewhere**. Of course, you can save yourself many hairaches by letting the company handle the distribution to a writer's dozen of online bookstores, for a commission.

What magic can D2D perform? Let's look at a sample from my novel Cyberspiracy with many of the common issues found in manuscripts.

Chapter 1 (Centered)¶
(No indent) Hacking computers can end your life. Permanently. I survived cause I have a friend in the highest place, and she mega owes me.¶
(1 space) Besides living through it, I know all the details from the top-secret Fibbie report.¶
(2 spaces) The girls and boys from the Federal Bureau interviewed everyone who knew anything.¶
(3 spaces) They also grabbed recordings that anybody made out of sheer stupidity or to cover their butt.¶
→ (tab) I know the truth, the whole truth, and nothing but the truth. So if you want to hear the story, raise your right hand.¶
→ (space + tab) Cross your heart and hope to die.¶
→ (tab + space) It all began on a dark and warm (in my room) October day. I rarely go outside. (2 returns)¶
¶
¶
I love my room. *It's safe—the way hacker girls like it* (Italics). At least, I think so. I don't know many hacker girls.¶
Actually, none besides me. More precisely, I met none in real life. (line feed)↵
Online, girly profile pics, avatars, or handles prove nothing but earn (hard return)¶
mega mean comments. Many hacker boys look down or despise us. Girls can't (hard return)¶
hack. Or code. So they say. (2 returns)¶
¶

---

1 Common formatting issues found in manuscripts

THE TEXT HAS **paragraphs without indents**, i.e. flush on the left, as well as some that **start with spaces or tabs**. The sample also includes groups of multiple **blank lines** and **returns and newlines or line feeds that split up sentences.** For the image, I've turned on Show/Hide in MS Word (Toggle Formatting Marks in LibreOffice, Show add-on in Google Docs) to make nonprinting characters visible.

The industry **standard for narrative calls for indents of paragraphs except the first one after a chapter or scene break**. D2D takes out all the extra leading spaces and tabs to produce a clean, consistent look.

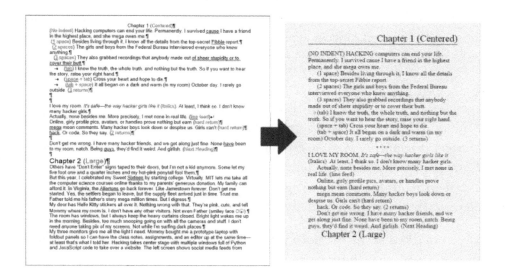

2 Draft2Digital cleans up many common formatting problems

THE CONVERTER TAKES a stab at other formatting problems to the best of its ability. Unfortunately, up to now the fabled WAMM (Writers & Authors Mind-Reading Module) has failed testing. Three problems areas may remain and require your intervention.

Chapter Starts

THE CONVERTER **needs to know how you marked a chapter title**. As the word "chapter" could occur within the narrative, the self-publishing platforms have adopted certain conventions.

If your current titles lack formatting, **apply the style Heading 1** to each to ensure the best results. Amazon supports this convention, too.

Draft2Digital gives you considerable leeway by allowing heading styles **or combinations of bold, centered, and larger fonts**, as long as you are consistent. You can see from the example above, if you centered some titles and enlarged the font on others, you end up with mixed results.

Make sure that every title shares *one* formatting option that you can specify as the criterion, e.g. all are centered regardless of font size. Bold alone is not enough, since it appears frequently in the body of fiction. If you enlarge the text, D2D recommends at least a four-point difference.

Scene Breaks

SINCE **D2D cleans up errand returns** created by accidentally hitting [**Enter**], it requires you to **mark scene breaks with *two* or *three* blank lines**. If you select a theme that includes a graphic, as in the example above, you can also mark a break with one or more asterisks (*) on a line by themselves. The converter will replace the placeholder with the scene break image.

If you marked scene breaks with one blank line, you can use advanced find and replace techniques to double them.

MS Word

- Open **Find and Replace** with [**Ctrl+H**].

- Find "**^l**" (caret with lower-case L) and replace all with "**^p**" to change all newlines to returns. Word distinguishes between the two in the following searches.

- Find "**^p^p**" and replace all with "**^p^p^p**" to change two paragraph marks to three, thus creating two blank lines at the end of the preceding paragraph.

TIP In Word's **Find and Replace**, click [**More >>**], then [**Special**] **to insert nonprinting characters** when you don't know the code.

LibreOffice/Google Docs

- Open **Find & Replace** with [**Ctrl+H**].

- Click **Regular expressions** to enable use of special character combinations that represent nonprinting characters.

- Find blank lines with "^$" (caret with dollar sign) and replace all with "\n\n" to change a paragraph marks on a line by itself to two, thus creating two blank lines.

Note: Older versions of LibreOffice do not support regular expressions in the **Replace** field. Google Docs requires an add-on.

Return at the end of every line

TEXT THAT ORIGINATED in an editor or email may contain hard returns (created by [**Enter**]) or soft returns (line feed or newline created by [**Shift+Enter**]) **at the end of every line**. Since paragraphs with only one line appear frequently in narrative with dialogue, the converter can't determine which lines need fixing.

If the text has no blank lines between paragraphs, unfortunately you'll need to find and delete the hard returns one by one.

If a blank line separates paragraphs, you can use advanced find and replace techniques to reformat the text.

MS Word

- Open **Find and Replace** with [**Ctrl+H**].

- Find "^l" (caret with lower-case L) and replace all with "^p" to change all newlines used by UNIX and Linux systems to returns. Word distinguishes between the two in the following searches.

- Find blank lines created by two successive returns with "^p^p" and replace all with a combination that does not occur in your manuscript, e.g. "%%%".

- Find remaining returns with "^p" and replace all with a **space**.

- Now find the combination from the above step, e.g. "**%%%**", and replace with "**^p**" to end the paragraphs.

LibreOffice/Google Docs

- Open **Find & Replace** with [**Ctrl+H**].

- Click **Regular expressions** to enable use of special character combinations that represent nonprinting characters.

- Find blank lines with "**^$**"(caret with dollar sign) and replace all with a combination that does not occur in your manuscript, e.g. "**%%%**".

- Find remaining returns or newlines with "**$**" (dollar sign) and replace all with a **space**.

- Now find the combination from the above step, e.g. "**%%%**", with "**\n**" to end the paragraphs.

Note: Older versions of LibreOffice do not support regular expressions in the **Replace** field. Google Docs requires an add-on.

Don't add blank lines after every paragraph. In fiction, they mark a scene break. D2D hence removes them. If you actually want one in the book, you need to add two or three blank lines.

H acking computers can end your life. Permanently. I survived cause I have a friend in the highest place, and she mega owes me.

Besides living through it, I know all the details from the top-secret Fibbie report.

The girls and boys from the Federal Bureau interviewed everyone who knew anything.

They also grabbed recordings that anybody made out of sheer stupidity or to cover their butt.

I know the truth, the whole truth, and nothing but the truth. So if you want to hear the story, raise your right hand.

Cross your heart and hope to die.

It all began on a dark and warm (in my room) October day. I rarely go outside.

I LOVE MY ROOM. *It's safe—the way hacker girls like it.* At least, I think so. I don't know many hacker girls.

3 Drop cap, phrase cap, and scene break graphic in action

4. Log in to your Draft2Digital account. Create one if needed.

5. **Upload Book File**. D2D generously accepts popular Microsoft Word old **DOC** and new **DOCX** files and OpenDocument (**ODT**) used by Apache OpenOffice, LibreOffice, Google Docs. You can even send the Rich Text Format (**RTF**) from early word processors like WordPad.

6. While the converter does its work, whip the cookie mix into batter, spread on a baking sheet, and shove into pre-heated oven.

7. Celebrate your efficiency and productivity with a sip of your favorite beverage.

8. **Fill in the information needed for the sales page**.

9. **Select the front and back matter** you want. D2D takes care of another hair-loss-inducing task by generating and formatting the common pages found in books such as the table of contents, dedication, or copyright page.

10. **Choose one of 21 themes** (what D2D calls a style) for your book. The tool adds a title graphic and optionally drop caps, a large first letter, to the beginning of every chapter. A graphic may mark a scene break and phrase caps begin the next sentence.

11. Preview the book. **Make sure every chapter title was detected and every page looks right**.

12. If you become so engrossed in the preview that you forget the cookies, vent the smoke from the kitchen. Offer the charred remains to the firefighters called by concerned neighbors.

13. Drink sips of your fav beverage to calm your nerves or wash down the cookies.

14. **Approve the galley proof**.

15. For a print book, **approve the automagically created wrap-around cover**.

16. Take a deep breath. You face your biggest decision now.

The BIG Decision

UNLIKE OTHER PLATFORMS, Draft2Digital doesn't lock you into their channel. **Buttons on the preview pages of both formats let you download the finished digital products**. You can upload the MOBI e-book to the Kindle store and the EPUB to Apple Books, Kobo, Google Play, and many other sites. KDP Print, IngramSpark, and other print on demand (POD) services will accept the print-ready PDF.

Why pay Draft2Digital a commission to distribute your book to more than a dozen vendors and online reading services the world over?

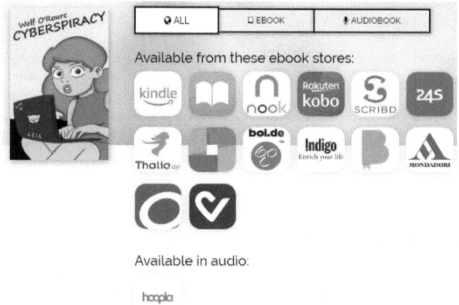

4 Online stores covered by Draft2Digital

TIME AND YOUR HAIR.

Going it alone means uploading the books and creating sales pages separately on all the different platforms. Learning the idiosyncrasies and requirements of each program. And replicating the work over and over every time something changes. Such as a Holiday price promotion.

International sites also mean **dealing with many different foreign tax laws** and reconciling them with your jurisdiction. Or tracking sales and resolving problems in various time zones.

An aggregator like Draft2Digital makes these mundane and frustrating tasks easier. Such as **aggregating access to all the sales channels onto a single landing page with a universal book link**, so customers can easily choose their preferred store.

On the other hand, **you may lose access to a vendor's exclusive promotions**, such as Amazon's KDP Select or Apple Book's coupons. Draft2Digital makes it easy to take a road in between.

Upload the D2D MOBI file to take advantage of the promotional opportunities at KDP Select. Once their 90-day exclusivity ends, relaunch wide to other vendors through an aggregator. If you add a paperback version three months later, you have yet another excuse to throw a launch party and get not drunk on your favorite beverage.

D2D also makes deals with vendors to give their authors access to promotions.

Finally, consider the relationship. Do you prefer to deal with a giant company who considers readers its primary customers? Or a **small outfit where key people hold monthly Ask Us Anything video conferences** and implement authors' suggestions? And the same customer service rep stays on your case from start to finish.

Of course, if you just want to offer e-books from your own website or hand out author copies of print books to friends and family, you've reached your destiny. Skip to step 20.

———————

17. **Select the stores** and territories.

18. **Set the prices** for each channel.

19. Click the [**Submit**] button.

20. Stop your 15-minute timer. **You've published your book**.

21. Take another sip to celebrate your accomplishment.

22. Thank me for the advice and recommending a non-alcoholic beverage.

Part II

2. Don't Rip Your Hair Out While Self-Publishing

———

S elf-publishing requires gazillion steps using half a gazillion different tools. Ripping out your hair in frustration at some of these steps will leave you bald at the end of your career. Fear not. One company has as its mission to save authors from this traction alopecia amazonia. No, *not* the Zon. In fact, the industry's 6,000-pound dinosaur does everything in its power to ensure that no writer can maintain a mane like Beethoven.

For starters, what looks like a **giant bookstore in reality breaks down into two separate and disjoint channels**—"Books" for print and "Kindle Store" for e-books. You can easily verify that the same search terms used in both do not produce the same results.

Worse, **Amazon cobbled together disparate programs into the semblance of a platform**: Kindle Direct Publishing (KDP), Author Central (AC), CreateSpace/KDP Print, **KDP Select**[1], Kindle Unlimited[2], Amazon Advertising. Each has its own website, and one digital hand doesn't know what the other one does.

TIP Finding the right article across the different help systems can lose you more hair than publishing a single book. Instead, ask your question in Google Search, add "site:amazon.com" and you shall receive the best matches across *all* Amazon websites in one results list.

Even if you find the right tool for the job, **clumsy procedures and quirky behavior** will leave you bald in no time.

Save your hair by **starting your book production with free publishing tools like Draft2Digital**'s (D2D) revamped platform **to simplify creation of e-books, paperbacks, audiobooks, or sales pages.**

1. https://kdp.amazon.com/en_US/help/topic/G200798990#eligibility

2. https://kdp.amazon.com/en_US/help/topic/G201537300

Like Amazon, **this aggregate publisher or aggregator can distribute the different versions** (other than hardcover) of your books. The similarities end there. Unlike the **KDP self-publishing platform with its proprietary MOBI format**, author-friendly **D2D doesn't lock you in**. In fact, you can avail yourself of their tools whether you publish with them or not. **You get to keep your e-books in both MOBI and EPUB (used by every other vendor) and the PDF of the print book**. Take them to whomever you like.

Or distribute through D2D to various retailers the world over, including Amazon, Apple Books, and Barnes & Noble. Let them deal with differing guidelines for each website.

2.1. Zon Defense

FOR THE CONVENIENCE, **D2D does charge a commission of 10% of the retail price** (about 15% of your royalties for most e-books). And since its print books always include the high wholesale discount for physical bookstores, your royalties will be considerably less than KDP Print selling through Amazon.

As far as KDP goes, **D2D becomes the publisher of record. Your books will *not* show up on your KDP bookshelf.** That has three important consequences.

> 1. **You cannot change the sales page from the KDP tools**, so you can't customize it with elements specific to Amazon (see 6.5). Its author-marketing platform Author Central (AC)[3] does allow editing the description for books that list you as author (see 12.3). In typical *one hand doesn't know* fashion (see above), that editor doesn't support the same formatting as KDP.

> 2. **You cannot enroll your e-book in KDP Select**[4], Amazon's exclusivity program with its **Kindle Countdown Deals** (see 12.4), or the popular **Kindle Unlimited (KU)**[5] flat-rate

---

3. https://authorcentral.amazon.com

4. **https://kdp.amazon.com/en_US/help/topic/G200798990#eligibility**

subscription service. A good portion of Amazon customers only read titles from KU.

3. **You cannot use Amazon Advertising**[6] (see 12.5) for those books.

Particularly new authors who most benefit from the visibility given by KDP Select and KU **opt for the 90-day exclusivity initially**. If the books get traction, they can always **worry later about going wide** (selling at other vendors).

TIP I based this guide on the **KDP US sites**. The **Resources** link to KDP US help pages, which usually match **other English-speaking countries, but some features may differ.**

2.2. The D2D Experience

HERE'S THE RUB. MIXING platforms only works in one direction. For the Zon, exclusivity is a mindset. **You can't move your work from KDP elsewhere**. Its free International Standard Book Numbers (ISBN) don't port. Its tools won't create an EPUB version.

TIP In the USA, a monopoly sells **ISBNs**. The number identifies its *owner* whom retailers consider the *publisher* even if you do most of the work. You can't take one company's ISBN to another one. Of course, you can **republish** that same book somewhere else **with a different free ISBN**. Since vendors consider it a different book, metadata, sales statistics, and reviews don't carry over. If you want the **flexibility** of moving a book from one platform to another or selling it on unsupported vendor sites (eg Google Play), **get your own ISBN**.

By starting the process at D2D, you can easily move the books to Amazon for an initial 90-day exclusive. If you go wide later, all the hooks

---

5. https://kdp.amazon.com/en_US/help/topic/G201537300

6. https://kdp.amazon.com/en_US/help/topic/G201499010

will be in place and you'll have consistency among *all* stores (more on that later).

Most important, the company aims to take the headache out of publishing your book and managing it out in the wild. So they've created tools for the most common items needed and thrown in a few little surprise freebies to make **their self-publishing platform easier to use than anything else out there**.

Anybody who had to deal with an ongoing support issue that bounced from one rep to the next in a large organization will also appreciate much smaller D2D (around 20 employees). **The same customer service rep usually answers follow-ups**. Responses can come quickly. During the monthly Ask Us Anything on Facebook, the audience pointed out that the Universal Book Links (UBL) (see 12.1) didn't cover audiobooks. One month later, they did.

So why not go with someone who's Head & Shoulders above the rest? Your hair will thank you eternally.

2.3. What about Other Companies?

BEFORE WE ENTER THE barbershop of self-pub wonderland, let's make a courtesy visit to other hairdressers. A confusing array of offerings make comparisons hard. Printers differ. Distribution models diverge. Costs vary. Only a few offer Print on Demand (POD) paperbacks or hardcover books.

Nevertheless, many bloggers have weighed in. Spoiler alert: most like D2D.

- British author services firm Reedsy chose the "12 BEST Self-Publishing Companies of 2020[7]."

- Reedsy also gives a cost comparison in "What is the Best Service for Print on Demand Books?[8]"

---

7. https://blog.reedsy.com/best-self-publishing-companies

8. https://blog.reedsy.com/print-on-demand-books

- Kindlepreneur's Dave Chesson tried out three of the aggregators in "Smashwords vs Draft2Digital vs PublishDrive Review[9]".

- New Shelves Books' Amy Collins does a comparison in her video Ebook Distribution. IngramSpark, Smashwords, Draft2Digital? Which one?[10]

- Smashwords veteran Derek Haines detailed why he switched to D2D[11].

- Self-Publishing with Dale praised D2D in his video Draft2Digital Review 2018 - Is Draft2Digital Worth It?[12]

- Jane Friedman does a deep dive in her video Navigating Self-Publishing Services[13] including services for kids' books.

- Self-Publishing School releases a comparison of author service firms under "Best Self-Publishing Companies[14]."

- Emma Rosen explains her choice in the video Publishing an ebook - KDP and Draft2Digital[15].

Some people won't buy from Amazon. Other vendors dominate in different countries. Keep in mind, though, that distribution doesn't equal sales. Unless you're willing to market your books in a region, wider availability may not help your earnings.

Publishing the exact same book at two sources, resulting in a double listing, is an industry no-no. Publishing platforms generally won't accept a book with an ISBN already in use at another service. Besides, you'd have to

9. https://kindlepreneur.com/smashwords-vs-draft2digital

10. https://www.youtube.com/watch?v=yk4LB4D-ewc

11. https://justpublishingadvice.com/draft2digital-vs-smashwords-review-one-clear-winner/

12. https://www.youtube.com/watch?v=vD1HqvlIxYg

13. https://www.youtube.com/watch?v=zD4dPtcOHa4

14. https://selfpublishing.com/self-publishing-companies

15. https://www.youtube.com/watch?v=tf-yhXjbmIg

do the setup work twice for little additional benefit. **You *can* have a MOBI version through KDP and a separate EPUB through someone else.**

Although D2D works with partners for additional services like editing, cover design, and marketing, they don't offer everything. For special needs, Table 2-1 gives a comparison to other choices.

Table 2-1: Publishing Services Comparison

	Commission	POD	Hardcover	E-book Themes	Editing, Design	Book-store
Draft2Digital	15%	√	X	√	partners	X
Smashwords	10%-15%	X	X	X		√
PublishDrive	flat fee	X	X	X		X
IngramSpark	varies	√	√	X	partners	X
Lulu	20%	√	√	X	fee	√
Bookbaby	varies	√	√	N/A	fee	√
Bublish	varies	√	√	√	fee	X

Smashwords[16]

THE ORIGINAL E-BOOK aggregator with more distribution channels than D2D.

Successful conversion requires following a 170-page style guide.

PublishDrive[17]

THIS AGGREGATOR OFFERS extensive international distribution for e-books and advanced marketing features.

---

16. https://www.smashwords.com/
17. https://publishdrive.com/

IngramSpark[18]

THE SELF-PUBLISHING arm of Ingram, one of the world's largest distributors and wholesalers of print books, offers the most comprehensive services including bulk orders.

Competitive e-book services, including free ISBNs and a WYSIWYG description editor.

Each book has fees for setup and maintenance. You can regularly find discounts, and IS waives the fees for members of the Alliance of Independent Authors (ALLi)[19].

Because of its complex worldwide distribution network, comparing costs becomes impossible. The fee schedule goes on for eight pages. In some markets, I had to set a minimum print price considerably above that at D2D.

Expects print-ready PDF for POD.

Has an option to return unsold books, a requirement for many physical bookstores.

Lulu[20]

ONE OF THE OLDEST SELF-publishing companies that distributes to their own bookstore, retailers, and other distributors like Ingram.

Free e-book conversion tool requires a 32-page E-book Creation Guide.

Separate e-book and print publishing tools (like Amazon).

Offers xPress App for direct sales from your Shopify[21] store with fulfillment by Lulu.

---

18. https://www.ingramspark.com
19. https://selfpublishingadvice.org
20. https://www.lulu.com
21. https://www.shopify.com/

Bookbaby[22]

ASSISTED SELF-PUBLISHING company that distributes to their own BookShop bookstore and other retailers.

No free tools.

Offers free e-commerce option for direct sales from your website.

Bublish[23]

ASSISTED SELF-PUBLISHING company that converts an EPUB file into Book Bubbles for sharing to social media with built-in marketing tracking.

Offers online eBook Creator word processor for e-book creation.

Does channel marketing through Amazon or Facebook ads, email to bookstores & libraries.

Gumroad[24]

E-COMMERCE PLATFORM that allows you to sell PDF, EPUB, MOBI or print books from one website.

Unbound[25]

CROWDFUNDING PUBLISHER who goes through a traditional publishing process once a book meets its pledge target.

Inkshares[26]

GOES THROUGH A TRADITIONAL publishing process once a book meets its pre-order threshold.

---

22. https://www.bookbaby.com
23. https://bublish.com/
24. https://gumroad.com/
25. https://unbound.com/
26. https://www.inkshares.com/

Distributes through Ingram.

3. Self-Publishing Checklist

3.1. The What

O nce you've written hundreds of pages, you've already accomplished a feat worthy of praise in story and song. But you've only taken the first step on the self-publishing path.

This guide has one purpose and one purpose only.

3.2. The How

A THREE-TIER APPROACH guides you as quickly and efficiently along the self-publishing path.

1. The following **list shows you an overview of the steps** from pages to book. If you know what to do, tick off items as you go.

---

1. https://books2read.com/Cyberspiracy

2. Need more details? Most steps in the list **link to brief instructions** on how D2D, Amazon, and other tools fit into the process.

3. Need even more details? The following **links and those in each Resources** section of the brief instructions point to **organizations** who can help and **in-depth articles and videos**.

• IBPA: Industry Standards Checklist for a Professionally Published Book[2],

• Jane Friedman: Self-Publishing Checklist[3],

• ALLi: What are the Industry Standards for Paperback Books[4]

• ALLi: Book Production : 12 Avoidable Rookie Errors[5]

• BookBub: How to Self-Publish a Book: Tips from Indie Authors[6]

• Reedsy: How to Self-Publish a Book: 7 Simple Steps to Success[7]

• The Creative Penn: How To Get a Book Published: Traditional, Self-Publishing, Print-on-Demand, Ebooks And Audiobooks[8],

• Mark Coker: How to Get People to Read Your Book[9],

---

2. https://www.ibpa-online.org/page/standards-checklist-download

3. https://www.janefriedman.com/self-publishing-checklist/

4. https://selfpublishingadvice.org/paperback-books

5. https://selfpublishingadvice.org/book-production-rookie-errors

6. https://insights.bookbub.com/how-self-publish-book

7. https://blog.reedsy.com/how-to-self-publish-a-book/

8. https://www.thecreativepenn.com/publishing

9. http://www.huffingtonpost.com/david-henry-sterry/mark-coker_b_2594203.html

- Chris Robley: From first draft to book launch: how to publish a novel[10],

- Debbie Young: Book Production: 12 Avoidable Rookie Errors[11],

- Draft2Digital: 9 Most Common Self Publishing Mistakes You Should Avoid

- Begin Self-Publishing Podcast: How to Use Draft2Digital with Dan Wood[12]

- Carla King: Self-Publishing Boot Camp[13]

- Self Publishing Formula: The Knowledge Vault[14]

- Free Advice Friday: People We Like[15]

- The Creative Penn: Professional Editors To Help With Your Book[16]

- The Creative Penn: How To Find And Work With A Book Cover Designer[17]

- Draft2Digital's Partners page[18].

---

10. https://blog.bookbaby.com/2015/05/how-to-publish-a-novel/

11. https://selfpublishingadvice.org/book-production-rookie-errors

12. https://www.youtube.com/watch?v=nWGMMBb4t-o

13. https://books2read.com/SelfPubBootCamp

14. https://books2read.com/KnowledgeVault

15. http://freeadvicefridays.com/index.php/peoplewelike/

16. https://www.thecreativepenn.com/editors

17. https://www.thecreativepenn.com/find-and-work-with-a-book-cover-designer

18. https://www.draft2digital.com/partners/

3.3. The When

YESTERDAY. SERIOUSLY, yesterday. It's never too early to plan your book launch. **Many steps require considerable lead-time.** For quality work, you can't rush hairstylists, cover designers, illustrators, editors, beta and proof readers. Many reviewers need the book months in advance. Some vendors take as long as two weeks to create a sales page from your details page. Amazon requires 24-hour reviews every time you submit a revised manuscript or cover. Some advertising, like BookBub Featured Deals, involves a long process. Give yourself the time to produce a quality product with a workable marketing plan behind it.

Some recommend a **lead-time to launch of as long as six months** so you can incorporate editorial reviews and publicity into your book and marketing collateral. A longer pre-order phase also gives you a bigger chance to make a splash. Amazon reports all pre-orders as sales on launch day, making it easier to hit a bestseller list during those 24 hours.

Need to get your baby out there quickly? **Cover as many steps as you can.** Remember, **you can always relaunch later.** Many midlist authors had success rebooting an old book with a revised manuscript, new cover, better description, or improved marketing plan.

Or **launch the print book later.** The more complex production and longer delivery times take their toll. A paper product is final, whereas most vendors automatically update bought e-books. Launching the two formats months apart gives you the chance to refine pieces for a second shot at a marketing splash. I changed my YA thriller Cyberspiracy to the pink-bow theme and updated all the e-books before the paperback officially launched. The new version also corrected mistakes reported by early readers.

Resources

STEVEN SPATZ: Budget Enough Time (And Patience) For Your Book Promotion[19]

---

19. https://blog.bookbaby.com/2015/10/budget-enough-time-for-your-book-promotion

Apple Books: Planning for Your Book Launch[20]

Jane Friedman: Self-Publishing Checklist[21],

BookBub: How to Promote a Book Launch[22]

BookBub: How to Launch a New Book Using BookBub's Marketing Tools[23]

BookBub: How to Promote a Book Launch (and How BookBub Can Help!)[24] (VIDEO)

3.4. The Checklist

YOU MAY NEED TO GO through some of these steps multiple times or in a different order. Some differ for print and e-book. Others only apply to fiction or nonfiction.

A color code and letter organize related entries into topics.

MetaData Body End Matter Cover Marketing

☐ **M Create book marketing plan.**

☐ **M Create book launch roadmap.**

☐ **M Assemble your street team.**

☐ **M Run a title poll or contest.**

☐ **D Set title and subtitle.**

---

20. https://authors.apple.com/market-your-book/502-planning-for-your-book-launch

21. https://www.janefriedman.com/self-publishing-checklist/

22. https://insights.bookbub.com/promote-book-launch-video

23. https://insights.bookbub.com/launch-book-using-bookbub-marketing-tools

24. https://insights.bookbub.com/promote-book-launch-video

☐ **B Create editorial stylesheet**[25]: important style rules, timeline, setting/locations names, character names, and a list of words whose spellings could be unclear to insure consistency during editing.

☐ **B Content/developmental/structural editing**[26]: detailed critique of story structure, plot, pacing, characterization, setting, timeline by critique groups, beta readers, and professional editors.

☐ **B Revise content**[27].

☐ **E Create glossary/appendices.**

☐ **B Copy/line editing**[28]: going through the text line by line to find typos, spelling mistakes, grammatical errors, inconsistencies, redundancies, repetitions and improve flow, syntax, and formatting.

☐ **B Address copyedit issues**[29].

☐ **B Beta-publish** (blog, social media, sharing sites, forums, e-zines, anthologies)

☐ **C Write cover design concept.**

☐ **B Write interior design concept**[30].

☐ **D Research and determine sales categories.**

☐ **D Research and set the prices** for all formats and territories.

---

25. https://rachellegardner.com/create-a-style-sheet-for-your-manuscript

26. https://www.thecreativepenn.com/writing-book-after-first-draft

27. https://www.jessicabrody.com/2020/01/5-tips-for-revising-a-first-draft

28. https://selfpublishingadvice.org/the-ultimate-guide-to-self-editing-your-manuscript

29. https://www.thecreativepenn.com/2010/12/11/beta-readers-copyediting

30. https://scribewriting.com/interior-book-layout

☐ D **Research and determine keywords.**

☐ D <u>**Determine imprint**/publishing company name.</u>

☐ D **Get your ISBNs**: the universal number bookstores use to order a book.

☐ D **Get your catalog information**: the data needed by libraries to include your book in their catalog (in the USA, this includes the Library of Congress Control Number (LCCN) or the Preassigned Control Number (PCN) and the Cataloging in Publication (CIP) record.)

☐ D **Collect endorsements** and blurbs.

☐ D **Create metadata list**: a single file for quick reference with all the collected metadata, the sales information that help identify the book, such as description, genre categories, search keywords.

☐ C <u>Get Industry-standard EAN **bar code**.</u>

☐ E **Write the copyright page.**

☐ E **Write dedication, acknowledgments.**

☐ D <u>**Write author bio**/About the Author.</u>

☐ D **Take author headshot.**

☐ D **Write book description/back cover copy.**

☐ E **Write book Q&A**[31].

☐ C <u>**Create front cover** designs.</u>

---

31. https://buildyourbrandacademy.com/blog/9460/

suggested-interview-questions-ultimate-guide-to-creating-an-author-media-kit-3-of-10

☐ **M Create an author website**[32] with About, Books, and Media pages.

☐ **M Create author pages**: your author listing at D2D, Amazon, GoodReads, BookBub, etc.

☐ **M Run cover-selection ads**[33], **polls, or contests.**

☐ **C Create back cover + spine design.**

☐ **D Enter metadata** (title, authors, keyword, categories, description, pricing)

☐ **M Setup preorder.**

☐ **M Create details pages**: your book listing at your website, D2D, Amazon, GoodReads, BookBub, etc.

☐ **M Link e- and print book** in KDP Bookshelf.

☐ **M Update central book database**: in the USA, if you use your own ISBN, update its Bowker Books In Print© entry.

☐ **B Format interior.**

☐ **E Create index.**

☐ **E Create table of contents.**

☐ **M Cover reveal** on social media, blog, newsletter.

☐ **M Create universal book link** if not done by D2D.

☐ **M Setup preview sample.**

---

32. https://www.thecreativepenn.com/authorwebsite

33. https://insights.bookbub.com/boosted-series-sales-testing-cover-designs

☐ M Share samples or promo codes.

☐ M Create book trailer[34]: marketing video showcasing highlights from the story.

☐ M Create media kit[35]: collection of publicity materials related to your book for use by media.

☐ M Create tip/sell/one-sheet[36]: one-page version of your media kit for use by event planners, libraries, or booksellers.

☐ E Write book review page[37] with Universal Book Link for the end matter.

☐ M Send out new release notices.

☐ M Send out launch party invites[38].

☐ M Guest-blog[39] about your book.

☐ M Make Advanced Reader Copies available for Review[40].

☐ M Request additional Amazon categories.

☐ B Import mansucript.

☐ B Layout e-book.

---

34. https://www.thecreativepenn.com/tag/book-trailer
35. https://buildyourbrandacademy.com/blog/8606/
    the-ultimate-guide-to-creating-an-author-media-kit
36. https://buildyourbrandacademy.com/blog/13184/
    creating-your-one-sheet-ultimate-guide-to-creating-an-author-media-kit-9-of-10
37. https://kindlepreneur.com/how-to-get-book-reviews-with-no-blog-no-list-and-no-begging
38. https://www.mailerlite.com/ultimate-guide-to-email-marketing
39. https://writingcooperative.com/
    how-to-be-a-welcome-guest-poster-a234a85b0a3e?gi=f20f6dbecbd6
40. https://kindlepreneur.com/how-to-get-book-reviews-with-no-blog-no-list-and-no-begging

☐ **B Layout paperback.**

☐ **E Create end matter.**

☐ **B Preview final pages** and adjust as needed.

☐ **C <u>Create print-ready cover.</u>**

☐ **B Create EPUB/MOBI files.**

☐ **B Create print-ready PDF.**

☐ **B Proofreading**[41]: final check of formatted print and e-book files intended to pick up typos, spelling mistakes, hyphenation problems, and formatting issues.

☐ **B <u>Publish MOBI</u>** <u>files to Amazon KDP.</u>

☐ **B <u>Publish EPUB</u>** <u>files to other sites</u> (D2D, Google Play)

☐ **B Order print proof copy.**

☐ **B Review proof copy.**

☐ **M Run social media posts and/or ads** using Universal Book Link (Amazon, BookBub, Facebook, etc.)

☐ **M Pitch your book to media**[42].

☐ **M Add reviews to book description** on details pages.

☐ **M Add editorial reviews** on details pages.

☐ **M <u>Put book on sale.</u>**

☐ **M Launch party.**

41. https://selfpublishingadvice.org/the-ultimate-guide-to-self-editing-your-manuscript

42. https://buildyourbrandacademy.com/blog

☐ M **Virtual or actual book tour**.

☐ M **Run price promotion**.

☐ M **Run giveaways**.

☐ M **Enroll your book in subscription services** (KU, ScribD, etc.).

☐ **Register copyright (USA[43])**. You have copyright protection from the moment you create the work. Registration gives you additional rights. US law requires submitting a finished electronic or print copy, so registering after publication allows you to complete the process all at once.

☐ M **Make final book available for Review**.

☐ **Create audio book**.

With that out of the way, let's get down and dirty with creating the pieces needed for self-publishing. In staying with the ever-popular ratings on the web, each section comes with a scalps number depending on how hairy its process is.

The images use my Young Adult (YA) Thriller Cyberspiracy[44] for illustration.

---

43. https://www.copyright.gov/registration/
44. https://Books2Read.com/Cyberspiracy

Part III

4. What You Need

———

The major self-publishing services have more or less agreed on these three pieces to sell a book in any of the formats.

1. A product, sales, or **details page**,

2. A **cover file**.

3. An **interior file**,

The **changes you make ripple through to various websites**—dozens if you publish wide. **Save yourself extra work**, like multiple updates and checks of results, by **having everything ready before you start data entry**. KDP and IngramSpark won't even let you save the first page until you filled in *all* the required fields.

D2D creates your back cover and Books2Read page from the data you enter on the [**Details**] page. If you update it later, you'll have to take additional steps. Amazon more or less keeps KDP and AC in synch, but updates may produce surprises—besides requiring 24-hour approval.

4.1. Details Page ⌐⌐⌐⌐

A PRODUCT, SALES, OR details page **displays the sales information**, also known as the **metadata**, *about the book*, such as description, genre categories, search keywords, and ISBN. Both KDP and D2D label the webpage for entering the data "Details," so I've adopted that name in the following procedures.

The text you enter here is **vital to sell your book. Carefully consider the right information ahead of time and write copy following marketing principles.** If you haven't done so yet, **create a list of all metadata in one file** for quick reference.

Many have written extensively about the **art and science of picking titles, keywords, genre categories, or writing book descriptions**. Free and paid tools exist. Every section comes with a sprinkling of resources I've used.

Metadata include the **title, series, author, and Publisher**. Some sales pages contain additional items such as digital rights management (DRM). D2D strikes a balance between its various vendors, lacking information for some special cases. Table 4-1 shows the differences for selected metadata.

Table 4-1: Book Details Comparison

	Subtitle	Edition	Contributors	Pre-order	DRM	ISBN
Amazon	√	√	√	√	√	√
D2D	X	X	√	√	X	√

Resources

JENNIFER DUNHAM: How To Write Killer Blog Post Titles That Convert[1]

Screencraft: How to Write Screenplay Titles That Don't Suck[2]

Ellen Violette: Why Writing a Great Title is More Important than Writing a Great Book[3]

Ellen Violette: 7 Bestseller Title Mistakes Authors Make & How to Avoid Them[4]

Description ⌒⌒⌒⌒

ON A SALES PAGE, **after the cover, the book description has the most impact on conversion** from browser to buyer. The text, also known as ad copy, needs to **entice the reader** and **give search engines keywords** that help

---

1. https://happinessmatters.com/how-to-write-killer-blog-post-titles-that-convert

2. https://screencraft.org/2017/06/12/how-to-write-screenplay-titles-that-dont-suck

3. https://medium.com/@ellenviolette_5197/
   why-writing-a-great-title-is-more-important-than-writing-a-great-book-a16036b0fbcd

4. https://www.linkedin.com/pulse/7-bestseller-title-mistakes-authors-make-how-avoid-them-violette

discovery. D2D recommends including the series, volume number, and the book's approximate length, as some vendors don't show that information at the top of the page the way Amazon does.

Format the description for easy reading. The first seven words matter the most. **Set off an attention-grabbing first line** by itself. Break the rest into short paragraphs surrounded by **blank lines**. The beginning, the most exciting part, can also go on the back of print books. D2D copies your book description as starting point for the cover blurb.

Look inside ↓

Wolf O'Rourc
CYBERSPIRACY

LEIA

Cyberspiracy (Cyber Series Book 1)

Kindle Edition

kindle

by Wolf O'Rourc ˅ (Author)

☆☆☆☆☆ ˅   3 ratings

Hot pink hair can't hide you from high-tech hitmen.

A timid and lonely sixteen-year-old girl hides from bullying in her dream world of dashing **master spy dolls**, blue-haired **Katy Perry Barbies**, and pink **Hello Kitty dresses**.

24S

Cyberspiracy - Cyber Series #1

Wolf O'Rourc

Summary

Hot pink hair can't hide you from high-tech hitmen.

A timid and lonely sixteen-year-old girl hides from bullying in her dream wor dolls, blue-haired Katy Perry Barbies, and pink Hello Kitty dresses.

Cyberspiracy (Cyber Series, #1)

by Wolf O'Rourc

nook **BARNES&NOBLE** Ove

Hot pink hair can't hide you from high-tech hitmen.

A timid and lonely sixteen-year-old girl hides from bullying in her dream pink Hello Kitty dresses.

Cyberspiracy: Cyber Series, #1

By Wolf O'Rourc

SCRIBD

Hot pink hair can't hide you from high-tech hitmen.

A timid and lonely sixteen-year-old girl hides from bullying dashing **master spy dolls**, blue-haired **Katy Perry Barbies**, dresses.

Cyberspiracy (Cyber Series, #1)

boi.de

Hot pink hair can't hide you from high-tech hitmen.

A timid and lonely sixteen-year-old girl hides from bullying in h dream world of dashing master spy dolls, blue-haired Katy Perr Barbies, and pink Hello Kitty dresses.

Cyberspiracy ♥

by Wolf O'Rourc ♣

Synopsis   Product Details   Delivery

Hot pink hair can't hide you from high-tech hitmen.

A timid and lonely sixteen-year-old girl hides from bullying in her dream Hello Kitty dresses.

Cyberspiracy

Wolf O'Rourc

Publisher Description

Hot pink hair can't hide you from high-tech hitmen.

A timid and lonely sixteen-year-old girl hides from bullying in her dream w haired **Katy Perry Barbies**, and pink **Hello Kitty dresses**.

And she hacks her way across the Net behind the avatar of a six foot four Dude.

 **Apple Books**

Cyberspiracy

Cyber Series, #1

Rakuten kobo

Synopsis

Hot pink hair can't hide you from high-tech hitmen.

A timid and lonely sixteen-year-old girl hides from bullying in her drean world of dashing **master spy dolls**, blue-haired **Katy Perry Barbies**, pink **Hello Kitty dresses**.

Cyberspiracy (Cyber Series, #1)

Hot pink hair can't hide you from high-tech hitmen.   Thalia

A timid and lonely sixteen-year-old girl hides from bullying in her c world of dashing master spy dolls, blue-haired Katy Perry Barbies, pink Hello Kitty dresses.

CYBERSPIRACY: CYBER SERIES, #1

Kobo ebook | August 31, 2019

 Indigo Enrich your life

ABOUT

Hot pink hair can't hide you from high-tech hitmen.

A timid and lonely sixteen-year-old girl hides from bullying in her are Perry Barbies, and pink Hello Kitty dresses.

Cyberspiracy

by Wolf O'Rourc

pubblicato da RoRo

 MONDADORI

Descrizione   Dettagli   Recensioni

Hot pink hair can't hide you from high-tech hitmen

A timid and lonely sixteen-year-old girl hides from bullying in her dream world

Figure 4-1: Different Vendor's Cyberspiracy Details pages

YOU CAN FURTHER **highlight key lines**, like the first one and a call to action. Most sales pages support **bold** and *italics*. As you can see from Figure 4-1, **vendors agree on little, including how they treat blank lines.** As shown in Table 4-2, Amazon Author Central[5]'s (AC) formatting differs from KDP's, and the latter's doesn't agree between Kindle and Books stores!

Table 4-2: Description Editor Comparison

	Bold	*Italics*	<u>Underline</u>	List	Heading	URL
KDP	√	√	√	√	√	X
AC	√	√	code	√	√	√
D2D	√	√	√	√	X	√

D2D and AC's (see 12.3) What You See Is What You Get (WYSIWYG) editors **format to the lowest common denominator** (another reason to start with D2D). KDP's editor allows additional HTML code, but doesn't show you the results. If you update the description in AC, it will remove unsupported codes. **For wide distribution, stick with the common formatting.**

Neither editor converts Uniform Resource Locator (**URL**) to clickable web addresses. **Amazon prohibits them in product descriptions, as well as phone numbers, mail addresses, or spoilers.**

Resources

KARON THACKSTON: How To Write Fascinating Amazon Book Listings To Sell More Books[6]

BlueInk Review: Four Mistakes Indie Authors Make With Their Book Description[7]

BookBub: 8 Book Description A/B Tests You Need to See[8]

---

5. https://authorcentral.amazon.com

6. https://thefutureofink.com/fascinating-amazon-book-listings

7. https://blog.bookbaby.com/2015/12/book-description-mistakes-indie-authors-make

The Creative Penn: Attract Readers with a Great Book Sales Description[9],

CoSchedule: <u>How to Write Emotional Headlines That Get More Shares</u>

CoSchedule: The #1 Free Headline Analyzer[10]

Romance Rehab: The top 10 romance novel blurb blunders we NEVER want to see again[11]

The Creative Penn: How To Write Your Book Sales Description With Bryan Cohen (VIDEO)[12]

Reedsy: How to Write a Book Blurb: A Guide for Novelists[13]

Reedsy: Rewriting your Book Description with Bryan Cohen[14]

ALLi: Best Selling Book Descriptions: A Visual Analysis[15]

Marisa Murgatroyd: The 4 Essential Copywriting Habits of Rich and Successful Entrepreneurs[16]

Marisa Murgatroyd: How to Instantly Infuse Emotion into Your Marketing Copy[17]

Brian Meeks: Mastering Amazon Descriptions: An Author's Guide: Copywriting for Authors[18]

---

8. https://insights.bookbub.com/book-description-ab-tests-you-need-to-see

9. https://www.thecreativepenn.com/book-sales-description

10. https://coschedule.com/headline-analyzer

11. http://www.romancerehab.com/blog/
    the-top-10-romance-novel-blurb-blunders-we-never-want-to-see-again

12. https://www.youtube.com/watch?v=HV28It4Kf7w

13. https://blog.reedsy.com/write-blurb-novel

14. https://blog.reedsy.com/live/rewriting-book-description-bryan-cohen/

15. https://selfpublishingadvice.org/best-selling-amazon-book-descriptions/

16. https://www.liveyourmessage.com/
    7-figure-society-the-4-essential-copywriting-habits-of-rich-and-successful-entrepreneurs

17. https://www.liveyourmessage.com/how-to-instantly-infuse-emotion-into-your-marketing-copy

Bryan Cohen: How to Write a Sizzling Synopsis: A Step-by-Step System for Enticing New Readers, Selling More Fiction, and Making Your Books Sound Good[19]

Keywords

WHAT D2D CALLS **Search Terms** are phrases up to 50 characters in length that should closely match what a reader looking for your book **would type into a search field**. You need to balance highly searched terms against the competition for them, so your book has a **chance of showing up at the top of the results list**. In addition, Amazon publishes a list of unacceptable keywords.

Table 4-3: Keywords Comparison

	Keywords	Comma-separated Entry	Reorder
Amazon	7	X	X
D2D	unlimited	√	√

As Table 4-3 shows, D2D allows as many phrases as you want, but **most vendors use the top five or fewer**. Amazon uses all seven of its keywords, so their order doesn't matter.

Keywords to Pick

CONSIDER SHORT PHRASES that readers would use to **describe the type of book they're looking for**. Any of the major story elements or non-fiction topics can work. Searching the web for **broad categories**, for example "popular story settings for romance," may give you starting points and commonly used wording. **Adding modifiers** to fit your story can **narrow searches** and help your book show up higher on the results list.

- Activities: career change, knitting, anger management

- Setting

---

18. https://books2read.com/u/bzo1GE

19. https://books2read.com/u/4j2gdv

o geographical locations: Scottish Highlands, African jungle

o immediate surroundings: neighborhood bar, big law firm

o social environment: Amish romance, Nazi plot

o historical time: Regency romance, Ming dynasty

o time of year: Halloween, summer vacation

o weather: big storm, tropical heat

- Character types: strong female lead, billionaire, Navy SEAL

- Objects: ancient artifact, sports cars, swords

- Plot themes: coming of age, everlasting love, vengeance

- Tone: dark, funny, inspirational

Do test searches on book sites, such as the various Amazon stores or BookBub, **using the keywords** you're considering.

TIP Because **Amazon remembers your search history** and tailors results accordingly, **for keyword research use the incognito or private mode of your browser** and don't log in to your Amazon account.

Incognito or Private browsing[20]

---

20. https://www.digitalcitizen.life/how-browse-web-incognito-all-big-browsers

GOOGLE CHROME: vertical dots menu at top right | **New incognito window**

or [CTRL+SHIFT+N]

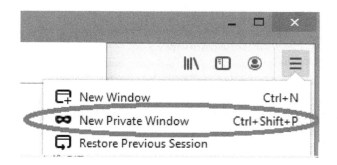

FIREFOX: hamburger icon at top right | **New Private Window**.

or [CTRL + SHIFT + P]

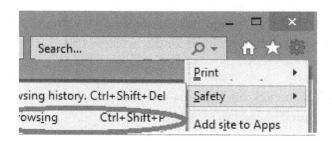

INTERNET EXPLORER: gear menu at top right | **Safety** | **InPrivate Browsing**

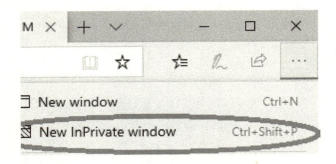

EDGE: ... (Settings and more) at top right | **New InPrivate window**

or [CTRL+SHIFT+P]

Opera: Customize and control Opera button at top left | **New private window**

or CTRL+SHIFT+N

Amazon's **auto-completion may suggests additions** to create popular search terms, such as "vengeance in death." If you get irrelevant or unsatisfying results, refine, rephrase, or discard keywords.

TIP For bestseller lists curated by readers **search for a keyword on Goodreads**[21] then click on **Listopia** above the results. They may give you ideas for additional phrases to research.

Keywords to Avoid

YOU HAVE A LIMITED number of keywords to work with. **Don't waste them on information covered elsewhere in the metadata**, such as title, authors, or genre categories. Vendors already use those terms.

Depending on the website, if you can **work a keyword naturally into the book description**, you could **free up a slot** for something that doesn't fit as well. Similarly, you could leave off any phrases already **mentioned in**

---

21. https://www.goodreads.com

editorial reviews. Since the vendors generally do not release such details on their algorithms, you'll have to run your own tests for each platform. See 6.2 for my results for Cyberspiracy.

Terms **common to the genre** such as "finding love" for romance novels won't gain your book an edge in searches.

Search engines have the **smarts to match variants and common misspellings** of terms, so don't waste a slot on them.

- Spacing: cyberthriller = cyber thriller

- Punctuation: U.S.A. = USA

- Capitalization: President = president

- Pluralization: Viking = Vikings

Except you may want to **include variants of foreign words with drastic spelling differences**: Hanukkah <> Chanukah

KDP has a **zero-tolerance policy for keywords meant to advertise, promote, or mislead**.

- Subjective claims about quality: best novel ever

- Time-sensitive statements: new, on sale, available now

- Amazon program names: Kindle Unlimited, KDP Select

- Misrepresentations: an author not associated with your book

For better results, Amazon also recommends you **leave out quotation marks**, so customers can search for any of the words in a phrase. Kindlepreneur found some advantage repeating keywords that appear in titles or subtitles.

Resources

GOOGLE'S KEYWORD PLANNER[22] helps you determine the popularity of a keyword.

A freemium tool, AnswerThePublic[23], scrapes Google's autosuggestions for related keywords.

A paid tool, Kindlepreneur's Publisher Rocket[24], simplifies keyword research on Az.

KDP: Make Your Book More Discoverable with Keywords/Keywords to avoid[25]

AC: Categories and Search Terms[26]

Kindlepreneur: How To Choose the Right Kindle Keywords[27]

Kindlepreneur: 7 Kindle Keywords: Use All 50 Characters or Not?[28]

The Creative Penn: Choose The Right Categories And Keywords for Your Book[29]

WritePublishSell: Choosing categories and keywords for books (VIDEO)[30]

Categories ⌒⌒⌒⌒⌒

CATEGORIES DESERVE a baldness award for the bushels of hair they will cost you. Libraries have dedicated cataloguing staff to figure out categories.

---

22. https://ads.google.com/home/tools/keyword-planner/

23. https://answerthepublic.com/

24. https://publisherrocket.com/

25. https://kdp.amazon.com/en_US/help/topic/G201298500

26. https://authorcentral.amazon.com/gp/help?ie=UTF8&topicID=201231280

27. https://kindlepreneur.com/how-to-choose-kindle-keywords/

28. https://kindlepreneur.com/7-kindle-keywords

29. https://www.thecreativepenn.com/book-categories-keywords/

30. https://www.youtube.com/watch?v=rJAZA9a1Y5I

The Zon makes it ten times harder by superimposing its own inconsistent and hard to use system. If categories didn't matter so much for the search algorithm and Amazon Advertising (AA), I'd dispense with them.

The Book Industry Study Group (BISG) publishes a **long list of categories to help standardize shelving** of books in stores and libraries. Start with these <u>Book Industry Standards and Communications (**BISAC**) codes</u>[31].

Since a **subcategory automatically includes the broader category above it**, drill down as finely as you can. Similarly, if you find a good subcategory match, including the catchall "General" at the same level or above gains you nothing.

Table 4-4: Categories Comparison

	Categories	Same for Print	Reorder
Amazon	2 + 10	X	X
D2D	5	√	√

As you're dealing with two distinct stores, Amazon allows two categories each for e-book and print. By comparison in Table 4-4, D2D five total. Again, **some vendors only accept one or two off the top**. Pick five BISAC codes, then order them. **Put the best match first.** For sensitive genres like *erotica*, some vendors require the primary code to identify the book as such. Second, add the next best match or the best match in a different broad category for more visibility. You can rearrange the order at D2D afterwards by dragging entries up or down. Amazon uses all categories, so their order doesn't matter.

You can use D2D's **Filter BISACS** field to find categories to start with as described in 6.3.

Categorically Zonsense

THE ZON STARTED DOWN the standard path but hasn't kept up with changes. Worse, the company **introduced its own system that doesn't map**

---

31. https://bisg.org/page/BISACEdition

to **BISAC**. Or map from the **Books to the Kindle store or across international stores**.

For each format's details page, you can select two BISAC codes that best approximate your book's subgenre. **Searches display the matching Amazon browse categories**, however. On the left of the results, under **Department**, an expandable menu tree shows **different categories based on the store the reader entered**.

TIP If you enter an **ASIN** (Amazon Standard Identification Number) or **ISBN** into the search bar, the **Department** list will narrow to only the sub-categories assigned to that book.

Since the Zon has many more categories than BISAC, you can only get some by specifying keywords. The lists are no longer in the help path. You can still search for them, though. It is possible the category request procedure below has replaced this crutch.

Teen & Young Adult Keywords For Selecting Categories[32]

Literature & Fiction Keywords For Selecting Categories[33]

Romance Category Keywords For Selecting Categories[34]

Science Fiction & Fantasy Keywords For Selecting Categories[35]

I'll See Your 4 and Raise You 20

IF YOU PUBLISH SEPARATELY through KDP, once your book is in the system, **you can email or call support to request ten Amazon categories for Kindle and ten for Books**. Yes, that's on top of the two plus two from above. As you can see from the list in Figure 4-2**Error! Reference source not found.**, the Cyberspiracy e-book has twelve. Ignore the loooooong weird

---

32. https://kdp.amazon.com/en_US/help/topic/G201276770

33. https://kdp.amazon.com/en_US/help/topic/G201359210

34. https://kdp.amazon.com/en_US/help/topic/G201216130

35. https://kdp.amazon.com/en_US/help/topic/G201216150

one. Sometimes such artifacts show up. Amazon support doesn't see them on their screens.

Title : **Cyberspiracy (Cyber Series Book 1)**
Contributor : **O'Rourc, Wolf (Author)**
ASIN : **B07V1CHL27**
Type : **Kindle eBook**
Binding : **Kindle Edition**
Release Date : **26 Jul 2019**
Page Count : **295**

BKLNK link: https://www.bklnk.com/B07V1CHL27

Book Categories and Sales Rank

Sales Rank shown if available; 'Top 100' (Best Sellers) and 'New' (New Releases) icons link to the US Zon page for that category.

- Books » Literature & Fiction » Genre Literature & Fiction » Coming of Age Fiction

- Books » Teen & Young Adult Books » Teen & Young Adult Literature & Fiction » Teen & Young Adult Coming of Age Fiction

- Kindle Store » Kindle eBooks » Literature & Fiction » Humor & Satire Fiction » General Humorous Fiction

- Kindle Store » Kindle eBooks » Literature & Fiction » Genre Fiction

- Kindle Store » Kindle eBooks » Mystery, Thriller & Suspense » Thrillers » Technothrillers

- Kindle Store » Kindle eBooks » Mystery, Thriller & Suspense » Thrillers » Political Thrillers & Suspense

- Kindle Store » Kindle eBooks » Mystery, Thriller & Suspense » Thrillers » Domestic Thrillers **Sales Rank: 1,041**

- Kindle Store » Kindle eBooks » Teen & Young Adult eBooks » Teen & Young Adult Mysteries & Thrillers eBooks » Teen & Young Adult Romantic Mystery eBooks

Figure 4-2: Cyberspiracy E-Book Categories

EVERY CATEGORY GIVES you one more chance to rank as a #1 Bestseller. Realistically, though, finding 24 that fit your book will often be a stretch. If you look closely, my e-book has two from the Books Store. These will overlap with the paperback, unless I can find twelve additional categories.

Since **all linked formats of a book show up on the same details page in search results**, mixing stores doesn't affect discoverability. Whether it impacts ranking is less clear.

Do NOT specify inappropriate categories just to rank in them. If enough readers complain, **Amazon will delist your book**. Not worth it.

Getting Childish

YOU HAVE A CHANCE TO score two dozen, if you write for Young Adults (YA). Older people also read these books. **You can specify the same categories for both age ranges**, if they exist. Again, no zonsistency. I've listed Cyberspiracy in three adult thriller subcategories that have no match under Teen & Young Adult.

In another hair loss incident that took me four support calls to resolve, a rep discovered another *one hand doesn't know* problem.

Although you can send a single request to cover both formats, **Kindle Direct Publishing handles category updates for e-books, Author Central for paperbacks**. Since KDP help doesn't mention the procedure, I presume eventually AC will get it all. For now, we have a mixed system.

The **BISG split off Young Adult Fiction** (ages 13-18) **from Juvenile Fiction** (12 and under) years ago. Amazon still hasn't and may never.

Until it does, they implemented another crutch on the details page. **To specify YA**, you select **Juvenile Fiction** categories from the BISAC lists, **then set the Children's book age range to 13 to 18** (see 6.3).

One line at the bottom of a long help article mentions this.

I'm laughing all the way to the barbershop. But it gets better.

You cannot set an age range for paperbacks.

Seriously (more hair silently drops to the ground)?

Someone at Amazon has to synchronize the two. Remember the warning about gathering *all* the details and entering them once? This is another reason why. Changing the age range later may not update the print book to match.

Without the correct age range, none of the YA categories will take.

Mix and Match (Sorta)

BISG **best practices discourage mixing juvenile, YA, and adult BISAC codes. D2D and IngramSpark now enforce this.** You can't mix and match.

Provided you set the correct age range as mentioned above, **Amazon still lets you match YA and adult** categories. Figure 4-3 clearly shows that.

Title : **Cyberspiracy (Cyber Series)**
Contributor : **O'Rourc, Wolf (Author)**
ASIN : **1951187016**
Binding : **Paperback**
Release Date : **15 Aug 2019**
Page Count : **293**

BKLNK link: https://www.bklnk.com/1951187016

- Books » Humor & Entertainment » Humor » Computers & Internet Humor
- Books » Literature & Fiction » Genre Literature & Fiction » Coming of Age Fiction
- Books » Mystery, Thriller & Suspense » Thrillers & Suspense » Spies & Political Thrillers
- Books » Mystery, Thriller & Suspense » Thrillers & Suspense » Technothrillers
- Books » Mystery, Thriller & Suspense » Thrillers & Suspense » Domestic Thrillers
- Books » Teen & Young Adult Books » Teen & Young Adult Literature & Fiction » Teen & Young Adult Action & Adventure » Teen & Young Adult Mystery & Thriller Action & Adventure
- Books » Teen & Young Adult Books » Teen & Young Adult Literature & Fiction » Teen & Young Adult Girls & Women Fiction
- Books » Teen & Young Adult Books » Teen & Young Adult Literature & Fiction » Teen & Young Adult Social & Family Issue Fiction » Teen & Young Adult Fiction about Bullying
- Books » Teen & Young Adult Books » Teen & Young Adult Literature & Fiction » Teen & Young Adult Coming of Age Fiction
- Books » Teen & Young Adult Books » Teen & Young Adult Mysteries & Thrillers » Teen & Young Adult Romantic Mysteries & Thrillers

Figure 4-3: Cyberspiracy Paperback Categories

But How?

SO WHAT'S THE SECRET method to getting 20 extra categories? The AC Search Results FAQs[36] (makes sense in a Wizard of Zon logic) gives the gory details under **Categories**. Ignore the confusing contradictions. The short version follows.

1. Search the appropriate store for a category, eg "YA thrillers."

2. Under **Department** to the left of the search results, **poke around the expanding tree**, highlight all lines from the desired subcategory to the store. Copy each of these browse paths and reformat them into a single line with ">" as separator.

3. Rip your hair out in frustration because the Zon can't provide a @#!X easy-to-use tool to pick 10 out of 16,000 categories.

4. Switch to a better procedure than this zonsense.

If you have no hair left at this point, **let D2D distribute to the Amazon stores and worry about mapping their five BISAC codes to categories**.

Should you persist in going down the hair-robbing path of KDP publishing, here's a much **better procedure for finding categories**. The Resources section has direct links for most of the English stores.

1. Go to the Amazon Best Sellers list[37] of a store. **These books most likely already have requested additional categories**.

2. Under **Any Department** on the left, drill down to a category that fits your book, eg for the *Cyberspiracy* e-book I selected Any

---

36. https://authorcentral.amazon.com/gp/help/

ref=AC_CU_Books-update-browse-categories-dyk?topicID=200513090

37. https://www.amazon.com/Best-Sellers/zgbs

Department > Kindle Store > Kindle eBooks > Teen & Young Adult > Mysteries & Thrillers.

3. Pick one of the best sellers, preferably a book with a comparable style, eg I chose Karen McManus's *One of Us Is Lying*.

4. Check its **Product details**, **Amazon Best Sellers Rank**. If you see **three categories**, the publisher has obviously requested more than two. If not, pick another book.

5. Copy the **ASIN** (Amazon Standard Identification Number) for e-book or the **ISBN-10** for paperback/hardcover, eg B01M98J44U or 1524714682.

6. Search Amazon for that number. With an **exact match** in the results list, the **Department tree only shows the categories applicable to that book**. You'll have to use the browser's back button to go back to the original search result to traverse the tree, but it's still less to wade through.

Or

Enter the number into a tool like BkLnk's category finder[38] and spit out a report like Figure 4-4.

Title : **One of Us Is Lying**
Contributor : **McManus, Karen M.** (Author)
ASIN / ISBN-10: **B01M98J44U**
Type : **Kindle eBook**
Binding : **Kindle Edition**
Release Date : **29 May 2017**
Page Count : **359**
Store Sales Rank: **3,111**
Zon Country Store Product Page

BKLNK link: https://www.bklnk.com/B01M98J44U

Book Categories and Sales Rank

Sales Rank shown if available. Read about the other icons below.

- Books » Books » Teen & Young Adult Books » Teen & Young Adult Literature & Fiction » Teen & Young Adult Social & Family Issue Fiction » Teen & Young Adult Friendship Fiction NEW! CATALIZE

- Books » Books » Teen & Young Adult Books » Teen & Young Adult Mysteries & Thrillers » Teen & Young Adult Romantic Mysteries & Thrillers **Sales Rank: 4** NEW! CATALIZE

- Books » Books » Teen & Young Adult Books » Teen & Young Adult Mysteries & Thrillers » Teen & Young Adult Mysteries & Detective Stories NEW! CATALIZE

- Books » Books » Teen & Young Adult Books » Teen & Young Adult Mysteries & Thrillers » Teen & Young Adult Thrillers & Suspense NEW! CATALIZE

- Kindle Store » Kindle Store » Kindle eBooks » Teen & Young Adult eBooks » Teen & Young Adult Mysteries & Thrillers eBooks » Teen & Young Adult Detective Story eBooks **Sales Rank: 3** NEW! CATALIZE

- Kindle Store » Kindle Store » Kindle eBooks » Teen & Young Adult eBooks » Teen & Young Adult Mysteries & Thrillers eBooks » Teen & Young Adult Thrillers & Suspense **Sales Rank: 6** NEW! CATALIZE

- Kindle Store » Kindle Store » Kindle eBooks » Teen & Young Adult eBooks » Teen & Young Adult Literature & Fiction eBooks » Teen & Young Adult Social & Family Issues Fiction » Teen & Young Adult Fiction about Friendship NEW! CATALIZE

- Kindle Store » Kindle Store » Kindle eBooks » Teen & Young Adult eBooks » Teen & Young Adult Social Issues eBooks NEW! CATALIZE

Results in Copyable Text Format

Click to select text, then Copy. Paste into your spreadsheet or text file.

```
One of Us Is Lying by McManus, Karen M. (Author) (B01M98J44U)
Books » Books » Teen & Young Adult Books » Teen & Young Adult Literature &
Fiction » Teen & Young Adult Social & Family Issue Fiction » Teen & Young Adult
```

Figure 4-4: One of Us Is Lying E-Book Categories

NOT ONLY CAN YOU SEE a list of categories, professionally researched by the publisher and in the format needed, the same results in **copyable text format** follow below. Beats drilling down in the **All Departments** tree and reformatting the path to each subcategory. The blue and orange buttons let you jump to the corresponding **Best Sellers** and **Hot New Releases** pages, so you can quickly gather more titles to research. Or rejuvenate your hair with one click on the **Catalize** button to get all categories used by the Top 25 books in that grouping. Of course, you can also copy related subcategories at the same level in the expanded **All Departments** tree and add them to the ends of the paths in your copied list.

TIP For bestseller lists created by readers **search for a subgenre on Goodreads**[39] then click on **Listopia** above the results.

7. Repeat this procedure with other books until you have enough categories for each format.

8. **Repeat this procedure with the stores in every region** you want updated. You may have to rely on the browse path trees in those markets, as BkLnk can't get information from all of them.

9. **Separate your entries into lists named region + "Kindle Store" + your ASIN and region + "Books Store" + your ISBN-10.** As *Cyberspiracy* shows, this really doesn't matter in the end, but Amazon specifies it. And each list goes to a different place for the updates. No point giving customer service a reason to reject your request.

10. Finish setting up your book.

Once your details pages are live in every needed store, email your lists following this procedure.

1. Log in to your AC account if you have one, otherwise use KDP.

---

39. https://www.goodreads.com

2. Go to the [**Help**] system and click the [**Contact Us**] button or use the link to the AC contact form[40] at **My Books | Update information about a book | Browse Categories | I want to update my book's browse categories** or the KDP contact form[41] at **Manage books on your [Bookshelf] | Enter book details and upload book content** shown in Figure 4-5.

3. Unless you feel like reading browse paths to the rep for half an hour, select **Email**.

4. Request that they add the categories to your book and paste in the lists.

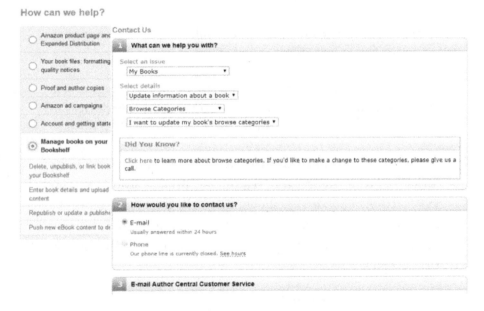

Figure 4-5: KDP + AC Contact Form

ACCORDING TO AMAZON, the changes can take 72 hours. I've seen results in BkLnk within minutes of the confirmation email arriving. You can also search the stores for your book by ASIN or ISBN to verify that the Department tree shrinks to the categories you specified.

40. https://authorcentral.amazon.com/gp/help/contact-us

41. https://kdp.amazon.com/en_US/contact-us

Resources

THE PAID TOOL Publisher Rocket[42] also simplifies category research.

BISG: Selecting A BISAC Code[43]

KDP: Browse Categories[44]

AC: Categories and Search Terms[45]

AC: Search Results FAQs[46]

Kindlepreneur: Secret Method to Choosing the Best Amazon Categories[47]

The Creative Penn: Choose The Right Categories And Keywords for Your Book[48]

Marylee MacDonald: New Categories for YA Authors | How to Rank on Amazon[49]

WritePublishSell: Choosing categories and keywords for books (VIDEO)[50]

Amazon: US Books Store Best Sellers list[51]

Amazon: US Kindle Store Best Sellers list[52]

Amazon: UK Books Store Best Sellers list[53]

---

42. https://publisherrocket.com/

43. https://bisg.org/page/BISACSelection

44. https://kdp.amazon.com/en_US/help/topic/G200652170

45. https://authorcentral.amazon.com/gp/help?ie=UTF8&topicID=201231280

46. https://authorcentral.amazon.com/gp/help/
    ref=AC_CU_Books-update-browse-categories-dyk?topicID=200513090

47. https://kindlepreneur.com/how-to-choose-the-best-kindle-ebook-kdp-category/

48. https://www.thecreativepenn.com/book-categories-keywords/

49. https://maryleemacdonaldauthor.com/categories-metadata-bisac

50. https://www.youtube.com/watch?v=rJAZA9a1Y5I

51. https://www.amazon.com/best-sellers-books-Amazon/zgbs/books

52. https://www.amazon.com/Best-Sellers-Kindle-Store/zgbs/digital-text

Amazon: UK Kindle Store Best Sellers list[54]

Amazon: Canada Books Store Best Sellers list[55]

Amazon: Canada Kindle Store Best Sellers list[56]

Amazon: Australia Books Store Best Sellers list[57]

Amazon: Australia Kindle Store Best Sellers list[58]

Pricing ⌒⌒⌒◯

BECAUSE OF THE COMPLEXITY involved, all platforms have a separate page for entering prices. Yes, that's plural, even for one book. You start with a single list price for your print or e-book. Pre-programmed hair loss escalates from there.

E-book List Price

Table 4-5: E-book Pricing Comparison

E-book	Royalties	Delivery	Territory	Subs.	Library	Lend
Amazon	70 / 35%	√	√	√	X	√
D2D	59.5 / 29.7%	X	√	√	√	X

THE TWO PLATFORMS' pricing options differ in many respects, as Table 4-5 shows. Amazon pays **35% royalties for e-books priced below $1 or above $10** (or an equivalent range if you changed to a primary marketplace with a different currency). **In between, they pay 70% minus delivery charges based on the file size, if you live in** certain countries including

---

53. https://www.amazon.co.uk/Best-Sellers-Books/zgbs/books

54. https://www.amazon.co.uk/Best-Sellers-Kindle-Store/zgbs/digital-text

55. https://www.amazon.ca/Best-Sellers-Books/zgbs/books/

56. https://www.amazon.ca/Best-Sellers-Kindle-Store/zgbs/digital-text

57. https://www.amazon.com.au/gp/bestsellers/books

58. https://www.amazon.com.au/gp/bestsellers/digital-text

Australia, Canada, the UK, and the US[59]. Promotional pricing by you or Amazon below the lower threshold earns 35%, except on Count Down deals.

Net of their commission, **D2D pays the same 59.5% for all retail channels except Amazon**, where prices outside the 70% range earn 29.7%. For more details, see 10.1.

Territorial Pricing

IF YOUR HEAD IS SMOKING already, your hair will soon catch fire. Both platforms will convert your list price to the currencies of other marketplaces automatically. You *can* override these territorial prices. *Should you?*

The USA calculates **sales taxes on top of the list price**. Many European countries **include a value-added tax (VAT) in the list price**. During currency conversion, neither KDP nor D2D factor in that reduction in net. To avoid a haircut on your royalties, you must manually set the price of your book higher. The Eurozone doesn't have a single VAT rate, but D2D allows only one Euro amount. Amazon lets you override the price separately for different Euro markets and shows you the royalties in each. You get to decide whether regularly adjusting all these prices is worth the hassle. For more details, see 10.1.

Subscription Pricing

BOTH PLATFORM OFFER **subscription services where customers pay a flat fee to read** as much as they want. Table 4-6 shows the choices.

Table 4-6: Subscription Services Comparison

	Program	Royalties
Amazon	Kindle Unlimited	Flip a coin
	Kindle Owners' Lending Library	Ditto
	Lending for Kindle	0
D2D	Scribd	59.5%
	24 Symbols	59.5%
	Kobo Plus	Varies

Amazon's has Kindle Unlimited (KU)[60] for the general public and Kindle Owners' Lending Library (KOLL)[61] for Amazon prime members. Both programs pay authors royalties from a pool that varies monthly with the combined revenue and page reads[62]. Lending for Kindle[63] allows customers to send their books to friends and family for up to 14 days without any payments.

D2D's offers a straightforward royalties rate, although Kobo's also varies with the number of subscribers.

Library Pricing

FINALLY, D2D LETS YOU **charge libraries a higher price for e-books** through OverDrive, Bibliotheca, Baker & Taylor, and Hoopla—more than double by default. You only earn 46.8% on that higher price, however. A library can opt for a cost per checkout model at OverDrive and Hoopla.

Amazon doesn't offer library pricing.

Paperback List Price

THE SIMPLICITY OF PAPERBACK pricing in Table 4-7 seems quaint by comparison. A few large players dominate. Independent Publishers Group

---

60. https://kdp.amazon.com/en_US/help/topic/G201537300

61. https://kdp.amazon.com/en_US/help/topic/G201392160

62. https://kdp.amazon.com/en_US/help/topic/G201541130

63. https://kdp.amazon.com/en_US/help/topic/G200652240

(IPG) handles the printing for D2D. Like other publishing services, **their Extended Distribution uses Ingram to deliver paperbacks to bookstores, online retailers, libraries, and academic institutions.** You reach the same downstream outlets, but with fewer choices—Ingram ultralight as D2D calls it.

Table 4-7: Paperback Pricing Comparison

Paperback	Royalties	Territories	Distribution	Returns	Copies
Amazon Store	60%	8	Amazon	X	√
Amazon Expanded Distribution	40%	1	Ingram	X	√
D2D Extended Distribution	45%	1	Ingram	X	√

In its Books stores, Amazon pays 60% royalties on paperbacks. To allow the customary 55% discount, royalties drop to **40% in US-only Expanded Distribution** to wholesale clients.

D2D pays 45% in its US-only print distribution.

TIP Since D2D only offers **Extended Distribution**, its **minimum prices will exceed those for Amazon.com without Expanded Distribution.** If you don't care about sales to stores and libraries in the USA, you can offer your paperback for less by publishing the print-ready PDF through KDP.

Most stores can't afford the risk of a book not selling. Unlike publishers, **neither Amazon nor D2D have a facility for accepting returns of unsold inventory.** You probably have to negotiate with individual stores to get them to take a chance on yours. Libraries usually don't bother with returns. If their acquisition departments has access to the Ingram catalogue, **Expanded/Extended Distribution** makes it easier for them to order your book.

Both platforms offer US author copies at cost. If you can sell them at list yourself, you earn both your royalties and the discount.

TIP Print prices differ by printer and may vary between Amazon, Draft2Digital, and Ingram.

Setting a Price

SO WHAT LIST PRICE do you enter? You could ask a barbershop oracle or **look at comparable books** for each format at different vendors.

Obviously, new authors can't charge as much as bestselling ones.

Don't underprice either. If similar books cost considerably more, potential buyers may dismiss your book as inferior. **Amazon enforces minimum prices** in all territories and D2D does for pre-orders.

TIP You **can't set Amazon's e-book list price to free permanently**. Once published, **you can do so at D2D**. They'll still list the minimum at Amazon, which then usually **price matches the book to zero**.

No platform will let you specify a paperback price below cost. In addition, with the 70% royalties option, Amazon requires the e-book to cost at least 20% less than the print book.

Set the price high enough to allow retailer discounting. Online vendors like Amazon may choose to discount a book to increase sales based on their algorithms, or you can temporarily enter a discounted price.

Neither Amazon nor D2D allow returns of unsold books. Without this option, only available from Ingram directly, few physical bookstores will stock your book. So why brother with print at all? Local venues may order limited quantities, if you hold events there. And libraries don't usually care about returning books.

Resources

WRITEPUBLISHSELL: How to price your book for retail (VIDEO)[64]

The Creative Penn: Pricing Books And The Use Of Free[65],

ALLi: Amazon's Unwritten Print Pricing Rule[66],

---

64. https://www.youtube.com/watch?v=-LdL64pwkv8

65. https://www.thecreativepenn.com/pricing-books

KDP: Royalties in Kindle Unlimited and Kindle Owners' Lending Library[67]

4.2. Cover

FORGET THE OLD SAYING. **We *do* judge a book by its cover**. Marketing people believe it contributes to 50% of sales. Don't skimp.

Your target audience has **expectations specific to a subgenre**. Compare your ideas to bestsellers in your subcategory. You want your cover to standout, but not so much that it doesn't belong.

Unless you **understand the psychology of a cover design**, such as a Z layout, hire a professional or buy premade covers.

Finding quality cover art takes time. Various sites offer free or low-cost images. **Read the license agreement to ensure that it allows your chosen pictures on book covers**. Pexels[68], for instance, requires you to add value to images that you use on a physical product. A costly copyright infringement lawsuit may force you to destroy all produced books.

Keep in mind that most prospects' **first impression comes from a small thumbnail** in a search result. Size every element—like title, author name, or images—big enough for readability when shrunk down.

If the cover incorporates photographs, opt for a **high-resolution to avoid display problems** on larger screens and for best printing results. The resulting file will increase the size of your e-book considerably, but the few cents in delivery charges may avoid disappointment among readers. For an eBook cover, as you can see from Table 4-8, Amazon considers a **height/width ratio of 1.6:1 ideal**. For every 1,000 pixels in width, the image should be 1,600 pixels in height, with a minimum height of 2,500 pixels.

Table 4-8: Cover Comparison

---

66. https://selfpublishingadvice.org/amazon-kdp-unwritten-print-pricing-rule

67. https://kdp.amazon.com/en_US/help/topic/G201541130

68. https://www.pexels.com/

	File Type	Recommended size (width x height px)	Wrap-around	Barcode
KDP	JPG, TIF	1600px x 2560px	√	√
D2D	JPEG, GIF, PNG, TIF, BMP	1600px x 2400px	√	√

Upload files in RGB (Red-Green-Blue) color mode even for paperbacks. PC-based graphics programs default to RGB. According to D2D, a CMYK (Cyan, Magenta, Yellow, and Key) image used for printing will produce poor results.

KDP only accepts cover files in JPEG and TIFF formats, no PNG or BMP.

You **can't finish a wraparound cover for a paperback until you have converted your interior file** and know the exact page number. Amazon and D2D provide tools that help with the final layout of your chosen design. Customarily, the **back contains blurbs**, information printed on the cover to describe the book and make it attractive to buy, **such as the description and your author bio, plus your headshot**. You should already have prepared these pieces for the details page.

Retail channels also require a **barcode with the ISBN**. Amazon and D2D will provide it, but you need to block that area in the lower right corner of the back cover. The two platforms don't agree on the exact dimensions. If you publish separately through both, you'll need to plan for two slightly different covers.

Many versions of Microsoft Windows include the **Paint graphics program** that lets you do simple tasks like resizing or changing formats.

Free graphics programs like Paint.Net[69] or Canva[70] (see 5.3) help with placing text on graphics.

A number of sites offer free images under various terms.

---

69. https://www.getpaint.net

70. https://www.canva.com

- Pexels[71]

- Unsplash[72]

- Wikimedia Commons[73]

- Pixabay[74]

- Free Images[75]

- Free Digital Photos[76]

- morgueFile[77]

- Death to the Stock Photo[78]

A couple search engines, search.CreativeCommons.org[79] and PhotoPin.com[80], help you find creative commons licensed photos for reuse. For inclusion in a book project, check the [**Use commercially**] option.

Resources

D2D: The Psychology of a Good Book Cover[81]

KDP: Cover Creator[82]

---

71. https://www.pexels.com/

72. http://unsplash.com

73. http://commons.wikimedia.org/wiki/Main_Page

74. https://pixabay.com

75. http://freeimages.com

76. http://www.freedigitalphotos.net

77. http://www.morguefile.com

78. https://deathtothestockphoto.com/join

79. http://search.creativecommons.org

80. http://photopin.com

81. https://www.draft2digital.com/blog/the-psychology-of-a-good-book-cover

82. https://kdp.amazon.com/en_US/help/topic/G201113520

KDP: Paperback Cover Resources[83]

Apple Books: Designing a Great Digital Book Cover[84]

Sara F. Hawkins: Law and Etiquette for Using Photos and Images Found Online[85]

Sara F. Hawkins: The Insider's Guide to Online Photo Use[86]

MeetEdgar: 3 Killer Sources of Copyright-Free Images to Avoid Getting Punched in the Face with a Lawsuit[87]

Emily Temple: Are Book Covers Different for Female and Male Authors?[88]

BookBaby: Judging a Book by Its Cover[89]

Avvo: Model Releases, Copyrights, and other Intellectual Property Concerns for Photographers and Models[90]

4.3. Interior File

INDUSTRY CONVENTIONS demand **additional parts beyond your manuscript in the interior text of a book.** It will **look more professional if you stick to the guidelines** given by the Independent Book Publishers Association (IBPA)[91]. Put considerable thought into pieces that affect your

---

83. https://kdp.amazon.com/en_US/help/topic/G201834210

84. https://authors.apple.com/prepare-your-book/508-designing-a-great-digital-book-cover

85. http://sarafhawkins.com/blog-law-photo-use-and-etiquette

86. http://sarafhawkins.com/insiders-guide-proper-online-photo-use

87. https://meetedgar.com/blog/
    2013103-killers-sources-copyright-free-images-avoid-getting-punched-face-lawsuit

88. http://flavorwire.com/275360/are-book-covers-different-for-female-and-male-authors

89. http://blog.bookbaby.com/2015/02/judging-book-cover-book-publicists-media-want-see-outside-book

90. https://www.avvo.com/legal-guides/ugc/
    model-releases-copyrights-and-other-intellectual-property-concerns-for-photographers-and-models

91. https://www.ibpa-online.org/page/standards-checklist-download

book sales and **write the copy following marketing principles.** If you need professional help with items like a headshot, figure on weeks of lead-time.

End Matter

THE **front matter precedes your manuscript or body** text and includes things like the title and copyright pages and the table of contents (TOC). Naturally, the parts after the body become the back matter. With the emergence of Look Inside features, most marketing related pages such as author bio and additional books in your catalog, your backlist, end up here. For simplicity, I've adopted the D2D practice of calling all the pages outside the body "End Matter."

The customary order in the US is as follows

Introductory Pages

Title Page

Copyright Page

Dedication

Table of Contents

Acknowledgments

Promotional Pages

[Body]

Promotional Pages

About the Author

About the Publisher

Historically, creating end matter for print books guaranteed *alopecia areata*, or spot baldness. Some page numbers require lowercase Roman numerals. Other parts have blank pages without headers or footers. You have to go through hair-losing contortions in a Samsonean effort to get all-purpose word processors like Microsoft Word to **implement the correct conventions**. If you can even remember them.

E-books simplified those tasks, but brought new problems. In order to accept manuscripts with simple formatting, **D2D and Smashwords treat blocks of blank lines as scene or page breaks**. As a result, laying out something as simple as a title page becomes a nightmare.

TOCs create their own problems, particular in print, where small formatting differences add up to shifting page numbers.

Some publishing platforms took the easy way out (for them). They expect a print-ready file, usually Adobe PDF, already formatted the way readers expect a book to look, including headers and page numbers. Most, KDP included, will convert a single Word document that contains *all* the required pages into a print-ready format, sometimes with considerable effort from you.

Dream2Dream

NOT SO D2D. SEEING the tragic hair loss suffered by modern authors, Draft2Digital came up with an innovative process. **A few clicks lets you create common end matter** elements from data entered on the [**Details**] and [**Layout**] tab. The website **formats the pages properly, puts them in the expected sequence, and adds page numbers as needed.** A ⌒⌒⌒⌒⌒ procedures turns into ⌒.

Complex chapter detection allows **generation of a TOC for print books that actually agrees with the body**.

With their integration of Universal Book Links, D2D can **generate marketing freebies** like "Also By," "New Release Email Notifications Signup," and "Teaser."

Such flexibility and ease of use comes at a price. The **conversion works best for the most common book formats**, stories and narrative non-fiction like memoirs, in simple chapters.

The multi-level structure and large images used in this guide, for instance, overburden the algorithms. I chose to publish it as I describe in this text to exercise the tools and show the results with all the limitations. Both KDP and D2D accept a print-ready PDF that would have produced paperbacks looking almost exactly like the underlying Word document, and cost me bushels of hairs to produce.

Amazon has since added similar end matter creation to the stand-alone Kindle Create (KC) program, their next generation conversion software. It follows a more labor-intensive path, though, lacking access to the metadata in KDP. And chapter formatting requires annoying amounts of manual intervention.

KC does allow more customization of end matter, in particular the copyright pages. D2D opted for the simple version common in many traditionally published books now. Without a custom field, you can't enter the **Cataloging in Publication (CIP)** record found in older books. It includes data **helpful for librarians when adding books to their catalog**, like the Library of Congress Control Number (LCCN) and our fiend, the BISAC code.

Nowadays, however, many download the information. Rather than pay for a CIP block, wine and dine a certified catalog librarian to put your book into WorldCat.org[92]. The **world's largest bibliographic database itemizes the collections of thousands of libraries** in MAchine Readable Cataloging (MARC) format. All alcohol aside, companies like the The Donohue Group[93] can create both CIP and MARC data for a fee. Your local library may do it for you as well, if they carry your book.

---

92. https://www.worldcat.org

93. https://dgiinc.com/

Resources

IBPA: Industry Standards Checklist for a Professionally Published Book[94]

Library of Congress: Preassigned Control Number Program[95]

Chris Robley: How to write a great author bio that will connect with readers[96]

Marisa Murgatroyd: 5 Credibility Boosters to Supercharge Your Website's About Page

Chris Well: The Ultimate Guide to Creating an Author Media Kit[97]

---

94. https://www.ibpa-online.org/page/standards-checklist-download

95. http://www.loc.gov/publish/pcn

96. http://blog.bookbaby.com/2014/03/how-to-write-a-great-author-bio

97. http://buildyourbrandacademy.com/blog/568404/the-ultimate-guide-to-creating-an-author-media-kit

5. Tools

———

Before we cover KDP and D2D in detail, let's look at some other tools you might want to consider for making your life easier.

5.1. Conversion

MOST SELF-PUBLISHERS only need to worry about converting a **word processor formats like DOCX or ODT** to the two **main e-book formats MOBI and EPUB**. If you download books from websites, you may encounter formats optimized for particular devices. To update these files, some of the following tools can also convert them to the main MOBI or EPUB.

Amazon's **Kindle e-readers use AZW** files. They offer better compression and additional features like bookmarks, annotations, last known page, and digital rights management (DRM). Fourth generation devices switched to the **AZW3** format, also called AZW8. The seventh generation introduced **KFX**.

Similarly, the EPUB eBook specifications contain the Open Packaging Format. **OPF** files store metadata like the title, the language, creator, reading order, and book ID in Extensible Markup Language (XML).

Mobipocket created the **PRC** and **PDB** formats specifically for Palm devices and its Reader Desktop. Some Kindle devices can decode them.

You may also find books in other general-purpose formats used on the Internet, such as plain text (**TXT, ASC**), Hypertext Markup Language (**HTM, HTML**) for webpages, Adobe's Portable Document Format (**PDF**), and Rich Text Format (**RTF**). Table 5-1 shows which tools accept which formats.

Table 5-1: Conversion Tools Comparison

	Input File Type	Output Format	Operating System	Preview	Theme Image
Kindle Create	DOC, DOCX, PDF	KPF	Windows, Mac	√	√
Calibre	DOC, DOCX, PDF, EPUB et al, MOBI et al, ODT, HTML, RTF, Plain Text, Comics	EPUB, MOBI, PDF, DOCX, ODT, HTML, RTF, Text	Windows, Mac, Linux	√	X
Scrivener	DOC, DOCX, PDF, EPUB, MOBI, ODT, HTML, RTF, Plain Text, FDX	EPUB, MOBI, PDF, DOC, DOCX, ODT, HTML, RTF, Plain Text	Windows, Mac	X	X
Vellum	DOCX	EPUB, MOBI, PDF	Mac	√	√
Word	DOC, DOCX, PDF, ODT, HTML, RTF, Plain Text, XPS	PDF, DOC, DOCX, ODT, HTML, RTF, Plain Text, XPS	Windows, Mac, browser	√	X
LO Writer	DOC, DOCX, PDF, ODT, HTML, RTF, Plain Text, UOT	PDF, DOC, DOCX, ODT, HTML, RTF, Plain Text, UOT, EPUB	Windows, Mac, Linux	√	X
Docs	DOC, DOCX, PDF, ODT, HTML, RTF, Plain Text	EPUB, PDF, DOC, DOCX, ODT, HTML, RTF, Plain Text	Windows, Mac, Linux	√	X
Pages	DOC, DOCX, PDF, RTF	EPUB, PDF, DOC, DOCX, RTF, Plain Text	Mac, browser	√	√
Sigil	EPUB, HTML,	EPUB	Windows,	√	CSS

| Plain Text, (DOCX, ODT, MOBI plugin) | Mac, Linux |

Kindle Create (KC)[1]

AMAZON'S SECOND-GENERATION conversion program that supports customizable themes, automatic end matter, and image placement. The built-in Kindle Previewer lets you see how the e-book looks on various devices. With a superior experience to KDP, I use it in the conversion procedures below. In typical Zon fashion **only KDP and Kindle Previewer can read and convert its proprietary KPF output format.**

Calibre[2]

CALIBRE IS A FREE PROGRAM for managing and converting e-books. It supports just about any format under the reading light. You can edit various parts of an e-book, remove unwanted elements, and output it in different basic formats. Calibre comes with a viewer that can display most e-books.

Scrivener[3]

A **paid** word processor specifically for authors and screenwriters that includes a number of tools, such as a storyboard for scenes, character bios, and folders for research like images and notes. Scrivener can store individual chapters and compile them into different output formats including MOBI and EPUB. To use the output effectively with many tools, however, you need to use at least version 3, which supports styles. Large learning curve.

---

1. https://www.amazon.com/Kindle-Create/b?ie=UTF8&node=18292298011
2. https://calibre-ebook.com
3. https://www.literatureandlatte.com/scrivener/overview

Vellum[4]

A **paid** book formatting and design tool (for **Mac only**) that supports customizable themes (called styles). It can generate **print-ready** PDF, MOBI, EPUB, and formats specific to certain stores like Apple or Kobo, for instance to deal with size limitations. The **preview mode allows you to see how your book will look on various e-readers**, like Kindle Fire, Apple iPad, and Android tablet.

Word Processors

PAID Microsoft Word 365[5] and many of its free alternatives (Apache OpenOffice Writer[6], LibreOffice Writer[7], Google Docs[8]) have **some abilities to output in PDF or e-book format**. For instance, I formatted the complex interior of my *Word Wizardry for Writers* guide and output it as print-ready PDF completely in Microsoft Word at the low, low price of only 37.6% of my hair. Publishing add-ons available.

Apple Pages[9]

FREE WORD PROCESSOR for **Mac, iPad, iPhone, and PC web browsers** that can save to Microsoft Word or EPUB format. Replaced **Apple iBooks Author**. Publishing add-ons available.

Sigil Ebook[10]

SIGIL IS A FREE, OPEN-source, multi-platform EPUB e-book editor, which can **convert HTML and plain text files to EPUB**. It does not come with themes, but will format the manuscript according to HTML cascading

---

4. https://vellum.pub/

5. https://products.office.com/en-us/word

6. https://www.openoffice.org/

7. https://www.libreoffice.org/

8. https://docs.google.com/

9. https://www.apple.com/pages/

10. https://sigil-ebook.com

style sheets (CSS) you provide. Plugins available for various advanced functions.

5.2. Preview

WITH EPUB THE STANDARD everywhere but The Marvelous Land of Zo, tools to read that format abound. Only the Kindle Previewer, though, shows how an e-book will look on various devices. Few other than Amazon provide tools for its MOBI format.

Adobe Digital Editions[11]

A POPULAR FREE **EPUB viewer** with features like **search**, the ability to **borrow** e-books from public libraries, **bookmarking**, **highlighting**, or notes.

EPUBReader for Firefox[12]

A FREE **add-on for the Firefox browser for previewing** EPUB files.

EPUB Reader for Chrome browser[13]

A FREE **add-on for the Google Chrome browser for previewing** EPUB files.

EPUB Validators

NOT PREVIEWERS FOR human eyes, but websites like Epub Validator[14], ePub Validator[15], or EPUBCheck[16] determine if your e-book passes strict EPUB validation requirements enforced by retailers like Apple.

---

11. https://www.adobe.com/solutions/ebook/digital-editions.html
12. https://addons.mozilla.org/en-US/firefox/addon/epubreader
13. https://chrome.google.com/webstore/detail/epub-reader/
    mbcgbbpomkkndfbpiepjimakkbocjgkh
14. https://www.ebookit.com/tools/bp/Bo/eBookIt/epub-validator
15. https://www.epubconversion.com/epub-validator/
16. https://epubcheck.mebooks.co.nz/

Kindle Previewer[17]

A FREE PROGRAM TO PREVIEW how e-books will appear on various Kindle devices with different screen sizes, display orientations, and font sizes. Absolutely shocking for the Zon, the Previewer not only supports various newer **MOBI formats like AZW8, PRC, and KPF**, but **also EPUB**. My go-to previewer now.

Kindle Cloud Reader[18]

A WEBSITE FOR READING in your browser MOBI e-books in your Amazon account or downloaded to your device.

Kindle App[19]

A FAMILY OF **free programs to read MOBI e-books** on iOS, Android, Mac, and PC.

5.3. Images

BOOK PRODUCTION COMMONLY requires manipulating pictures in multiple ways. A simple graphics editor suffices to resize images to fit the interior layout. To create complex designs for covers requires a program that can layer elements on top of each other. You may also need one to convert the lesser-known formats listed in Table 5-2 to the ones acceptable in self-publishing.

Table 5-2: Graphics Tools Comparison

---

17. https://www.amazon.com/gp/feature.html?ie=UTF8&docId=1000765261
18. https://read.amazon.com/
19. https://www.amazon.com/b?ie=UTF8&node=16571048011

	Input File Type	Output Format	Operating System	Layers	Stand-alone
Paint	BMP, JPEG, PNG, GIF, TIFF, ICO, WEBP, HEIC	BMP, JPEG, PNG, GIF, TIFF, ICO, HEIC	Windows	X	√
Paint.NET	BMP, JPEG, PNG, GIF, TIFF, ICO, WEBP, TGA, DDS, PDN	BMP, JPEG, PNG, GIF, TIFF, ICO, WEBP, TGA, DDS, PDN	Windows	√	√
Paintbrush	BMP, PNG, JPEG, GIF, TIFF	BMP, PNG, JPEG, GIF, TIFF	Mac	√	√
GIMP	BMP, JPEG, PNG, GIF, TIFF, EXR, ICO, WEBP, TGA, DDS, HEIF, PSP, PSD, EPS, PS, XWD, XPM, PCX, DNG, SVG, MNG, PDF, DCM, PIX, FLI, WMF, GBR, XCF, raw	BMP, JPEG, PNG, GIF, TIFF, EXR, ICO, WEBP, TGA, DDS, HEIF, PSD, EPS, PS, XWD, XPM, PCX, PDF, DCM, PIX, FLI, HTML, GBR, XCF, raw	Windows, Mac, Linux	√	√
OIE	BMP, JPEG, PNG, GIF	BMP, JPEG, PNG, GIF	Windows, Mac, Linux	√	X
Canva	BMP, JPEG, PNG, GIF, TIFF, SVG	BMP, JPEG, PNG, GIF, TIFF, PDF, PPTX	Windows, Mac, Linux	√	X
Photoshop	BMP, JPEG, PNG, GIF, TIFF, EXR, PSD, PSB, EPS, PBM, DNG, PIC, PICT, PDF, DCM,	BMP, JPEG, PNG, GIF, TIFF, EXR, PSD, PSB, EPS, PBM, DNG, PIC,	Windows, Mac	√	√

raw	PICT, PDF, DCM, raw

Paint (Paintbrush for Windows)

MICROSOFT WINDOWS INCLUDES the **granddaddy of free raster graphics (bitmap) editing programs** since 1.000 B.C. It comes with many of the commonly used functions to manipulate images and a full RGB color palette. Great for cropping, quick touch ups, and overlaying text, if you don't need multiple layers for that perfect placement.

Paint.NET[20]

THE FREEWARE PROGRAM offers everything you missed in Paint and then some. Support for layers and the magic wand lets you create complex compositions from multiple images. If you look closely at my cover image, you may notice the individual layers used. Many plugins that offer new or enhanced features.

Paintbrush[21]

MAC USERS DESPAIRING over the loss of MacPaint can download **this free equivalent to Paint** that adds layers to a similar tools arsenal.

The GIMP[22]

AS THE NAME GNU IMAGE Manipulation Program implies, this stand-alone app is part of the free and open-source GNU software collection, around since the antiquity of desktop computers. Lots of tools and layers for everyone including your inner Linux lover. Great if you need to convert an esoteric format into something a web browser will understand.

---

20. https://www.getpaint.net/
21. https://paintbrush.sourceforge.io/
22. https://www.gimp.org/

Online Image Editor[23]

IF YOU PREFER ONLINE tools, **this free browser-based equivalent to Paint** offers lots of tools, layers, and conversion functionality.

Canva[24]

YOU CAN USE **browser-based** freemium Canva for free, but you need to upgrade to the premium version to unlock more features. A **large template library** has gained it a following for book cover and other design.

Adobe Photoshop[25]

LIKE OFFICE 365, THE **de facto industry standard in raster graphics editing now comes as a monthly subscription service**, if you need its advanced features. Many plugins that offer new or enhanced features.

Resources

ALLI: 48 Best Writing and Self-Publishing Tools for Authors: Jay Artale[26]

The Creative Penn: How To Format Your Ebook And Print Book with Vellum[27]

Once you have all your pieces and tools together, wash and style your hair in celebration. You're ready to enter the wonderland of Draft2Digital.

---

23. https://www.online-image-editor.com/

24. https://www.canva.com/

25. https://www.adobe.com/products/photoshop.html

26. http://selfpublishingadvice.org/
   best-tools-of-the-self-publishing-trade-running-an-author-business-jay-artale

27. https://www.thecreativepenn.com/2018/02/21/
   how-to-format-your-ebook-and-print-book-with-vellum

6. Creating Your Sales Page

———

The previous sections showed how **many pieces have to come together to publish a book**. The journey starts with the dreaded metadata on the details page. Naturally, the tools challenge your hairline.

At the Zon, you get to rip your thatch out before you even reach the fun part of converting your book. Start at D2D. But if you must publish at KDP, the following chapters will guide you through the major steps for either.

Both Draft2Digital and Amazon have released many blogs and videos with detailed instructions. I've included a sprinkling in the **Resources** sections.

If you haven't done so yet, **create accounts for Draft2Digital, KDP, and Author Central (AC)**[1]. All Amazon services share the same credentials, but you have to log in separately at every website.

Resources

WRITEPUBLISHSELL: Setting up your Amazon Author Central Account (VIDEO)[2]

TIP D2D colors the most commonly used button orange and the less common one gray. Even though for Windows users the gray buttons may look inactive, they're fully functional.

To add a new book, both platforms have big buttons at the top of their [Bookshelf], called [**My Books**] at D2D and **Your Books** at KDP.

---

1. **https://authorcentral.amazon.com**

2. https://www.youtube.com/watch?v=TSD0PICo8cc

D2D

THE [**Add New Book**] button covers both electronic and print versions. If you plan to let D2D distribute to Amazon for you, you can save yourself the *hairache* and skip the **Zon** steps.

Figure 6-1: D2D Add New Book Button

Resources

D2D: Setting Up a New Book (VIDEO)[3]

D2D: Exploring the Ebook Tab on the View Book Details Page (VIDEO)[4]

D2D: D2D Print - Starting a Print Book Project from Scratch (VIDEO)[5]

Zon

IF YOU WANT TO PUBLISH separately at KDP, start with the [**+ Kindle eBook**] button. You'll have to enter the same data for the paperback separately or copy it from one format to another with the buttons that appear later.

---

3. https://www.youtube.com/watch?v=zevfgrLVq90

4. https://www.youtube.com/watch?v=BL06yohC8Kc

5. https://www.youtube.com/watch?v=ST27j8eTXFQ

Figure 6-2: KDP New Book Buttons

TIP Don't leave a page without clicking the buttons to save or go to the next step. You may lose your entries. Don't worry about questionable data. Nothing is final until you publish. Of course, having everything ready will let you zip through.

6.1. Metadata

BOTH KDP AND THE STREAMLINED D2D start with the metadata, the **sales information that help identify the book. You have to enter title, author, and at least one BISAC code as category** before you can proceed to the next step. Like IngramSpark, D2D won't even let you save your work without these minimum entries. KDP has a [**Save as Draft**] button.

Worse, every time you update certain information that impacts later steps, you must go through the preview and acceptance all over. I'll say it again. **Have all the metadata including prices ready, enter everything at once, and save yourself extra work and hair loss.**

D2D

D2D ADDED A NEW WRINKLE in their latest revamp. Without a front cover image, you can merely set your book for preorder. Since the **sales pages only need a thumbnail derived from the cover**, you can upload a work in progress. It should reflect your final design, though. Do you see the pattern? **Producing pieces in the order of the Self-Publishing Checklist makes the process more efficient.**

The next fields in Figure 6-3 require little explanation. You may still want to hover the cursor over the question mark in a yellow circle ❓. The **help bubbles often include tips to optimize your data selection**.

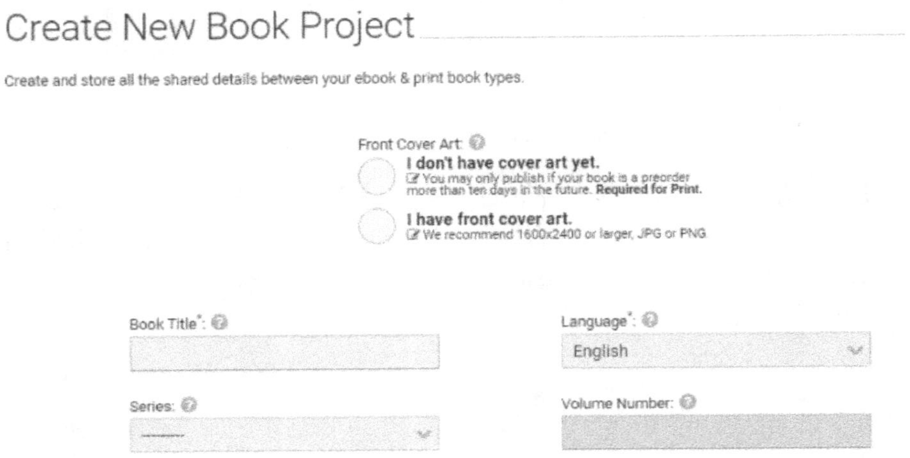

Create New Book Project

Create and store all the shared details between your ebook & print book types.

Front Cover Art: ❓
I don't have cover art yet.
☑ You may only publish if your book is a preorder more than ten days in the future. **Required for Print.**

I have front cover art.
☑ We recommend 1600x2400 or larger, JPG or PNG.

Book Title*: ❓

Language*: ❓
English

Series: ❓

Volume Number: ❓

Figure 6-3: D2D Metadata Entry

UNLIKE AMAZON, DRAFT2DIGITAL **doesn't give you the option to specify an edition or subtitle**. The book's publishing history with D2D determines what edition they list on their copyright page. Some of the bigger vendors, Amazon included, check for a **match between the metadata and the text on the cover. Don't fudge a subtitle into the title or series name**. If you *must* have that feature, publish elsewhere.

D2D's simple process aims to save the locks of most authors, who write in narrative style with few pictures or highlights. Subtitles matter more for non-fiction books like how-to manuals. D2D's converter doesn't do well with their complex formatting. The full-color print version of this guide, for instance, comes from KDP. IngramSpark also supports subtitles and editions.

Language defaults to English. D2D lets you pick many more than KDP, including regional or historical dialects, such as Old French from before 1400, Swiss German, or South American Indian Languages.

TIP Don't get cute with the selected language. Amazon, for example, removes e-books in languages that Kindle doesn't support.

Optionally, you can enter a **Series** name, which joins a list for use with future books, and the **Volume Number, the order of the book within the series.** Many vendors show that information on the sales page. Some do not, so D2D recommends **repeating that data in the description.**

TIP Unlike the freeform **Series field** at most vendors, **D2D uses a dropdown list, thus ensuring consistent spelling** across books and **correct creation of series pages.**

Zon

OTHER THAN THE DIFFERENCES mentioned, KDP data entry in Figure 6-4 matches D2D's.

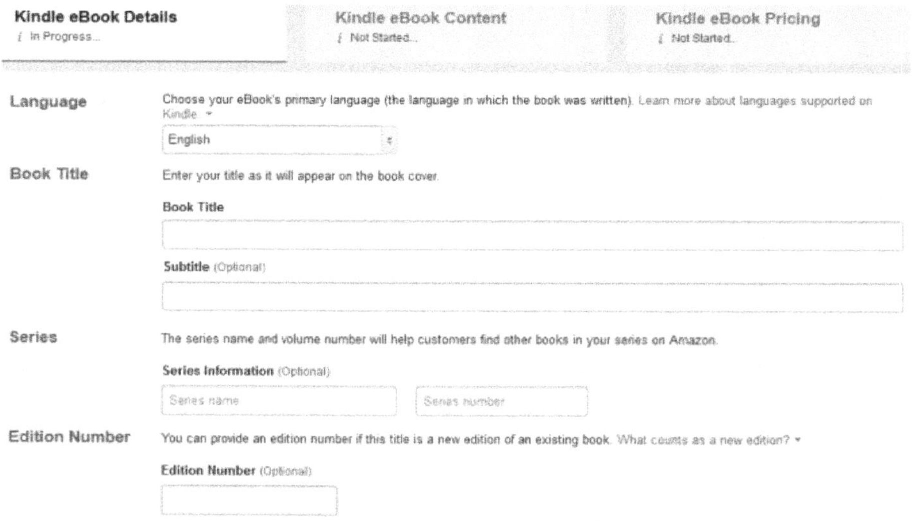

Figure 6-4: KDP Metadata Entry

D2D

IF YOU PUBLISH UNDER an imprint, you can add it under **Publisher** in Figure 6-5. The name shows up on the generated End Matter pages **Title** and **About the Publisher**.

Figure 6-5: D2D Authors, Publisher, and Keywords Entry

D2D USES A **prioritized list to specify names** from a list maintained under [**My Account**] | [**Contributor Profiles**]. The top entry becomes the primary authors listed first on sales pages. Search engines don't care about the order, so list everyone who contributed. If one of your cohorts threatens to scalp you over the top honor, you can rearrange the list by dragging the names up or down. Once you've settled the matter in a barbershop quartet sing-off, you can remove the loser by clicking the [**X**] next to the name.

TIP You only specify the author names here. The selection of the displayed profile information happens separately for end matter (see 8.1) and on the back cover (see 9.3).

Unlike KDP, **non-author contributors have their own lists below the Description** as shown in Figure 6-13. I could tell you the reason why, but then I'd have to shear you.

Zon

SINCE KDP DOESN'T USE the **Publisher** information, the print book has no entry field for it. You can optionally specify one on the [**Content**] tab of the e-book. **Kindle Create will ask for the information** if you add a Title page under **Frontmatter**.

The **Primary Author has separate entry fields**. All other authors and contributors share an expanding list. Click the button to select a type, then fill in the fields. The data saves with the rest of the page when you click the buttons at the bottom. To add more names, click [**Add Another**]. If someone loses a sing-off, click [**Remove**].

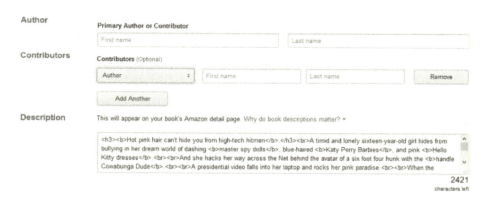

Figure 6-6: KDP Authors, Publisher, and Description Entry

TIP The **Paperback Details tab** has a **separate field for the primary author's middle name**. The Kindle tab doesn't.

Resources

D2D: Complete Walk-Thru (VIDEO)[6]

D2D: Frequently Asked Questions (FAQ)[7]

---

6. http://d2d.tips/ebookwalkthru

7. https://www.draft2digital.com/faq

D2D: How to Convert Your Manuscript to eBook with Draft2Digital (VIDEO)[8]

D2D: Setting Up Your Ebook - Ebook Publishing Step 1: Details (VIDEO)[9]

D2D: D2D Print - Converting Your Ebook to Print - Step 1: Details (VIDEO)[10]

D2D: D2D Print - Step 1: Details (VIDEO)[11]

Keith Wheeler Books: How to Publish a Book | Draft2digital Tutorial[12]

Sean Dollwet How to Publish Your Books on Draft2Digital Step-by-Step

Author Business with Rebecca: How to Go Wide After Leaving Kindle Unlimited with Draft2Digital[13]

Emma Right TV: How to use draft2digital to format your ebooks and print books[14]

Anthony J. Fleischmann Jr.: How to Easily Format a Paperback book with Draft 2 Digital[15]

KDP: eBook Metadata Guidelines (VIDEO)[16]

KDP: Paperback Metadata Guidelines (VIDEO)[17]

Apple Books: Apple Books Formatting Guidelines[18]

---

8. https://www.youtube.com/watch?v=fE1VQd870Mg

9. https://www.youtube.com/watch?v=v4dLDKpZjVw

10. https://www.youtube.com/watch?v=iQyfSQQqsaY

11. https://www.youtube.com/watch?v=56JkPSYaDc8

12. https://www.youtube.com/watch?v=22aS2LSdiPU

13. https://www.youtube.com/watch?v=lbp86GTCzZQ

14. https://www.youtube.com/watch?v=veFWCWNVemg

15. https://www.youtube.com/watch?v=FqCIl7valzE

16. https://kdp.amazon.com/en_US/help/topic/G201097560

17. https://kdp.amazon.com/en_US/help/topic/G201953870

18. https://help.apple.com/itc/applebooksstoreformatting/en.lproj/static.html

Carla King: A Self-Publisher's Guide to Metadata for Books[19]

AC: Amazon Details pages[20]

6.2. Keywords

KEYWORDS, WHAT D2D calls **Search Terms,** are phrases up to 50 characters in length that should closely match what a reader looking for your book **would type into a search field**. The two platforms treat data entry differently, as shown in Table 6-1.

Table 6-1: Keyword Entry Comparison

	Keywords	Comma-separated Entry	Reorder
Amazon	7	X	X
D2D	unlimited	√	√

D2D

YOU CAN ENTER AS MANY phrases as you want to create a **prioritized list**. The field (see Figure 6-5) accepts multiple terms separated by commas, simplifying copying a list from a metadata file.

Vendors take categories off the top until they've maxed out their sales page entries. Even though Amazon could use more, they only accept five from D2D. Again, **some vendors only use one or two off the top. Put the most-searched keywords first**. See 4.1 for suggestions to optimize your selection.

Like other prioritized lists, dragging entries changes the order. The [**X**] button removes entries.

TIP You can't highlight D2D **Search Terms** to **copy** them because the entries are actually buttons. On the super-secret **Metadata pages**, you *can* **highlight the entire list** or use the [**Copy**] button. On the **My Books** or

---

19. http://mediashift.org/2010/10/a-self-publishers-guide-to-metadata-for-books285

20. https://authorcentral.amazon.com/gp/help/144-2626472-3329002?ie=UTF8&topicID=202209530

View Book page, click the cover thumbnail. Or, on the **Ebook** or **Print Details** pages click the red [Edit shared metadata and cover] link.

Zon

AMAZON USES ALL SEVEN of its keywords in Figure 6-7, so their order doesn't matter. Since each has its own field, you can only copy entries from a list one by one.

Keywords	Choose up to 7 keywords that describe your book. How do I choose keywords? ▾ Your Keywords (Optional)	Cyberspiracy Print Book
	cyberthriller	pink hair
	presidential election books	hacking stories
	young adult coming of age fiction	fun
	technothriller	

Keywords	Enter up to 7 search keywords that describe your book. How do I choose keywords? ▾ Your Keywords (Optional)	Cyberspiracy E-book
	teenage female protagonist	us presidential election
	cyberbullying	young adult thriller
	political thrillers fiction	action thriller
	young adult fiction for girls	

Figure 6-7: KDP Keywords Entry for Cyberspiracy

KDP MAINTAINS **separate keyword lists for the e- and print book**. You can see the different entries I made for Cyberspiracy. **Even if you link the two formats, searches will not work across all fourteen phrases.** For instance, typing in "cyberbullying pink hair" in either store will find neither edition. This example also shows the limits of including keywords in text on the sales page, since the heroine's pink hair appears at the beginning of the description in both stores.

6.3. Categories ∩∩∩

SUPERFICIALLY, ENTERING categories seems simple other than the gigantic BISAC list you have to wade through. Of course, if you want your twenty extra Amazon ones, you'll have to go through the hairy nightmare described in under I'll See Your 4 and Raise You 20 (see 4.1).

Table 6-2: Category Entry Comparison

	Categories	Same for Print	Reorder
Amazon	2 + 10	X	X
D2D	5	√	√

D2D

AS SHOWN IN Table 6-2 and Figure 6-8, you can **add up to five categories by selecting them from the expanding Subject List.** The BISAC code turns green and pops into the field to the right.

TIP If the short view with only 10 entries annoys you, do your research on the easily searchable Complete BISAC Subject Headings List[21] webpages. After an update, the vendor lists may lag behind.

Typing keywords into the **Filter BISACS** field and hitting [Enter] **narrows the list to applicable top-level categories.** The match is exact. The words "young adult" will find the matching category, whereas "adult young" displays "No results found." To reset the list, clear the field and hit [Enter].

Try all your keywords in the search field. You may be surprised what top-level categories come up. Searching their BISAC pages for those keywords may yield categories you never thought of.

---

21. https://bisg.org/page/BISACEdition

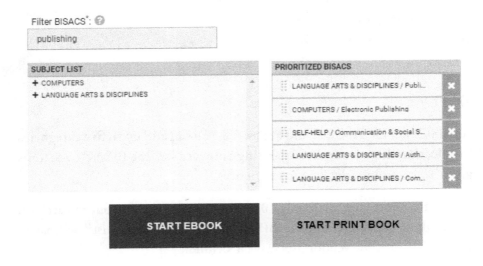

Figure 6-8: D2D Categories Entry

VENDORS TAKE CATEGORIES off the top until they've maxed out their sales page entries. Even though Amazon could use more, they only accept five from D2D. Again, **some vendors only use one or two off the top**. Pick five BISAC codes, then order them. **Put the best match first**, *especially for erotica* (see 4.1). Second, add the next best match or the best match in a different broad category for more visibility.

Like other prioritized lists, dragging entries changes the order. The [**X**] button removes entries, or you can click the green entry on the left again.

TIP You can't highlight D2D **BISAC Subjects** to **copy** them because the entries are actually buttons. On the super-secret **Metadata pages**, you *can* **highlight the entire list** or use the [**Copy**] button. On the **My Books** or **View Book** page, click the cover thumbnail. Or, on the **Ebook** or **Print Details** pages click the red [Edit shared metadata and cover] link.

Zon

TO PICK YOUR TWO CATEGORIES, click [**Set categories**] at the top of Figure 6-9 and select from the partial BISAC list. **Amazon uses all**

entries, whether from here or their special procedure, so **the order doesn't matter.**

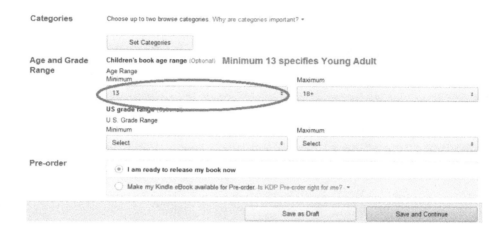

Figure 6-9: KDP Categories Entry (E-book Version)

TO REMOVE A CATEGORY, click [**Set Categories**] and then the appropriate Remove link at the bottom of the dialog box shown in Figure 6-10.

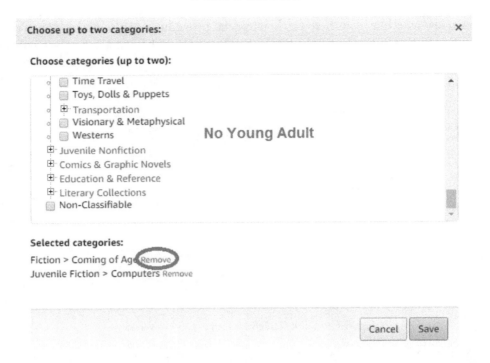

Figure 6-10: KDP Partial BISAC List

TIP You can highlight and copy the two categories from the book's KDP sales page. **To get a list of all the categories**, including those you requested through the special procedure, **you need to use a tool like BkLnk[22]** as shown in But How? (see 4.1)

The BISG **split Young Adult (YA) Fiction from Juvenile Fiction (JF)** years ago. As you can see from Figure 6-10, Amazon still hasn't updated their BISAC list. **To get into Amazon's YA categories**, select the best matches from **Juvenile Fiction *and* specify a Minimum of 13 for Children's book age range** in Figure 6-9. On Germany's Amazon.de, a minimum of 12 will put the book in YA. For the US and UK stores, 12 could go either ways depending on other factors that the Zon doesn't list in the help articles. Conversely, if you want **Children's categories**, you *must* **set the Minimum age to 11 or lower.**

---

22. https://www.bklnk.com/categories5.php

KDP gives no warning during data entry that the separate and *optional* **Age and Grade Range** section affects **Categories**. Yet, they enforce the separation of YA and JF categories. If you don't set the correct age, the Books Store won't show your book in *any* YA categories.

Confused? It gets worse. The **Paperback Details** screen shown in Figure 6-11 doesn't have an **Age** section, only one for **Adult Content**. Despite multiple support requests, my YA book never showed up in Teen & Young Adult. In another case of *one hand doesn't know*, AC took over paperback categories. KDP knows the age range for your e-book, but someone at AC needs to set it for paperbacks. What could possibly go wrong (for six months)?

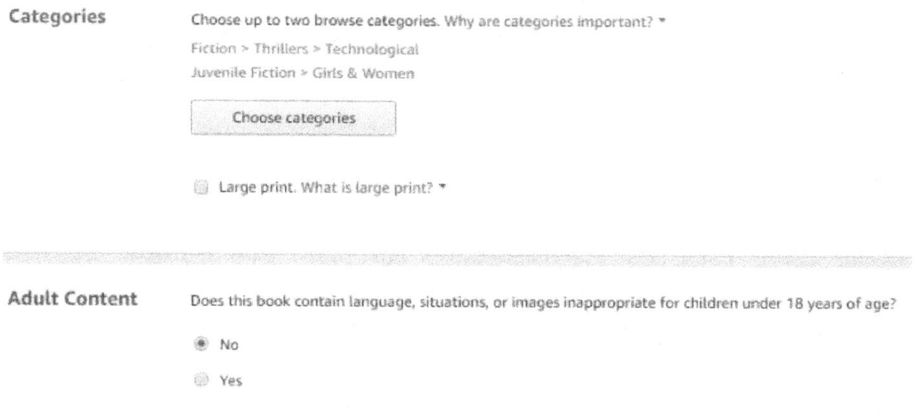

Categories
Choose up to two browse categories. Why are categories important? ▾
Fiction > Thrillers > Technological
Juvenile Fiction > Girls & Women

Choose categories

☐ Large print. What is large print? ▾

Adult Content
Does this book contain language, situations, or images inappropriate for children under 18 years of age?
◉ No
○ Yes

Figure 6-11: KDP Categories Entry (Print Book Version)

LINKING THE E- AND print book supposedly synchronizes the Age Range. Make sure to specify it before selecting **Link Books** in the [...] menu of the **Your Books entries**. If, after a few days, a tool like BkLnk doesn't show the correct categories for your print book, call Amazon to have them fix the Age Range.

BISAC category options displayed in KDP **won't match the store websites** exactly because the **Departments** shown follow Amazon proprietary browse categories.

Resources

KDP: Browse Categories[23]

With the general metadata entered, D2D's process now splits into print or e-book depending which button you hit to save your data. The next page for either formats looks similar and first asks for your manuscript. We'll cover that in 7.1.

TIP D2D buttons related to **e-books are blue**, those for **print gold**.

6.4. Pre-Order

THE **Release Date** comes next. Asking for one may seem odd. If you finish the **Publish step before the date in this field, the sales pages become active at all vendors that allow pre-orders.** Customers can buy the book, but won't receive it until the Release Date.

D2D

YOU CAN SPECIFY **separate dates for print and e-book** on their respective **Details** pages, for example in Figure 6-12. **Not all vendors support pre-orders.** D2D currently **can't set them up at Amazon.**

Figure 6-12: D2D Release Date Entry

---

23. https://kdp.amazon.com/en_US/help/topic/G200652170

Zon

TO SPECIFY AN E-BOOK Release Date, change the selection at the bottom of Figure 6-9 to **Make my Kindle eBook available for Pre-order**. You can enter a date up to one year later. KDP will calculate and show by when you must submit your final manuscript—basically three days earlier. Miss the deadline and Amazon cancels your pre-orders and bans you for a year. Keep in mind that the Zon rejects manuscripts for a variety of reasons. Don't wait until the last minute to find out.

Pick a realistic date. You can delay your release up to 30 days **one time without penalty** *per* **account**. Miss again on *any* book and the one-year ban goes into effect.

If all your hair loss made you doubt your age and reach for your reading glasses, despair not. You don't need to search Figure 6-11 for a Pre-Order section. The print book has none. **You can't put a paperback on pre-order in KDP**. All kinds of conspiracy theories abound as to why. My lips are sewn. Even a freshly sharpened razor can't cut this deep, dark secret out of me.

Resources

KDP: Kindle eBook Pre-Order[24]

ALLi: Should Indie Authors offer Pre-Orders?[25]

6.5. Description ⌢⌢⌢

ENTERING THE BOOK DESCRIPTION will certainly ruin the remaining rug you spared from writing the description in 4.1. Don't slack off just yet, though. After the cover and title brought the prospect to your book page, you want to **use highlights and white space to best effect to close the deal**, particularly with the few lines visible above the fold.

---

24. https://kdp.amazon.com/en_US/help/topic/G201499380

25. https://selfpublishingadvice.org/should-indie-authors-offer-pre-orders-elizabeth-s-craig

Sales pages use the HyperText Markup Language (HTML) underlying webpages. All the tools generate output in that format, but limit you to a basic subset of those codes.

Most, but not all, vendors support **bold** and *italics* on sales pages. They fail to agree on much beyond that including blank lines. As Figure 4-1 shows, **you can't create one single layout that will display the same on every website**.

KDP has more flexibility, needing to cater only to one vendor, and even they can't make their description work consistently across the different stores.

D2D's What You See Is What You Get (WYSIWYG) **editor limits you from the start to common formatting supported by** *most* **sites**.

Draft2Digital's and Author Central's editors look and function similarly. As Table 6-3 shows, their **output differs considerably**.

Table 6-3: Description Formatting Comparison

	Button	Hotkey*	D2D	AC	ABDG	KDP
Bold	B	[Ctrl+B]	\<strong>	\<b>	\<strong>	\<b>, \<strong>
Italics	I	[Ctrl+I]	\<em>	\<i>	\<em>	\<i>, \<em>
Underline		[Ctrl+U]	X	\<u>	\<u>	\<u>
"Quoted"			X	\<q>		\<q>
~~Strike~~			X	\<s>	\<s>	\<s>
Subscript			X	\<sub>	\<sub>	\<sub>
Super script			X	\<sup>	\<sup>	\<sup>
—Line—			X	\<hr>	\<hr>	\<hr>
Blank Line		[Enter]	\<p>\ 	\<div>	\<p>\ 	\<p>, \
Bullet	☰		\<ul>\<li>	\<ul>\<li>	\<ul>\<li>	\<ul>\<li>
Numbered	☰		\<ol>\<li>	\<ol>\<li>	\<ol>\<li>	\<ol>\<li>
Heading			X	\<h1>-\<h6>	\<h1>-\<h6>	\<h1>-\<h6>
Undo		[Ctrl+Z]	√	√	√	√
Select All		[Ctrl+A]	√	√	√	√

*For Mac the hotkey combinations uses [Cmd] instead of [Ctrl]

**FOR BLANK LINES, SOME vendor sites use paragraphs \<p> and others line breaks \
. To achieve a somewhat consistent look, D2D combines both in its description.** Sites that ignore one or the other will have narrow spacing. Pages that use both paragraphs and line breaks will have wider spacing. That's actually an advantage, since the text appears easier on the eyes.

AC uses dividers for blank lines. **Most vendor sites, Amazon stores included, do not understand them**. You can paste rich text containing <p> or type them into the **EDIT HTML** tab without a problem. **Hard line breaks only work with a terminating slash**
. If you copy text created with
s into AC, it will strip them out.

The Amazon stores support the most HTML formatting of any vendor. AC or KDP, which doesn't even have a WYSIWYG editor, provide no easy way to apply the additional formatting, however. You either enter the code, or create the formatted description in an HTML editor such as MS Word. **Most of the third-party word processors produce code that KDP, AC, or D2D don't support**. A free online tool, Kindlepreneur's Amazon Book Description Generator[26] (ABDG), provides buttons to apply almost all the formatting Amazon understands.

The safest route to a universally accepted description is to create it in D2D. To enhance it for the Zon, **copy the formatted text to an editor with an HTML view such as AC or ABDG, then copy the code from there to KDP**.

Of course, every time you update the text in D2D, you have to reapply any additional formatting in KDP. I know, I know, by now you can sing the mantra in four-part harmony while combing your remaining hair: Have all the metadata ready, enter everything at once, and save yourself extra work and hair loss.

Because of the differences in HTML, **you can't copy a description edited in AC back to D2D or KDP**.

TIP A bug in D2D prevents copying of formatted text from AC, or between the e-book and print descriptions. You can **copy it to MS Word** or another HTML editor first, which will reformat it with its own codes. If you **then copy what looks like the same formatted text from Word into D2D**, it will sometimes correctly convert it to its own simple HTML.

---

26. https://kindlepreneur.com/amazon-book-description-generator/

D2D

THE FUZZ-FRIENDLY DESCRIPTION editor has buttons for **bold**, *italics*, bulleted (?) and numbered lists (1.). Clicking the button again turns off that format.

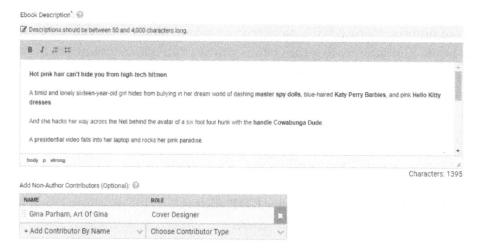

Figure 6-13: D2D Book Description Entry

A STATUS BAR BELOW the text shows the current HTML tags that apply to the cursor location. By using the same codes as websites, the editor's output works on the web in general.

TIP When **entering web addresses** or Uniform Resource Locators (URL), D2D requires the protocol (http:// or https://). **Avoid errors and extra typing by going to the page in a browser and copying the URL from the address bar**.

You can undo changes using [Ctrl+Z] in Windows and [Cmd+Z] in Mac. To cancel all modifications, click any of the blue buttons other than [**Save & Continue**] to go to a different page.

Zon

AS YOU CAN SEE FROM Figure 6-6, **KDP doesn't have a WYSIWYG editor.** You must enter any formatting as HTML code. Worse, the **Details** pages **don't have a preview function either.** To see how the formatted text will look, you have to enter enough data to publish the book at least in preorder. After a mandatory Amazon review, which may take 24 hours, the appropriate store's sales page will then show you the result. Do I have to spell out for you that this is a ~~stupid~~ inefficient process and to start at D2D?

Like other parts of KDP data entry, the editors **differ between print an e-book.** The latter renders the code as written. You can add returns to break up lines for readability without a problem. If you copy that formatted code to the **Paperback Details**, however, Amazon will render those returns as if they're *in the code.* The sales page thus contains extra blank lines.

Not surprisingly, the AC description editor doesn't add extra formatting for readability, as shown in Figure 6-14. Because of this inconsistency in formatting and the delay before seeing the results, **don't make changes to the description directly in either KDP editors.** Get the formatting right in D2D or ABDG and copy it from there.

You can undo changes using [Ctrl+Z] in Windows and [Cmd+Z] in Mac. To cancel all modifications, click any of the menu choices at the top and then [**Continue without Saving**] to go to a different page.

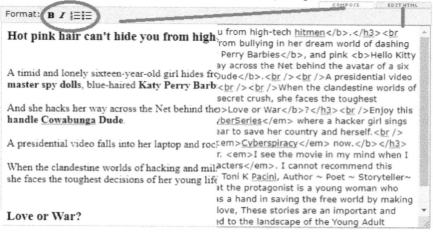

Figure 6-14: AC Description Editor

LIKE D2D, AC HAS BUTTONS for **bold**, *italics*, bulleted (•) and numbered lists (1.). Unlike D2D, the buttons don't adjust correctly to context as you move the cursor. They stay in the state you last selected.

AC supports the same tags that KDP does and then some. Select the [**Edit HTML**] tab to enter them as code.

You can undo changes using [Ctrl+Z] in Windows and [Cmd+Z] in Mac. Since the AC editor runs in a dialog box, you can't leave it by clicking on a link. To cancel all changes, click [**close**] or [**x**] at the top right. To save your work, click [**Preview**] to see the entire formatted description, then [**Save changes**].

Since D2D's editor doesn't have an HTML code view, you can't copy directly from it to KDP. Instead, paste the rich text description into AC, switch the view to the [**Edit HTML**] tab, then copy the code to KDP.

If you made changes in AC, the code may contain tags not supported by KDP like <div> or . Delete any code not listed in the above table before copying to prevent "Description contains an unsupported HTML tag" errors when saving. Since HTML codes come in pairs, you may want to remove the corresponding closing tag that starts with a slash, like . KDP does ignore any closing tags without a matching starting tag.

TIP The **data entry for a number of sections of the Amazon sales pages takes place at the much easier to use AC**. These include the **author page** and related items like **About the Author** or upcoming events, the back cover blurb, and the **editorial reviews**. See 12.3 for how to add books to your author page.

Resources

KINDLEPRENEUR: Amazon Book Description Generator[27], a free WYSIWYG editor

KDP: Supported HTML for Book Description[28]

AC: Editorial Reviews[29]

WritePublishSell: How to jazz up your book description on Amazon (VIDEO)[30]

---

27. https://kindlepreneur.com/amazon-book-description-generator/

28. https://kdp.amazon.com/en_US/help/topic/G201189630

29. https://authorcentral.amazon.com/gp/help?ie=UTF8&topicID=200649600

30. https://www.youtube.com/watch?v=JaellbQ6RKU

6.6. ISBN

AS MENTIONED IN 2.2, vendors use an International Standard Book Number (**ISBN**) **to identify a book worldwide.** That still holds true for paper, even for the Zon (check the URLs in their Book Store). When they started their Kindle Store, however, they decided to use their own Amazon Standard Identification Number (ASIN). Consequently, as Figure 6-17 shows, **you don't need an ISBN to publish an e-book on Amazon.**

You do at D2D to avoid duplications across its many vendors. If you don't provide an ISBN, the system assigns you one. Since D2D can distribute to Amazon, you can use that number across all vendors.

Unless the body differs significantly, you don't need separate IBSNs for the MOBI and EPUB versions. If you plan to go wide, get your ISBN from D2D. If you publish separately at Amazon, don't specify one.

A print book does requires a different ISBN from the e-book. To comply with industry standards, the Zon requires one too. If you don't want to purchase your own, let D2D distribute to Amazon. You could get away publishing with a KDP ISBN, but the industry frowns on the same book having two identifiers.

Resources

REEDSY: ISBN for Self-Publishers: The Complete Guide[31]

Draft2Digital: The Surprising Truth About ISBN[32]

D2D

THE ISBN CONCLUDES the **Details** section. You can provide your own or D2D will assign a free one of theirs, which identifies them as publisher for retail purposes. Once you published a format, you can't change its identifier.

---

31. https://blog.reedsy.com/how-to-get-an-isbn

32. https://www.draft2digital.com/blog/the-surprising-truth-about-isbn

If you want the ability to move the book to a different distributor, buy your own ISBNs.

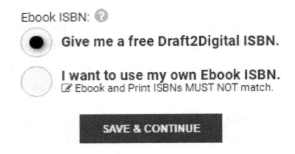

Figure 6-15: D2D ISBN Selection

[**Save & Continue**] takes you to the next page to complete the book's interior. You can return to [**Details**] by clicking [**Previous**] or the blue button on top.

Zon

THE ISBN ENTRY APPEARS on the **Content** page at different locations depending on the format, shown in Figure 6-16 and Figure 6-17. You can provide your own.

Otherwise, for print books, KDP will assign a free one of theirs, which identifies them as publisher for retail purposes. The ISBN becomes the ASIN. You can't change it once you published the paperback.

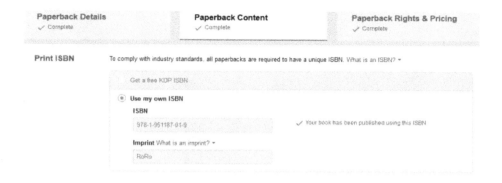

Figure 6-16: KDP Print ISBN Selection

FOR E-BOOKS, YOU CAN leave the field blank or request a free KDP one. Regardless, Amazon uses a separate ASIN as identifier in the stores.

Figure 6-17: KDP E-Book ISBN Selection

7. Interior

———

With the metadata done, we finally get to the fun part of book publishing—converting your manuscript. The procedure **takes a word processor format**—old and new Microsoft Word (DOC, DOCX), rich text format (RTF), and others—**to generate one of the common e-book formats** MOBI, EPUB, or PDF. The latter also serves as an input format for print on demand (POD).

You can use third-party tools like those given in Conversion. For most authors, the free, next-generation Draft2Digital and Kindle Create (KC) converters provide a good excuse to avoid hairline-raising Kindle Direct Publishing. Its upload functionality does *not* let you make any adjustments to the book's interior.

KC produces a proprietary KPF file format. You can't use the output with any platform other than KDP. At the risk of sounding repetitive: if you even think you may get within one hair's width of going wide with your narrative book, start at D2D.

7.1. Import

TABLE 7-1 shows the different file formats used by D2D and KDP. Both allow separate uploads for print and e-book. You can create two projects in KC or upload the same KPF file to KDP for the two formats. **For a narrative without complex formatting requirements, you usually don't need to upload separate files.**

Table 7-1: Manuscript Import Comparison

	File Type	Output Format	Max Size
D2D	DOC, DOCX, RTF, EPUB, ODT, PDF	EPUB, MOBI, PDF	50MB
KC	DOC, DOCX, PDF	KPF	
KDP	DOC, DOCX, RTF, EPUB, MOBI, AZW, HTML, Plain Text, KPF, PDF	MOBI, PDF, HTML	650MB / 8,000 pages

D2D

IN ADDITION TO MICROSOFT **Word**, you can upload **RTF**, and OpenDocument (**ODT**) formats. If you use the free Apache OpenOffice[1], LibreOffice[2], or Google Docs[3], you do *not* need to convert ODT to Word.

For an e-book, you can upload a finished EPUB, but you can't take advantage of the enhanced formatting D2D provides or generate end matter. You cannot upload PDF.

For print on demand (POD), you can upload a print-ready PDF, but you can't make changes to the interior in D2D. You cannot upload EPUB.

TIP D2D doesn't accept MOBI files. KDP does but only outputs MOBI and HTML. If you want to port a MOBI file to D2D, use Calibre to convert it to DOCX.

Imports take place at the top of each format's **Details** page (see Figure 6-12). Clicking on what looks like an entry field or the [**Browse**] button will let you select a document file. Once completed, the date and time of the upload and a [**Document on file download link**] appear. **The print book starts initially with the same file but doesn't update when you upload newer**

---

1. https://www.openoffice.org/

2. https://www.libreoffice.org/

3. https://docs.google.com/

versions of the e-book. You can click the [**Use Ebook File**] button to copy the newest one.

TIP By uploading your work in progress regularly, you can use **D2D as free cloud storage**. In the event you lose your computer and all your backups (you do have them, right?), you can download all your originals from D2D. KDP allows downloading MOBI and HTML (hidden in the Preview section) versions, but not the word processor files.

D2D allows a file size up to 50 MB. That may seem limiting. Even accounting for spaces and formatting, it still comes out to millions of words. Only a large number of high-resolution images can blow up a manuscript that much. For instance, the screenshots used in this guide averaged 125 KB or 0.125 MB.

Modern smartphones with their megapixel cameras routinely take pictures of 1 MB or more. For e-books, you can compress them to a smaller size without much loss using the tools in 5.3. In print, a lower resolution may result in fuzzy details. For example, inkjets produce the equivalent of 720 dots per inch (DPI) or more. At the minimum recommended 220 DPI (see 9.1), a five-inch wide image would require at least 1,100 pixels. If you need to include many large pictures where details matter, consider uploading a separate file for POD.

Resources

D2D: Setting Up a New Book (VIDEO)[4]

D2D: Setting Up Your Ebook - Ebook Publishing Step 1: Details (VIDEO)[5]

D2D: D2D Print - Converting Your Ebook to Print - Step 1: Details (VIDEO)[6]

D2D: D2D Print - Step 1: Details (VIDEO)[7]

---

4. https://www.youtube.com/watch?v=zevfgrLVq90

5. https://www.youtube.com/watch?v=v4dLDKpZjVw

6. https://www.youtube.com/watch?v=iQyfSQQqsaY

7. https://www.youtube.com/watch?v=56JkPSYaDc8

KC

Figure 7-1: Kindle Create Import

FOR BOOKS, INCLUDING narrative non-fiction, you **can only upload the two Microsoft Word formats** shown in Figure 7-1. If D2D's features don't satisfy your needs and you're starting with a different format, use one of the tools in 5.1 to convert the file to DOCX.

To publish graphic novels and multi-media books, KC will accept a **print-ready PDF**. You can't change formatting, only add advanced features such as a table of contents.

Resources

KDP: Kindle Create Tutorial[8]

---

8. https://kdp.amazon.com/en_US/help/topic/GYVL2CASGU9ACFVU

Zon

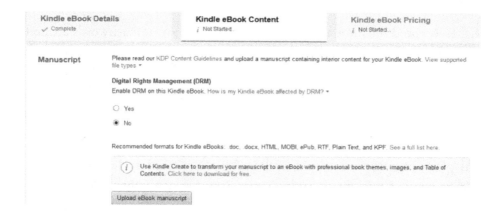

Figure 7-2: KDP E-Book Import

IN ADDITION TO MICROSOFT **Word**, KDP accepts **RTF**, **EPUB**, **MOBI**, even **HTML** formats. The latter comes in handy if you want to convert a blog saved from a webpage. Should you want to publish separately at Amazon to take advantage of its exclusive programs, you can ensure consistency in the look of your book by producing the MOBI with D2D and uploading it directly.

KDP also takes the intermediate **KPF** format produced by KC. No other platform does.

For POD, you can upload a print-ready PDF. You can upload EPUB, but **not classic MOBI**, only the more advanced **AZW** version.

KDP takes files as large as 650MB, a gigantic format for anything other than multi-media.

7.2. Document Formatting for E-book ◠◠◠◠

THE YOUNG DIGITAL PUBLISHING industry hasn't yet established universal standards. The deep chasm between MOBI and EPUB demonstrates that clearly. Apple Books added their own multi-media extensions that require a tool like Apple Pages to create.

KDP accepted the limited formatting of early e-books. Smashwords created its own conventions to add automatic formatting during conversion. KC now supports features like drop caps and ornamental scene breaks, bundled into **themes to quickly spruce up the interior** (see 7.5), but with a manual process. D2D chose a middle ground, combining automatic formatting through themes with some manual intervention.

All platforms agree on bold and *Italics*. MS Word styles became the recommended minimum body formatting, but even there the vendors' interpretations differ widely. If you insist on publishing separately at KDP, prepare yourself for extra work and author-pattern baldness.

I ran a test document formatted as paperback through the three converters to illustrate common issues you may have to deal with.

¶

Title Style

① *Cyberspiracy*¶

② 4 blank lines

Wolf· O'Rourc¶

③ 72 pt
Spacing ¶

④ Bold **RoRo¶**
Italic *Las·Vegas* ¶

Copyright¶

¶ ¶
------------Page Break------------

Figure 7-3: MS Word Document for Conversion Test

1. The Microsoft Word styles **Heading 1** and **Title**.

2. Four blank lines as **page break**.

3. Vertical **Spacing**.

4. **Bold** and *italics* formatting.

5. **Headers** and **Footers**.

6. **Drop caps**.

7. Two and three blank lines or three asterisks (***) as **scene breaks**.

8. **Images** in line with text.

D2D

TO ENSURE COMPATIBILITY across all devices, **Draft2Digital only supports basic formatting common in narrative books**. It can't properly convert advanced formatting such as vertical spacing, colors, lines, and tables.

The conversion follows the conventions established by Smashwords. Vertical spacing vanishes into thin hair. **Minimize your headaches by taking advantage of the formatting built into the generated end matter and themes**.

D2D automatically formats the paragraph following a chapter title or scene break with drop caps or phrase caps (see 7.5) as specified by the theme. You don't have to apply a style or formatting to every first paragraph. To turn off this behavior, select a minimalist theme without those frills.

Figure 7-4 and Figure 7-5 show the results for the test document.

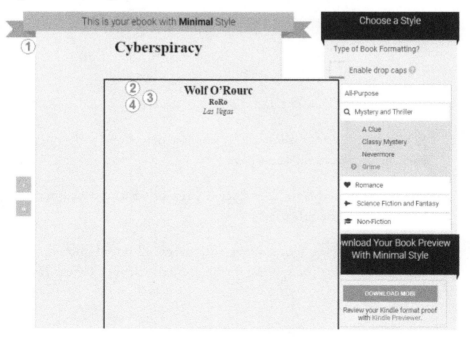

Figure 7-4: D2D Conversion Test Title

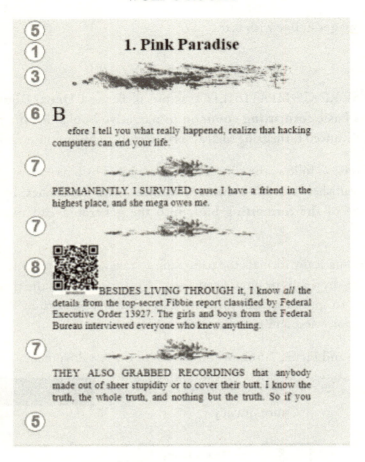

Figure 7-5: D2D Conversion Test Body

1. **Heading 1** and **Title** used for chapter detection by default. Each chapter starts on a new page.

2. Four or more blank lines force a **page break** and a **chapter break** even on the title page.

3. Vertical **Spacing** Ignored. On title pages, all lines bunch up. Chapter titles use the spacing specified by the theme (**Grime** in this example).

4. **Bold** and *italics* formatting converted.

5. **Headers** and **Footers** ignored.

6. **Drop caps** don't convert correctly. Specifying them as part of the theme overwrites the faulty import.

7. Two and three blank lines, or those with only asterisks (***) converted to **ornamental scene breaks** as specified by the theme.

8. **Images** in line with text screw up text reflow.

KC

AMAZON KEEPS UPPING automation capabilities in KC. Compared to D2D, the rudimentary chapter detection still requires considerable human intervention to clean up. In particular, KC requires you to designate each first paragraph if you didn't apply drops caps in MS Word.

As shown in Figure 7-6, KC supports most Word formatting, including vertical spacing, drop caps, colors, lines, and tables.

CYBERSPIRACY

Wolf O'Rourc

RoRo
Las Vegas

Figure 7-6: KC Conversion Test

1. **Heading 1** and **Title** used for chapter detection by default. Each chapter starts on a new page.

2. Four blank lines become vertical **Spacing**.

3. Vertical **Spacing** converted.

4. **Bold** and *italics* formatting converted.

5. **Headers** and **Footers** ignored.

6. **Drop caps** converted.

7. Two and three blank lines converted into vertical spacing that you can only remove by changing the paragraph **Spacing** under **Formatting**. Three asterisks (***) converted as is. You have to specify each line where you want an **ornamental scene break** specified by the theme.

8. **Images** in line with text screw up text reflow.

Zon

YOU GET THE BASIC FORMATTING you applied in MS Word. **KDP has no themes or capabilities to change the body after the import** and directs you to KC instead. That means no automatic page breaks, vertical spacing, or ornamental elements not created in the Word document.

As shown in Figure 7-7, KDP supports most Word formatting, including vertical spacing, drop caps, colors, lines, and tables, but often with a haircut to the dimensions.

Cyberspiracy

Wolf O'Rourc

RoRo
Las Vegas

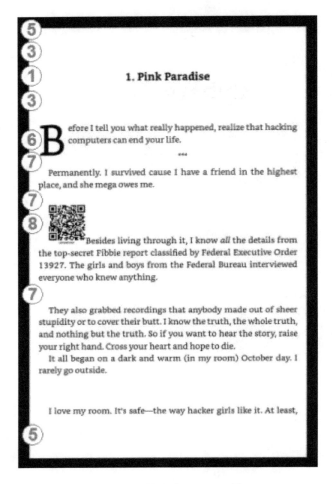

Figure 7-7: KDP Conversion Test

1. **Heading 1** and **Title** used for chapter title detection. Beyond formatting the line, KDP does *not* use the information for automatic page breaks or table of contents generation.

2. Four blank lines converted.

3. Vertical **Spacing** converted, but the dimensions don't match Word.

4. **Bold** and *italics* formatting converted.

5. **Headers** and **Footers** ignored.

6. **Drop caps** converted.

7. Two and three blank lines or three asterisks (***) converted as is. KDP has no **ornamental scene breaks.**

8. **Images** in line with text screw up text reflow.

7.3. Formatting Recommendations

The cleaner your starting document, the better your conversion results. Extra spaces or tabs may cause e-readers to reflow text incorrectly.

All Word documents start with the **Normal style** for the body. Most vendors agree with using the built-in **Heading 1 style for chapter titles.** Deviating from these conventions causes problems. I could write a whole book on formatting with word processors (and I did, *Word Wizardry for Writers*[9]).

TIP The major word processors have **functions to make formatting characters visible.** In MS Word, click the Show/Hide button ¶ or [Ctrl+*] (numeric keypad only).

The following list details common items to avoid.

- **Don't center text or images with spaces or tabs.** Create a **Centered** style based on **Normal** with a paragraph alignment of "centered" and *no indent*. Delete the spaces or tabs and apply the style instead.

- **Don't use tabs or spaces to indent paragraphs.** For consistency in the body text, set an indent by modifying the Normal style. If you used tabs instead of indents, remove them with a global search and replace. MS Word represents a tab character with "^t" in the **Find what** field. If you instead used spaces, search for them at the beginning of lines with "^p " (a paragraph mark followed

---

9. *http://www.wolforourc.com/writes/word-magic*

by a space) and replace with "**^p**" until Word finds no more. The Quick Guides give detailed steps for various word processors.

• **Don't use multiple blank lines for vertical spacing**. E-readers will separate paragraphs based on their own settings. To positions elements, for example on the title page, add **Spacing Before** or **After** in the **Paragraph** formatting. For chapter titles, add the **Spacing** to the **Heading 1** style. Any theme settings will overrides yours anyway.

• **Don't add drop caps**. In Word, you have to manually format every chapter. D2D lets you include them as part of the theme with one click.

• **Avoid uncommon symbols**. Although supported by word processors, wingdings or emojis may turn into question marks. Replace them with regular characters or insert them as inline images (as done in the **TIP** above).

• **Avoid uncommon bullet styles**. If the bullets disappear in the preview, type in a simple symbol that many devices can display such as a dash (-). If your book contains many lists, clicking on the triangle next to the **Bullets** button ( ) lets you **Define New Bullet** using regular text characters.

• **Don't place large images in line with text.** As you saw in the conversion test, e-readers have problems reflowing paragraphs with images taller than the line height. A centered image in a paragraph by itself looks best. For consistency, use the **Centered** style from above or create a separate **Image** style.

• **Place large images on the chapter title page**. The e-reader may reflow large images onto a new page, leaving lots of white space on the preceding page. Since a new chapter always starts on a fresh page, you minimize extra breaks.

- **Don't link images without inserting them.** To allow you to update images easily, MS Word lets you link to files stored in a folder without actually adding them to the document. That causes no problems when printing from your computer. The conversion of the uploaded file takes place on a server somewhere in the cloud. Since it doesn't have access to the images on your hard drive, it puts in placeholders such as red Xs. If you want to be able to update images without reinserting them, use the **Insert and Link** option. Field update functions such as [F9] will then refresh the document content from the external file. In case you're wondering, KC running on your computer does insert linked images during conversion.

- **Avoid unusual scene break symbols.** Two blank lines always work. Using three asterisks needlessly creates more work. First, you need to apply a Centered style to them each time. Second, if you type three asterisks and hit [Enter] afterwards, Word will convert them into a dashed border line. These are difficult to remove later, so use **Undo** immediately.

- **Avoid images as scene break symbols.** They create more work for you and the e-readers. First, you need to apply a **Centered** style to them each time or copy them from templates. Second, you add an additional image that the device needs to render and that increases the file size. Also, keep in mind that many devices don't use a white background. Some may not understand a transparent background (see 7.5) either. If you don't mind all the extra work, keep any images you use small and simple. Cyberspiracy's pink bow, for instance, only uses up about 200 bytes (0.0002 MB) each time.

- **Avoid columns and tables.** Many converters and e-book readers have problems with them.

The following recommendations apply to each tool specifically.

D2D

- Since D2D ignores **vertical spacing** and converts blank lines to something else, either use a simple layout for end matter or have it generated. Let the theme handle chapter title formatting and spacing.

- If you use the theme's **ornamental scene breaks**, create them from blank lines to save yourself the hassle of formatting asterisks. If you prefer them for visibility, you can avoid the occasional conversion to dash lines by only using two or one. D2D will convert *any number of* asterisks on a line by themselves into scene breaks, even if you leave them left aligned. You don't need extra spacing around them, as the theme adds that.

- If you use a theme **without ornamental scene breaks**, D2D will leave yours as is. If you prefer symbols to blank lines, three plus signs (+++) won't turn into a border line in MS Word. Three tildes (~), hash marks (#), asterisks (*), dashes (-), and equal signs (=) will.

- Since D2D can't convert **drop caps** (see 7.5), turn them on in the theme instead. Don't bother with the laborious process of adding them in the word processor.

- Since D2D has themes with **phrase caps** (see 7.5), you can save yourself the hassle of capitalizing the beginning of sentences in the word processor.

- Unfortunately, scientific authors will continue to suffer from traction alopecia. **The D2D conversion removes all lines and boxes**. Tables turn into left-aligned, borderless, tabbed text, which may spill across lines. See the example in Figure 7-16.

- **The converter only supports black and white text**. Any font and background colors disappear. Don't rely on color to distinguish text. For instance, this guide uses red and green for "yes" and "no" in tables, but also distinguishes the two through checkmarks and crosses. See the example in Figure 7-16.

• D2D will use any table of contents it finds, including a typed one with a title such as "Contents." If you want it to generate a table of contents with all the detected chapters hyperlinked, omit one in the manuscript.

KC

• KC does a poor job on chapter detection if the manuscript has multiple levels of headings like this guide does. If you want automatic end matter generation, use Draft2Digital. Otherwise, do all the formatting in the word processor and have KDP convert it as is.

• You have little control over KC's chapter detection other than unchecking unwanted ones. If you don't want to bother with applying **Heading** styles, let D2D handle the conversion.

• If you use the theme's **ornamental scene breaks**, don't use blank lines to mark them. KC converts them to vertical spacing. Adding a scene break does *not* remove that extra space. You have to change the paragraph **Spacing** under **Formatting** each time. A single symbol at the beginning of the line suffices as placeholder and causes you the least amount of work. **You have to add each scene break every time you upload a new version.** Unless you need KC's advanced features, use D2D for the conversion.

• Even though KC converts all **Heading 1** lines into chapter titles, it doesn't flag the following text as **Chapter First Paragraph**. Without that designation, KC won't apply **drop caps**. It will correctly convert Word's drop caps, but still won't flag the paragraph. The result looks the same. Unless you want to reuse the manuscript in D2D, apply drop caps in Word. Otherwise, you have to flag the first paragraph of every chapter every time you convert a new version of your manuscript.

• KC doesn't have a formatting option for **phrase caps**. Format them in your word processor or have D2D do it for you.

• **KC retains all lines, boxes, and table borders**. As the example in Figure 7-18 shows, tables are always left-aligned.

• **Font and background colors remain**. See the example in Figure 7-18.

Zon

• Although KDP will convert most of MS Word's formatting, it has its own funky interpretations of dimensions for features like **margins** or **drop caps**. Unless you want to rip out your hair *and* beard trying to determine what to change in the word processor to get the right result, take Amazon's advice. Use KC or switch to D2D.

Resources

D2D: Draft2Digital's Pocket Guide to eBook Layout[10]

Reedsy: What is Typesetting? Your Guide to Interior Book Design[11]

Smashwords: Smashwords Style Guide[12] (website)

Smashwords: Smashwords Style Guide[13] (e-book)

Apple Books: Designing Great Book Layouts and Interiors[14]

---

10. https://www.draft2digital.com/blog/the-pocket-guide-to-ebook-layout/

11. https://blog.reedsy.com/what-is-typesetting

12. https://www.smashwords.com/books/view/52

13. https://www.smashwords.com/books/view/52

14. https://authors.apple.com/prepare-your-book/509-designing-great-book-layouts-and-interiors

Wolf O'Rourc: Word Wizardry for Writers[15] (paperback)

ALLi: The Ultimate Guide to Self-Editing your Manuscript[16]

The Creative Penn: Book Formatting For Ebooks And Print[17]

7.4. Document Formatting for Paperback

THE *hairaches* from formatting for e-book conversion explode into full-blown *hairgraines* for print on demand (POD). Dealing with misinterpretations of margins, widows, orphans (see 7.5), and page placement in KDP will leave you hairless and headless. D2D really shines in this area, as Table 7-2 shows.

Table 7-2: Document Formatting Comparison

	Min Page	Remove tabs	Hyphenate	Widows/Orphans
D2D	64	√	√	√
KDP	24	X	X	X

Given the overhead involved, services impose a minimum size for print books. Spine text won't fit on books with fewer than 100 pages. So how will anyone find your book when it faces spine-out in bookstores and libraries? D2D discusses the psychology of page count in this video[18].

D2D

TIP A paperback must have at least 64 pages in the paper size you selected to preview and publish through D2D.

Since print uses the same converter as e-book, the above Formatting Recommendations apply equally. The following hair-saving suggestions concern only print.

---

15. http://www.wolforourc.com/writes/word-magic

16. https://selfpublishingadvice.org/the-ultimate-guide-to-self-editing-your-manuscript

17. https://www.thecreativepenn.com/formatting/

18. https://www.youtube.com/watch?v=9_XTlBaM0W8

• Unlike the e-book, you can turn **drop *and* phrase caps** on and off separately for any theme that includes them. Don't trouble yourself applying them in Word.

• The converter will ignore the **header and footer** text in your Word document. Since Draft2Digital automatically applies industry-standard header text and page numbering, you don't have to worry about it.

• Matching **widow and orphan** control (see 7.5) to Word will leave you bald in no time. Unless you do, however, page numbers will diverge between the two versions. Forget Word's count and **don't include its table of contents**. Let D2D generate one based on its own page numbering and get rid of that major hairache.

• Unless you have a good grasp of MS Word sections and a tolerance for pain, **let D2D generate the end matter and ensure that the body text starts on page 1.**

• Similarly, **no need to break chapters into their own sections to force them to start on the right**. Just check the box, and D2D will handle it.

TIP If you want Amazon paperbacks with the same theme, you can upload the D2D EPUB to KDP. Given its idiosyncrasies, the formatting may not be exactly the same. Of course, if you dream that big, you may want to consider a professional product like Vellum.

KC

SINCE PRINT USES THE same converter as e-book, the above Formatting Recommendations apply equally. The following hair-saving suggestions concern only print.

- The converter will ignore the **header and footer** text in your Word document. You can select from eight pre-defined layouts for author name, book title, chapter title, and page number.

- KC automatically optimizes widows and orphans. You have no control.

- Unless you have a good grasp of MS Word sections and a tolerance for pain, **let KC generate the end matter and ensure that the body text starts on page 1.**

- **Chapters start on the right.** You have no choice.

Zon

TIP A paperback must have at least 24 pages in the paper size you selected to preview and publish through KDP.

KDP excels in disagreeing with Word about margins, widows, and orphans. History is replete with tragic tales of authors who lost their headdress trying to capture the Zon's peruke.

For example, the converter will use the **headers and footers** as specified in your Word document. By industry conventions, most end matter pages and the first page of every chapter don't have headers. To achieve that effect in word, you must break up each chapter into a separate section, an advanced feature sure to turn most writers' hair snow white.

The fine print right above the [**Upload paperback manuscript**] button states "**For best results, we recommend using a formatted PDF file to create your paperback.**" That should tell you something. Unless you have a good reason—like certain balding writers who want to publish their guide in full color—send an SOS (Save Our Scalps) and let D2D handle formatting of your print book.

Or, break the Word document into sections, create all the end matter in the correct location and order, apply the correct headers, footers, and page numbering to each, create a table of contents in Word, and, if you can still stand, save all to a print-ready PDF.

7.5. Interior Formatting

KDP GIVES YOU NO FORMATTING options after the import. D2D really shines in this area, letting you apply themes with ornamental designs and other formatting that require considerable effort in word processors lacking specialized features for desktop publishing. KC includes a full-blown editor to change formatting, but with much less automation than D2D. Table 7-3 summarizes major differences.

Table 7-3: Enhanced Typesetting Features

	Themes	Drop Caps	Phrase Caps	Align	Space	Font Options
D2D	21	√	√	X	X	
KC	4	√	X	√	√	**B**_I_U Size Face
KDP	0	X	X	X	X	

Most important to authors' hair, both D2D and Kindle Create can add **drop caps**. This embellishment, popular in fiction, **makes the first letter of each chapter truly stand out**—bold, capitalized, oversized to cover up to three lines, and without indent, as shown in Figure 7-9. KC's implementation, though, hardly protects your scalp, requiring as much work as MS Word. The latter can partially automate drop caps through macros, making the manual intervention required in KC even less attractive.

D2D adds **phrase caps** as alternative for chapter and scene beginnings. These stand out less, using the regular font, covering one line height, only **capitalizing the start of the paragraph** without indent. D2D applies it across the first 20-30 characters, always including entire words. The variability in word length makes creating phrase caps through a Microsoft Word macro challenging. KC doesn't support this feature.

D2D

ONCE YOU'VE FINISHED the import and details, we reach the two areas where Draft2Digital really shines. For the first huge time saver, automatically generated end matter, see 8.

Next follows bulk interior formatting on the **Preview** (e-book) or **Inside** (print) tab. Enhanced typesetting that requires chapter by chapter formatting in word processors happens with one or two clicks.

You can **quickly spruce up the entire interior of a book by selecting one of more than twenty themes**, which D2D unfortunately calls template styles. I'll stick with "theme" to avoid confusion with MS Word styles.

Themes control the overall presentation in an e-reader including

- **ornamental designs** and **spacing around chapter titles,**

- ornamental designs for **scene breaks,**

- **drop caps** across the first two lines,

- **phrase caps.**

Draft2Digital groups themes by genre. Of course, you can pick any theme you like regardless. Look at a group as suggestions likely to appeal to that genre's readership.

The first theme, **D2D Simple**, shows the book as formatted in the word processor. **D2D Block** gives you the same with **indents removed** from all paragraphs. These two classic themes don't have drop caps or ornamental designs.

All other themes automatically turn on phrase caps at the beginning of every chapter and following a scene break. If you used multiple levels of headings, **one, usually Heading 1, becomes a chapter break**. You can select a different heading as shown in 8. All other levels become scene breaks with phrase caps.

One click on the **Enable drop caps** checkbox turns them on for every chapter beginning, instead of phrase caps. These remain after all scene breaks.

As shown in Figure 7-8, **Minimal** adds a line under the chapter title.

All remaining themes add ornamental graphics around the chapter title and as scene break. Figure 7-5 shows the result for **Grime**, Figure 7-8 for **Sweet Bow**. The vertical spacing adjusts to accommodate each design. D2D ignores any vertical spacing you specify in the word processor.

As discussed in 7.2, **two or three blank lines or a line with nothing but one or more asterisks (*) turn into an ornamental scene break**. D2D does *not* distinguish between hard ([Enter]) and soft ([Shift+Enter]) returns when counting blank lines.

Distinct from paid high-end programs like Vellum, Draft2Digital doesn't let you create a theme with your own images. You could embed them in the Word document. Unlike the quick application of a theme, you need to insert each graphic separately. And update each one, if you change your mind.

TIP If you **repeatedly embed the same ornamental graphics** in a Word document, **Insert and link** them. Should you need to modify the design, you can change all instances by updating the link instead of needing to reinsert them one by one.

Before rolling your own theme design, keep in mind that **you have no control over the background used by an e-reader.** For **images meant to blend into the page**, make sure they have a **transparent background**. Advanced graphics programs like Paint.NET have a Magic Wand tool to select all parts of an image with the same color. Deleting them creates transparent holes. Nonetheless, some e-readers don't understand the transparency attribute and may show the image with a white background.

The two non-fiction themes **D2D Block** and **Textbook** create block text without indents. All other themes use industry standard indenting of all paragraphs but the first after a chapter or scene break.

E-book

Figure 7-8: D2D E-Book Theme Selection and Preview

THE **Preview** page in Figure 7-8 shows all the **theme groups in the upper right**. Clicking on a white heading shows that genre's selection.

Unlike print, you can't turn off phrase caps other than by selecting one of the two classic themes.

To accommodate every possible reading device, D2D actually **embeds a separate graphic for each of these ornamental elements**. The size of the converted file goes up correspondingly, as much as 300 bytes or 0.0003 MB per instance.

Unlike KC, D2D has no option to change the font face or the font family. **All e-books generated will display in the system default serif font for the device**.

Resources

D2D: Creating your Ebook - Ebook Publishing Step 2: Layout (VIDEO)[19]

D2D: Preview and Choose a Template - Ebook Publishing Step 3: Preview (VIDEO)[20]

Print Book

THE **Inside** tab lets you customize many aspects of the book's look. Before you upload a custom PDF, play around with these settings. To accommodate the many hair-robbing challenges of a print layout, D2D breaks the options into sections.

---

19. https://www.youtube.com/watch?v=PtKydXLBeX4

20. https://www.youtube.com/watch?v=x0mmzBppaoQ

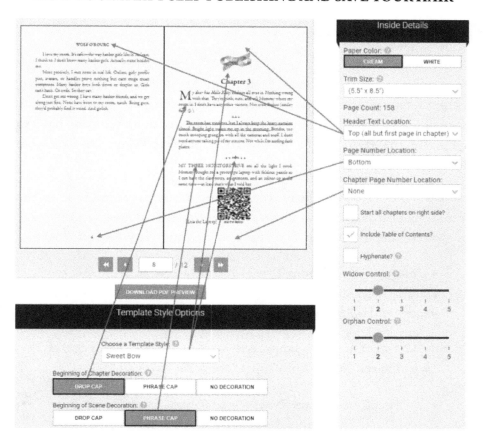

Figure 7-9: D2D Print Book Theme Selection and Preview

THE PAGE SHOWS ALL the themes in a drop-down list at the bottom left. Once you select one, the two rows of buttons below let you **customize drop caps and phrase caps separately** for chapters and scenes, unlike the e-book. If you select **No Decoration** for both, D2D only removes the indent from the first line of a chapter or after a scene break.

The **Inside Details** in the upper right let you easily adjust the layout without all the *hairscratching* required in Microsoft Word. With built-in chapter detection, you no longer need to break the manuscript body into sections to apply enhanced typesetting. Draft2Digital also has formatting options specific to print books that require other crutches in Word. Using the controls on the right can save you more hair than all the e-book *hairaches* combined.

First come the **paper settings**. Pagination, determined by the **Trim Size**, matters for a number of options. After a repagination, D2D displays the new **page count** below these controls. Because the **cover dimensions have to agree with the page size**, you can no longer change it if you upload a custom design.

Headers, the text above the body at the top of the page, and footers, the text at the bottom, follow industry conventions. They treat the first page of each chapter differently. D2D has easy options to handle the following.

- Unless you set [**Header Text Location**] to **None**, D2D uses the **Details** pages information to put the **primary author as left-page header** and the **book title on the right**.

- D2D automatically **suppresses headers on the first page of each chapter**, so they don't appear above the title.

- By default, the [**Page Number Location**] is centered in the footer. If you set [**Header Text Location**] to **None**, you can move the page number to the outside of the headers.

- D2D **automatically suppresses a page number above the chapter title**. Optionally, you **can suppress it at the bottom of a chapter's first page**.

You can't change the length of the header text, so my long title wrapped. Fortunately, moving the page number to the footer gave it the necessary space.

The remaining controls deal with pagination. **Because many settings and algorithms affect when MS Word breaks a page, you'll find it impossible to replicate the result in any of the converters.** Spare yourself a fright wig and **ignore the Word pagination. Adjust the D2D controls until all pages look okay.** Professional interior designers go to that length to ensure a good reader experience. If your book includes many images, you may have to move or resize some in your word processor to achieve optimal placement.

A simple click lets you [**Start all chapters on right side**], a hairy nightmare in MS Word. Yes, it really is that easy in D2D.

Should you want a table of contents, let D2D generate it by checking [**Include Table of Contents?**]. Only with short, simple books will you get agreement between D2D and Word's table of contents. In all other cases, don't bother trying. If you require a multi-level table of contents, like this guide, the complexity of your book suggest using a different platform anyway.

TIP Unlike Word, D2D normally **only includes lines with Heading 1 style in its table of contents**. If you **don't want a title line included, use a different style** or format it individually.

Conversely, if you want other headings included, **use the e-book's chapter detection to adjust the table of contents** to your needs, then copy the file to the print converter.

The remaining three controls deal with the issues most responsible for an army of bald interior designers.

The [**Hyphenate?**] checkbox matches an option in MS Word that turns on hyphenation of words at line ends. Particularly if you justify paragraphs for a smooth right edge, **lines with long words may create gaping whitespace in between**. Hyphenating them solves that problem at the expense of annoying those readers who hate words going across lines. Pick your hair tonic or rewrite the offending paragraphs.

[**Widows Control**] determines the **minimum number of lines of a paragraph that may appear at the top of a new page** by themselves. Setting it to "1" will allow a widow, a last line of a paragraph alone on the next page. Too high a number may create noticeably uneven bottom margins with much whitespace at the end of many pages.

Conversely, [**Orphan Control**] determines the **minimum number of lines of a paragraph that must stay together at the bottom of a page**. Setting it to "1" will allow an orphan, a first line of a paragraph alone at the bottom of a page. Too high a number may create noticeably uneven bottom margins with much whitespace at the end of many pages.

Although you have five levels *each* of widow and orphan control, setting both high will lead to conflicting rules with unpredictable results when short paragraphs fall at the bottom of pages.

Unlike KC, D2D has no option to change the font face or the font family. **All books generated will print in Garamond typeface.**

Resources

D2D: Converting your Ebook to Print - 2 Inside (VIDEO)[21]

D2D: D2D Print - Step 2: Inside (VIDEO)[22]

Author Level Up: Format Ebooks for Free with Draft2Digital (VIDEO)[23]

Emma Right TV: Using D2d To Format For MOBI, EPUB (VIDEO)[24]

KC ⌒⌒⌒⌒

YOU CAN **quickly spruce up the entire interior of a book by clicking the [Theme] button and selecting one of four themes**. They control the overall presentation in an e-reader including

- **font formatting and spacing** around **chapter titles,**

- **font formatting and spacing** around **chapter subtitles,**

---

21. https://www.youtube.com/watch?v=9_XTlBaM0W8

22. https://www.youtube.com/watch?v=9_XTlBaM0W8

23. https://www.youtube.com/watch?v=KLggrfffDX0

24. https://www.youtube.com/watch?v=QEC6wCZ37VI

- **font and paragraph formatting** of other **Standard Elements** including **Block** and **Opening Quotes**,

- **ornamental designs** for **scene breaks**,

- **drop caps** across the first three lines.

As shown in Figure 7-10, **Kindle Create's themes do not have ornamental designs for chapter titles**. You can create the effect by inserting chapter start images as described later. Given the amount of work involved, consider using D2D instead.

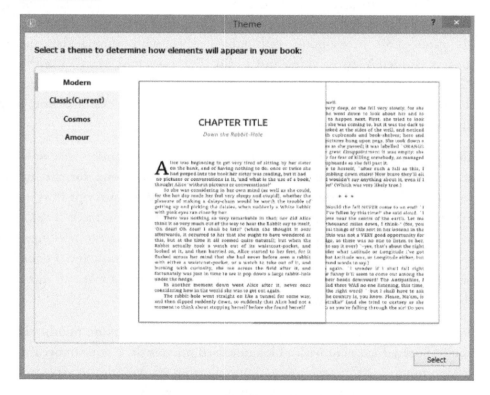

Figure 7-10: Kindle Create Theme Selection

UNLIKE D2D'S MINIMALIST options, KC does not offer a basic theme devoid of enhanced typesetting. You can achieve that by changing the formatting of titles and subtitles. No need to change other theme-dependent elements like **Chapter First Paragraph** and **Separator**, since you have to apply them by hand. They don't come into play automatically.

KC provides a full-blown editor that allows changing the body and formatting in a variety of ways. You can select text and change fonts or indents. At the moment, that power has little purpose, however.

TIP For e-books, any styling on body text overrides the user's preferred reading settings. Apply such formatting sparingly. Users report it as a poor reading experience.

If you selected the second or third choices in Figure 7-1 to publish print replicas of comics and nonfiction, you must import a print-ready PDF file. You cannot edit these e-books, only enhance them with optional elements such as **Guided View** or **video and audio**. The pages look exactly like the PDF. No reflowable or resizable text. Only certain Kindle devices support them. The reader *can* take advantage of optional features like notes, highlights, and synchronizing the last page read.

You can only use the editor if you select the first import option that **only accepts MS Word documents, which supports the same formatting features as KC.** And **you *cannot* re-upload a revised manuscript into its existing project.** Creating a new one loses any changes you made in KC. In other words, to preserve what you did in the editor, you can no longer work on the source document. You really need a good reason and a good hairdresser to go through all the effort in KC when you can make all those changes to the original just the same.

To add unnecessary work, **KC automatically appends a version number if you import a document with a filename used previously**. If you remove the version number, KC warns you without allowing an override. To replace a previous version, you have to remove it before saving the new import. Since the software doesn't have a menu choice to delete a project, you must find it in your file system. Look for a folder named after the source file plus a "_KC" suffix. KC will tell you the currently configured location in the dialog box to save a new project, where you can also change the name and directory (In Windows, usually **Documents**).

On top of the one way street, **applying enhanced typesetting like drop caps in KC takes the same effort**, if not more, as in MS Word. In its current incarnation, at best, KC lets you tinker with the text to make minor modifications without needing to upload a new manuscript to preview the results. If you forget to apply the same changes to the source document, you lose them.

TIP The current version of **KC does *not* let you edit or format bulleted or numbered lists, tables, separators, or footnotes.** Unless you have the leisure to redo work over and over, **make your edits in a word processor**.

If you ignore my warnings, to protect your hair, be sure to wear thick gloves first time you need to upload a revised manuscript into KC. That said, its editor has three panes, shown in Figure 7-11.

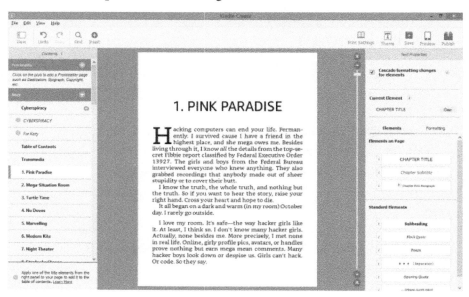

Figure 7-11: Kindle Create Editor

THE **Contents/Pages** pane on the left lets you **navigate chapters** in the body and **add front and back matter** (see 8). **Dragging a heading lets you**

reorder chapters similarly to dragging a heading in MS Word's Navigation pane. Right clicking a chapter brings up a context menu with these choices

- [**Delete Section**]: Removes the entire chapter without prompt or warning. If you made a mistake, [**Edit**] | [**Undo**], the [Undo] button, or [Ctrl+Z] will restore the section.

- [**Insert Chapter Start Image**]: Unlike D2D, **KC themes do not include a chapter title graphic.** You can insert any JPEG (no PNG) of at least 760 pixels width before the title. Since the image does *not* become part of the theme, you must repeat this process for every chapter. The effort is the same as in MS Word, but with fewer options.

- [**Convert to**]: Lets you **flag any chapter as a specific part of the end matter and move it** before or after the body.

- [**Add Page**]/[(+)] button: Lets you insert a blank page in the body or end matter.

- [**Merge with Previous**]/[**Next Section**]: Lets you combine chapters. Not available for end matter.

The editor in the **center pane** lets you **insert and delete text**, format it with the common hotkeys [**Ctrl+B**], *[Ctrl+I]*, [Ctrl+U] (Cmd for Mac), and **right-click selected text to create, edit, or remove external hyperlinks**. Right clicking without selecting text brings up a context menu with these choices.

- [**Split chapter here**]: Despite the name, it **merely adds a page break**. The new chapter has no title formatting, nor does it appear in the table of contents. Applying **Chapter Title** to a line does all that and adds a page break.

- [**Insert Image**]: Lets you **insert any size JPEG** (no PNG). Left clicking the image changes the right pane to **Image Properties**.

You can **replace the image**, add **Alt Text** describing the image to devices with screen readers for the visually impaired, select from four image **Size**s, and three alignment **Position**s relative to text. Right clicking lets you [**Delete**] or [**Replace Image**].

The WYSIWYG editor displays the changes in the generic format of the theme. To see the result for particular devices, use the [**Preview**] button to start the built-in Kindle Previewer (see 7.6).

TIP KPF files produced in **Kindle Create only work with KDP,** hence only display on Kindle devices. **You cannot necessarily replicate the same formatting in other platforms** such as D2D that have to cater to a broader range of e-readers.

With the cursor in body text, the right pane shows the **Text Properties** in Figure 7-12. These change dependent on the type of text, called **Elements on Page**, equivalent to MS Word styles. They cover the following formatting choices, with different default settings depending on element type and theme.

- [**Font**]: [**Bold**], [*Italic*], [Underline] (same as the shortcut keys), **size**, **color**, and **font face** (limited to Bookerly, Amazon Ember, Monospace). Some themes add their own font face for titles, but you can't apply them to other elements. **These options only activate with text selected.**

- **Advanced Font Options:** ~~Strikethrough~~, subscript, superscript, UPPER CASE, lower case, Title Case, and **Letter S p a c i n g**. **These options only activate with text selected.**

- **Paragraph** alignment.

- [**Apply Drop Cap**]: Sets the beginning letters of the paragraph to drop caps and activates controls that set the number of lines (max 5) and letters (max 3) covered.

- **Indents**: Separate settings for left, right, and hanging (first line only).

- **Spacing**: Allows setting the vertical spacing before and after a paragraph, and the line spacing within a paragraphs.

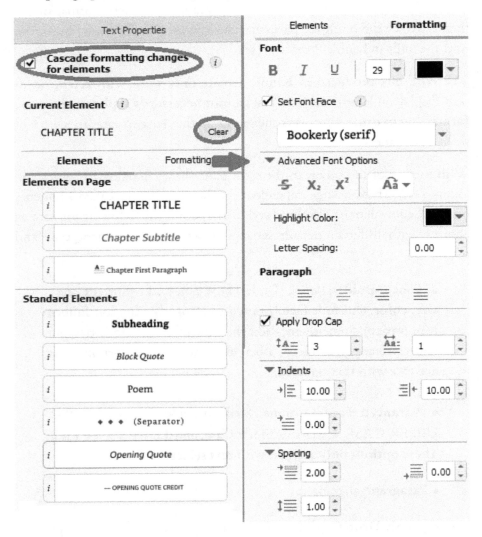

Figure 7-12: Kindle Create Text Properties

IF YOU LEAVE [**Cascade formatting changes for elements**] at the top checked, the formatting changes affect all paragraphs with that element type and subsequent applications, i.e. the equivalent of MS Word's **Update <style> to Match Selection**. The implementation is flaky. For instance, altering drop caps for **Chapter First Paragraph** does not cascade.

For each theme, KC provides the following elements with pre-defined font and paragraph formatting (style). Hovering over the [*i*] button to the left in Figure 7-12 displays effect and purpose. The most used styles have shortcut key combinations assigned to them.

- [**Chapter Title**] [CTRL+ALT+T]: Adds a page break and creates a table of contents entry.

- [**Chapter Subtitle**] [CTRL+ALT+S]: For descriptive text about the chapter below the title. Does not add a page break or create a table of contents entry.

- [**Chapter First Paragraph**] [CTRL+ALT+F]: Usually removes any indent and adds a drop cap.

- [**Subheading**]: For descriptive text about a section. Does not add a page break or create a table of contents entry.

- [**Block Quote**]: For highlighting long quotes or excerpts by indenting them left and right and changing the font formatting to distinguish from narrative.

- [**Poem**]: For highlighting a poem by changing the font and paragraph formatting to distinguish from narrative.

- [**Separators**] [CTRL+ALT+-(hyphen)]: A decorative element as scene break.

- [**Opening Quote**]: For highlighting a quote by changing the font and paragraph formatting to distinguish from narrative.

- [**Opening Quote Credit**]: For highlighting the source of a quote by changing the font and paragraph formatting to distinguish from narrative.

To apply one of these styles, **select *one* paragraph and hit a button in the Elements list or use its shortcut key combination.** If you select multiple paragraphs, only the first changes. You can't apply a style to text within a paragraph. For instance, the **Opening Quote Credit** must be on a separate line.

TIP Kindle Create lacks a button to apply the default style like Word's Normal. To do so, **use the [Clear] button** next to the **Current Element** name.

The automatic chapter detection *only* applies the **Chapter Title** element. For reasons only known to wig makers the world over, it will not format the immediately following text. If you pick a theme with drop caps, you must select each occurrence and make it a **Chapter First Paragraph**.

Unlike D2D, you can't specify different chapter detection criteria. To split off headings KC didn't detect, you have to individually select a line and format it as **Chapter Title. Chapter Subtitle** won't do.

In fact, **other than Chapter Title, the elements require manual application** and **can appear *anywhere* in the body.** You can use **Chapter First Paragraph** to get a drop cap after each scene break if you wish to go through that much trouble. For all practical purposes, there's no difference between a **Chapter Subtitle** and a **Subheading, Opening Quote** and **Opening Quote Credit**, or **Block Quote** and **Poem.** You merely have two different styles that you can use for different purposes.

KC also does not convert blank lines or three asterisks to Separators. You have to create them one by one where you want them. Worse, any placeholders for scene breaks remain in the text unless you remove them. KC has an [**Edit**] | [**Find**] function, but no replace. **For narrative fiction, the formatting power in KC takes way too much effort compared to the simplicity of D2D.**

Clicking the [**Print Settings**] button opens a dialogue box with eight page-layout options, shown in Figure 7-13. These only cover placement of author name, book title, chapter title, and page number. You have no further control. Page numbers use lowercase Roman numerals in front matter and switch to Arabic ones starting with "1" in the body. Chapters always start on the right side.

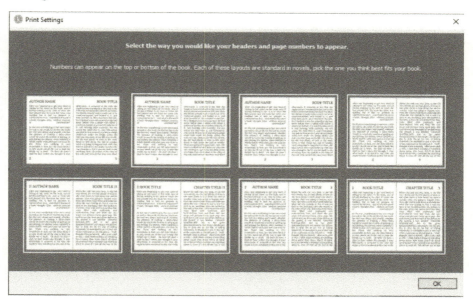

Figure 7-13: Kindle Create Print Settings

Zon

KDP PERFORMS A SPELL and format check during the import. You can correct the errors in your manuscript and re-upload, or tell KDP to ignore them as shown in Figure 7-14.

Figure 7-14: KDP Spelling Errors

YOU HAVE NO ABILITY to control the formatting. For e-books that means no themes, drop caps, or end matters unless you add them in MS Word the hard way. Your print layout options are limited to paper type and size, and bleed, as shown in Figure 7-15.

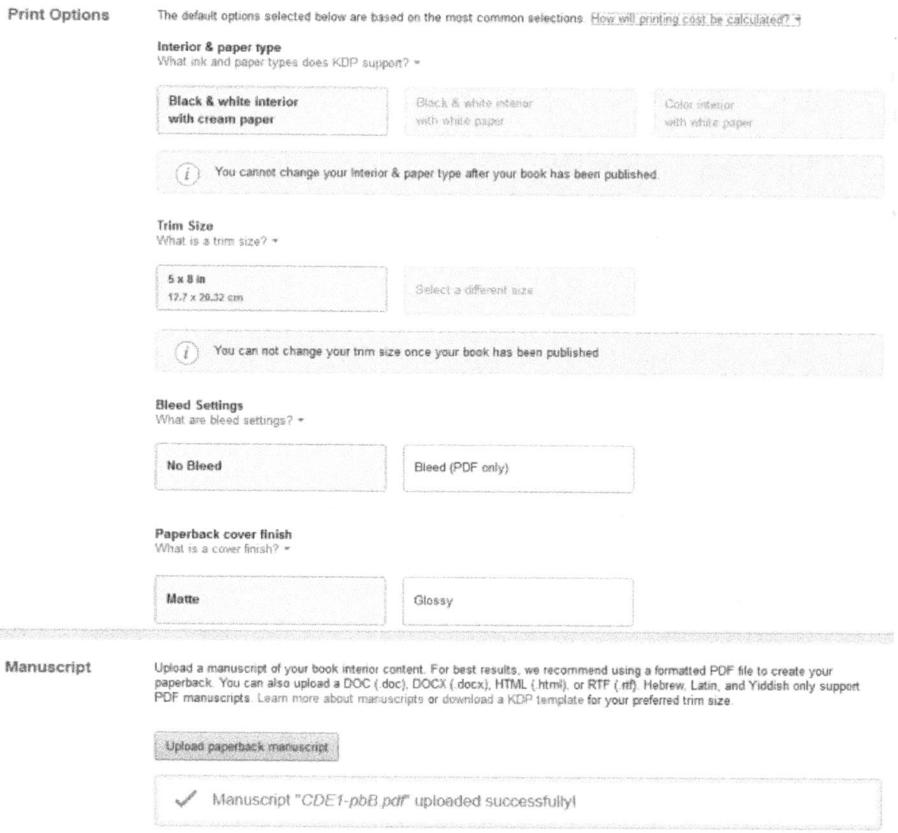

Figure 7-15: KDP Print Layout Options

PRINT BOOKS RUN INTO bigger problems. KDP's handling of margins, widows, and orphans differs from MS Word. Even if you set matching paper sizes in both, the probably that the pagination on a book with hundreds of pages will agree is zero to none. Images at the bottom may drift to the next page, leaving a gaping hole of whitespace behind. Word's table of contents will not agree with the page numbers assigned by KDP.

Just in case you haven't gotten the message by now. Save yourself. Save your hair. Import your book into D2D or KC and upload their end products into KDP, if you must publish directly through Amazon.

Resources

THE BOOK DESIGNER: Picking Fonts for Your Self-Published Book[25]

KDP: Paperback Interior Design[26]

KDP: Build Your Book (PDF)[27]

KDP: Paperback file setup calculator (Excel)[28]

KDP: Printing cost and royalty calculator (Excel)[29]

7.6. Preview

CONGRATULATIONS, YOU've imported and converted your manuscript. Now you get to stroke back your remaining hair and **review your book for any problems in the previewer**. Each platform has one, with their different options shown in Table 7-4. Of course, they each have various ways to steal your locks.

Table 7-4: Preview Options Comparison

25. https://www.thebookdesigner.com/2012/06/picking-fonts-for-your-self-published-book/

26. https://kdp.amazon.com/en_US/help/topic/GDDYZG2C7RVF5N9J

27. https://images-na.ssl-images-amazon.com/images/G/01/15/29/95/40/91/96/15299540919613.pdf

28. https://kdp.amazon.com/en_US/help/topic/G200735480#manuscript_ebook

29. https://kdp.amazon.com/en_US/help/topic/G200735480#manuscript_ebook

	Device Preview	Horizontal	Navigate	Auto
D2D	E-Reader	X	Page Chapter Link TOC	X
KC	E-Reader	√	Page Location TOC	√
Kindle Previewer	E-Reader Tablet Phone	√	Page Chapter Location Link TOC Image List Table	X
KDP	E-Reader Tablet Phone	√	Page Location TOC	X
Kindle PC	E-Reader	√	Page Location TOC Mark	X
ADE	E-Reader	X	Page Link TOC Mark	X

You can also use e-reader programs like Adobe Digital Editions (ADE) or the Kindle App mentioned in 5.2, to check a customer's experience.

Table 7-5: Preview Formatting Comparison

	Preview Font	Font Sizes	Table	Emoji	Hyperlink
D2D	Garamond	1	Spill	√	√
KC	Bookerly Amazon Ember Monospace	12	Shrink	X	√
Kindle Previewer	Bookerly Caecillia Palatino Baskerville Helvetica Georgia Light Lucida	12	Shrink	X	√
KDP	Bookerly Lucida Amazon Ember Baskerville	9	Shrink	X	√
Kindle PC	Bookerly Caecillia Georgia Helvetica OpenDyslexic Palatino	11	Cut	X	
ADE	Garamond	5	Cut	X	√

D2D and KDP also let you download proofs of the book, known as galleys. Particular for print books, you can hire professional proofreaders to check for layout and typesetting problems.

TIP You don't necessarily need to send out print copies for proofing and wait for slow mail. Using **Tools | Comment** in **Adobe Acrobat Reader**, proofreaders can mark up a print-ready PDF file, including strikeouts, inserts, and highlights.

Checklist

MAKE SURE TO COVER at least all applicable items on this checklist.

TIP Both D2D and KDP paperbacks **require bleed for the cover and interior graphics that reach to the edges of the page.** Due to slight deviations when cutting books to size, such **images need to extend 1/8 in (0.125" or 3.2 mm) beyond the trim lines** in a template to prevent white borders. Similarly, important **text should stay away that far from the edge.**

A color code and letter organize related entries into topics.

E-book **Paperback**

Entire Book - flip through every page

☐ **Page breaks** at correct location.

☐ **Title Formatting** correct.

☐ **Text Formatting** correct.

☐ **Regular body text distinct** from **bold** or *italics*.

☐ **P No content beyond trim line.**

☐ **E Font size change:** All text changes and reflows (test in Kindle Previewer or e-reader).

☐ **E Font typeface change:** All text changes and reflows (test in Kindle Previewer or e-reader).

☐ **E Background color change:** Text readable in in all modes (white, black, mint, and sepia)(test in Kindle Previewer or e-reader).

☐ **E Check MOBI file size:** Amazon may charge a delivery fee, depending on your royalty plan. For large e-books, you may want to select a different option. See **Resources** for details on the complex calculations.

Front Matter

☐ **No template text** on title or copyright page.

☐ **P No template text** in headers or footers.

☐ **Text legible** (7+ points, no overlap, distinct from background).

☐ **Title page** with Title, Author Name, Publisher.

☐ **P Title page has no header, footer, or page number.**

☐ **Copyright page** with copyright notice, ISBN.

☐ **P Copyright page has no header, footer, or page number.**

☐ **Information on Title and Copyright page matches metadata on Details tab exactly.**

☐ **Information on Title and Copyright page matches cover** (front, spine, back) exactly.

☐ **P Information on Title and Copyright page matches headers and footers in body.**

☐ **Dedication page.**

☐ **P Dedication page has no header, footer, or page number.**

☐ **Also By** with Author Name, other Titles.

☐ **P Also By has no header.**

☐ **Foreword.**

☐ P Foreword has no header.

☐ P Roman-numeral page numbers in sequential order.

Table of Contents

☐ **Text legible** (7+ points, no overlap, distinct from background).

☐ **Contains all chapters.**

☐ **E Each entry clickable and links to the correct location** in the book.

☐ **E Entries have no page numbers.**

☐ **P Page numbers match chapter title page.**

☐ **P No more than 2 consecutive blank pages.**

Chapter Title Pages

☐ **Text legible** (7+ points, no overlap, distinct from background).

☐ **Format consistent** throughout.

☐ **Chapter title correct** font typeface and size.

☐ **Vertical spacing** correct.

☐ **Theme graphic** correct.

☐ **First paragraph drop cap** or phrase cap.

☐ **First paragraph no indent.**

☐ **P Title page has no header, footer, or page number.**

Body Text

☐ **P No template text** in headers or footers.

☐ **Text legible** (7+ points, no overlap, distinct from background).

☐ **Format consistent** throughout.

☐ **Paragraphs indented** except chapter and scene start.

☐ **Justification** consistent.

☐ **Theme graphic for all scene breaks.**

☐ **P No widows.**

☐ **P No orphans.**

☐ **E Each hyperlink clickable and links to the correct target.**

☐ **P Arabic-numeral page numbers in sequential order.**

☐ **P No more than 2 consecutive blank pages.**

Images

☐ **Position correct.**

☐ **P Images meant to display completely outside inside trim line.**

☐ **P Images meant to reach to the edge of page extend beyond trim line.**

☐ **Size correct**, entire image displayed.

☐ **Alignment correct.**

☐ **Text in image is legible** (7+ points, no overlap text, distinct from background).

☐ **No pixilation.**

Tables

☐ **Text in table legible** (7+ points, no overlap, distinct from background).

☐ **Position correct**, outside bleed area.

☐ **Size correct**, entire table displayed.

☐ **Alignment correct.**

Back Matter

☐ **P No template text** in headers or footers.

☐ **Text legible** (7+ points, no overlap, distinct from background).

☐ **Review Request** with Universal Book Links.

☐ **P Review Request has no header.**

☐ **Also By** with Author Name, other Titles.

☐ **P Also By has no header.**

☐ **Email Signup.**

☐ **P Email Signup has no header.**

☐ **Teaser** chapter.

☐ **P Teaser has no header.**

☐ **About Author** with Author Name, Bio.

☐ **P About Author has no header.**

☐ **About Publisher** with Author Name, Bio.

☐ **P About Publisher has no header.**

☐ **P No more than 10 consecutive blank pages at the end.**

Cover

☐ **No template text** on front, spine, or back.

☐ **Text legible** (7+ points, no overlap, distinct from background).

☐ **Important text readable as thumbnail.**

☐ **P Cover sized for bleed.**

☐ **P No important text in bleed area.**

☐ **P Spine wide enough for text** (100+ pages).

☐ **P Spine text space on each side.**

Resources

KDP: Previewing and Publishing Your Kindle Create Book[30]

KDP: Digital Pricing Page[31]

KDP: The 2020 Guide to Amazon Fees and Royalties for Kindle eBooks and KDP Print[32]

---

30. https://kdp.amazon.com/en_US/help/topic/GRVZMSZ2THRTR5V9

31. https://kdp.amazon.com/en_US/help/topic/G200634500

32. https://www.authorimprints.com/amazon-kdp-royalty-pricing/

Apple Books: Ebook Proofreading Checklist[33]

D2D

AS SHOWN IN 7.5, **D2D integrates the previewer into its formatter.** The **e-book and print version differ considerably** in look and feel. Particularly for checking text, choose the one you prefer. Layout, obviously, differs between the two formats, so you may have to make separate passes through both. For an **e-book, the page view immediately reflects any formatting changes** you make. For a paperback, click the [**Apply Changes**] button at the bottom to **generate a new preview**.

TIP If you upload an EPUB, D2D disables formatting controls and the page viewer since you can't change the body text. The e-book will contain any end matter sections you selected on the **Layout** page. To preview them, download the MOBI or EPUB and use one of the tools in 5.2.

The simpler e-book previewer on the **Preview** page, shown in Figure 7-16, earns D2D its 2-scalp rating. An inability to jump around in the galley makes checking specific sections tedious. The buttons to the left and right of the pages view let you go forward and back by a page or chapter. For navigation, each different part of end matter counts as a chapter. Unlike KDP, the preview starts on the page 1 of the body. Use [<] or [<<] to see the front matter.

---

33. https://itunespartner.apple.com/books/articles/ebook-proofreading-checklist-2716

Others have "Don't Enter" signs taped to their doors, but I'm not a kid anymore. Some let my five foot one and a quarter inches and my hot-pink ponytail fool them.

Table 1

	Format	Image	Tables	Preview	For
KC	DOC, DOCX, PDF	√		X	8
D2D	MOBI, EPUB	√	Wrap	X	1

But this year, I celebrated my Sweet Sixteen by starting college. My family can afford it.

In Virginia, the Allertons go back forever. Like Jamestown forever. Don't get me started. Yes, the settlers began to leave, but the supply fleet arrived just in time. Trust me. Father told me his father's story mega million times. But I digress.

[Check the colony's history]

My door has Hello Kitty stickers all over it. Nothing wrong with that. They're pink, cute, and tell Mommy where my room is. I don't have any other visitors. Not even Father (smiley face ☺ 😻).

+++

The room has windows, but I always keep the heavy curtains closed. Bright light wakes me up in the morning. Besides, too much snooping going on with all the cameras and stuff. I don't need anyone taking pix of my screens. Not while I'm surfing dark places.

 I have reviewed this manuscript and approve it for release for distribution to any sales channels I select. ❓

Figure 7-16: D2D E-Book Previewer

THE PREVIEWER SHOWS the page in color. Theme graphics, images, and emoji appear as they are in the originals. Since D2D doesn't support font and background colors, text only displays in black Garamond typeface with a fixed size, as seen in Figure 7-16.

In e-books, tables wrap around in weird ways. Because of the many devices, the look for a reader may differ considerably from what you see. Adobe Digital Editions (ADE), the Kindle App, and the Kindle Previewer, mentioned in 5.2, hide columns on the right. D2D spills them onto the *facing* page. If you must include tables in your book, check them in as many different apps as you can.

Just like in an e-book, the hyperlinks are live and appear in blue. That does mean that internal links work, such as the table of contents. You can navigate from there to any chapter in the book. Unfortunately, D2D provides no easy means to jump back to the beginning.

TIP Preview doesn't include a **button to go to the beginning** of the book. Clicking [Previous] and starting the preview over will bring you back to the first chapter, but the converter will rebuild your book each time.

One of the previewer's bonuses comes to the rescue. As seen at the lower right of Figure 7-8, buttons let you download the MOBI and EPUB e-books. These immediately reflect any formatting changes you make.

Draft2Digital also includes links to the viewing tools Kindle Previewer and ADE. These offer full-blown navigation so you can move freely through the book. Of course, you can send the downloads to e-readers to check how they display on them. Since D2D gives you the actual e-books, you can review them with whichever font options a device offers.

TIP D2D doesn't have a device preview. You can open both the MOBI *and* EPUB file in Kindle Previewer 3 and look at them with different screen configurations.

The third button downloads a galley in print-ready PDF format. All URLs appear as footnotes at the bottom of a page.

TIP The PDF from this page is a preview version in a size selected by D2D, usually 5.5 x 8.5". **For a PDF that looks like your print book**, download it from the **Print Book**'s [**Inside**] tab or the **View Book** page's [**Print Book**] tab, where you can select a paper size.

To continue on to the [**Publish**] section, you must click below the page to acknowledge that you reviewed and approved the galley. The field resets every time you upload a copy of the manuscript. Stop pulling on your hair.

You *don't* have to go through the review to work on the pricing. D2D doesn't care if you looked at anything before you placed the checkmark.

TIP If you upload a manuscript and only want to check the body text, **you don't need to go through the Layout step**. Use the blue button on top to jump straight to **Preview**. If you do, D2D doesn't generate end matter for you to review.

The print previewer on the [**Inside**] page, shown in Figure 7-17, reflects the look and feel of a paperback with two pages side by side. Since D2D doesn't offer interior color print, everything appears in black and white. Like real paper, none of the hyperlinks work. Instead, for each, the galley has footnotes listing the targets.

The buttons at the bottom of the page let you go forward and back by a page or chapter, with each different part of the end matter counting like the latter. You can't navigate by table of contents. Instead, you can type in a number to jump to that page. The previewer starts the count with the front matter, so add its total to get to a numbered page in the body text.

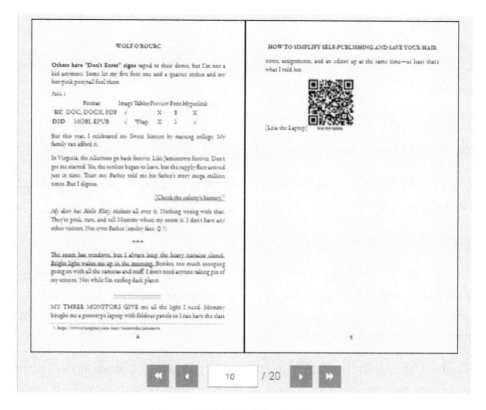

Figure 7-17: D2D Print Previewer

SINCE THE CONVERSION matches the e-book, the print version has no lines, boxes, or table borders either. As shown in Figure 7-17, symbols available in the font display correctly, but extended characters like emoji may appear as "?." Draft2Digital only offers print books in Garamond typeface.

As seen at the bottom of Figure 7-9, a button lets you **download the galley in print-ready PDF format**. You can send it to a proofreader for review.

The print previewer doesn't require a checkmark to proceed. Clicking the [**Save & Continue**] button suffices.

Resources

D2D: Preview and Choose a Template - Ebook Publishing Step 3: Preview (VIDEO)[34]

D2D: Converting your Ebook to Print - 2 Inside (VIDEO)[35]

D2D: D2D Print - Step 2: Inside (VIDEO)[36]

Kathrese McKee: Draft2Digital My Experience[37] (Previewing & Proofing) (VIDEO)

KC

AS SHOWN IN Figure 7-11, **Kindle Create's WYSIWYG editor offers a device-independent preview of the manuscript** with navigation features available through the menu. The page view immediately reflects any formatting changes you make.

To check the layout for different devices, the [**Preview**] button at the upper right lets you launch the Kindle Previewer, shown in Figure 7-18, as a separate app. The buttons to the left and right of the preview pane and in the **Inspector** let you go forward and back by the unit specified in the **Navigate By** field: page, table of contents entries (steps through end matter), chapter titles (ignores end matter), drop caps, images, links, and tables. The field next to the buttons displays the current location using the same units. A **slider** below it allows quick movement to different sections of the book.

The previewer does little to protect your scalp, but it guards against carpal tunnel syndrome by offering an **Auto Navigate** feature. Clicking its arrow button will advance the page by the unit selected above, at the **Speed** determined by the slider to the right.

---

34. https://www.youtube.com/watch?v=x0mmzBppaoQ

35. https://www.youtube.com/watch?v=9_XTlBaM0W8

36. https://www.youtube.com/watch?v=9_XTlBaM0W8

37. https://www.youtube.com/watch?v=Z_U7LfJSwjY

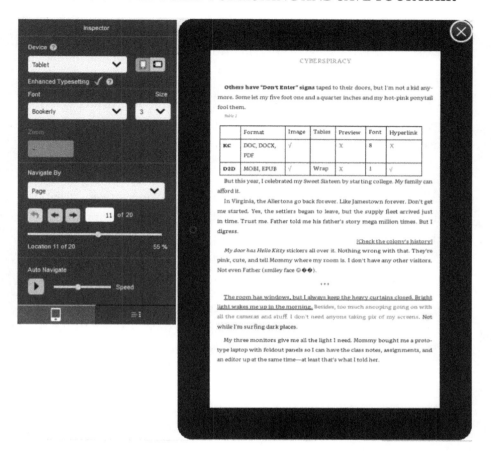

Figure 7-18: KC E-Book Previewer

THE BUTTON AT THE LOWER right of the **Inspector** switches to a table of contents view. Clicking an entry brings you to that chapter.

You can test different layouts by changing the **Device** selection between **vertical** or **horizontal views** of a **Tablet**, **Phone**, or **Kindle E-reader**.

The preview pane shows the page in color. Theme graphics and images appear as they are in the originals. As shown in Figure 7-18, symbols available in the font display correctly, but extended characters like emoji may appear as place holders. Kindle Previewer offers eight fonts in twelve sizes. These are for testing only, since the e-reader determines the presentation. For that reason, the same limitations on tables as in D2D apply.

Just like in an e-book, the hyperlinks are live and appear in blue. Internal links work, such as the table of contents. You can navigate from there to any chapter in the book.

TIP The full Kindle Previewer adds a pane with thumbnails of all pages, four background colors, multi-language support, quality checks, a command-line interface, and conversion from various e-book formats to KPF, MOBI, and AZK.

Unlike D2D, KC does *not* let you download the manuscript in an e-book format. The [**Publish**] button only generates an Amazon proprietary KPF file for upload to KDP, where you can download a MOBI file. To make an EPUB version, you must use a different tool like D2D or Calibre, as mentioned in 5.1.

Currently, **KC offers no print preview** to check on the page layout features you selected with [**Print Settings**]. You have to upload the KPF file into KDP and use the functionality there. This extra step earns KC an additional scalp over D2D.

Resources

KDP: Upload and Preview Book Content[38]

Zon

THE [**Launch Previewer**] button under the **Content** tab, shown in Figure 7-19 and Figure 7-21, **loads previewers for e-book and print**. The two **versions differ considerably** in look and feel. **Any time you upload a manuscript, KDP requires a preview** to continue, so you may have to make several passes through both.

A complete lack of formatting controls and limited functionality earns KDP its 5-scalp rating. **Even the smallest correction requires you to make changes in another program** like a word processor, D2D, or KC, upload

---

38. https://kdp.amazon.com/en_US/help/topic/G200641240

a new manuscript, and preview it again. Slow loading each time that you launch the previewer may not cost you hair, but adds wear and tear on twiddling thumbs.

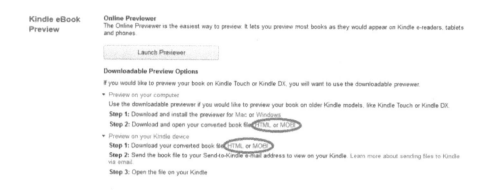

Figure 7-19: KDP E-Book Preview Section

THE E-BOOK PREVIEWER, shown in Figure 7-20, has the look and some functionality of the Kindle Previewer program. The buttons to the left and right of the preview pane let you go forward and back by a page. They only appear if the cursor hovers over the pane. The drop-down menu at the top offers you additional navigation options. [**Beginning**] brings you to the first page, usually the same as [**Cover**]. [**Table of Contents**] jumps to that section in the book, where you can use the hyperlinks. [**NCX View**] pops up an index of all sections, where you can double-click entries.

A field at the top shows the current **Location** in the file in device independent units. You can enter a number by guessing relative to the total size displayed to the right. Hitting [Enter] then jumps to that area.

The online previewer has no Auto Navigate feature.

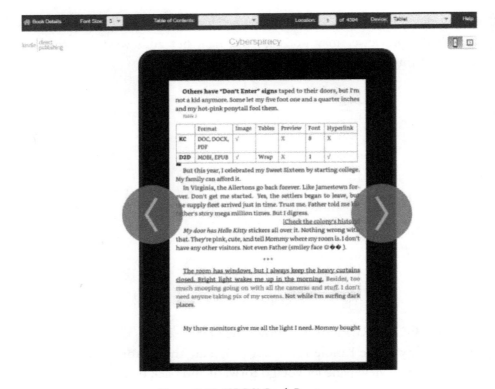

Figure 7-20: KDP E-Book Previewer

THE CONTROLS AT THE upper right let you test different layouts by changing the **Device** selection between **vertical** or **horizontal views** of a **Tablet**, **Phone**, or **Kindle E-reader**.

The preview pane **shows the page in color**. Theme graphics and images appear as they are in the originals. As shown in Figure 7-20, symbols available in the font display correctly, but **extended characters like emoji may appear as place holders**. Unlike KC, you can't change the base font, but can preview text in nine sizes. These are for testing only, since the e-reader determines the presentation. For that reason, the same limitations on tables as in D2D apply.

TIP Neither KDP or KC can import OpenOffice, LibreOffice, or Google Docs OpenDocument (ODT) files. Given Microsoft's secrecy about its format, these programs struggle with converting advanced features like auto numbering and cross-references to DOCX. If you publish text books through KDP, save your barnet and build manuscripts in MS Word[39].

Just like in an e-book, the hyperlinks are live and appear in blue. Internal links work, such as the table of contents. You can navigate from there to any chapter in the book.

Given all the shortcomings in the online version, for a thorough review, listen to the painful whispers of your hair and Amazon's recommendation and use Kindle Previewer or another tool. To do so, use the unassuming [**Book Details**] link at the upper left (or the browser's Back button) to return to the **Content** page.

To get to the actual e-book, click on [**Preview on your computer**] or [**Preview on your Kindle device**] below the [**Launch Previewer**] button. Each choice expands to give you two links to **download** identical copies of the [**HTML**] and [**MOBI**] **versions of the converted manuscript**. You get different instructions specific to the target devices.

TIP Unsure how to upload a MOBI file to a Kindle? The [**Preview on your Kindle device**] instructions include a link to Learn more about sending files to Kindle via email[40].

To make an EPUB version, you must use a different tool like D2D or Calibre, as mentioned in 5.1.

TIP Unlike MS Word, **KDP doesn't include custom formatting in its HTML version** of your manuscript. Once you search and replace unneeded general formatting tags, you're left with a **much cleaner starting point to post your book's content to a website** than the mess Microsoft creates. For comparison, the HTML file of "A 15-Minute Recipe" came out to 193 KB in MS Word and 43 KB in KDP. Incidentally, LibreOffice came out even cleaner at 28 KB.

---

39. https://products.office.com/en-us/word

40. https://www.amazon.com/gp/sendtokindle/email

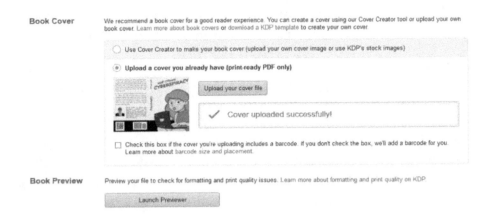

Book Cover   We recommend a book cover for a good reader experience. You can create a cover using our Cover Creator tool or upload your own book cover. Learn more about book covers or download a KDP template to create your own cover.

○ Use Cover Creator to make your book cover (upload your own cover image or use KDP's stock images)

◉ Upload a cover you already have (print-ready PDF only)

Upload your cover file

✓ Cover uploaded successfully!

☐ Check this box if the cover you're uploading includes a barcode. If you don't check the box, we'll add a barcode for you. Learn more about barcode size and placement.

Book Preview   Preview your file to check for formatting and print quality issues. Learn more about formatting and print quality on KDP.

Launch Previewer

Figure 7-21: KDP Print Cover and Book Preview Section

THE PRINT PREVIEWER page, shown in Figure 7-22, reflects the look and feel of a paperback with two pages side by side. The **Print Options** under the [**Paperback Content**] tab, shown in Figure 7-15, let you switch between [**Black & white**] and [**Color interior**]. The preview pane changes accordingly. Like real paper, none of the hyperlinks work. **Clicking instead zooms** in on the current location. While magnified, dragging the text lets you see other parts. To return to the page view, move the cursor outside the preview pane. KDP does *not* convert links. It simply removes the URL, leaves the formatting intact, and reports the problem as fixed in its **Quality Check**.

The buttons to the left and right of the preview pane let you go forward and back by a page. They only appear if the cursor hovers over the pane. You can't navigate by table of contents. Instead, you can type in a number in the **Page Range** field at the bottom to jump there. The previewer starts the count with the cover, so add two plus the front matter total to get to a numbered page in the body text.

The [**Thumbnail View**] button at the bottom shrinks each page view so you can see a grid that you can click to select a destination, similar to the Kindle Previewer. Using the [**Two Page View**] button switches back without changing location. Unchecking [**Guides**] removes the dashed lines that mark the bleed areas into which text should not extend.

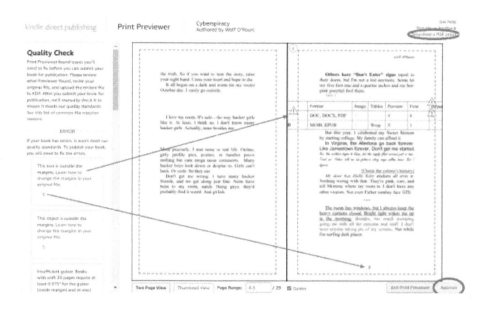

Figure 7-22: KDP Print Previewer

THE **conversion matches the e-book**. As shown in Figure 7-22, symbols available in the font display correctly, but **extended characters like emoji may appear as place holders. KDP prints the book in the closest match to the font typefaces you used in your manuscript**.

As seen at the upper right of Figure 7-22, a link lets you **Download a PDF proof** in print-ready format. You can send it to a proofreader for review.

To proceed to publishing, you must accept the proof by clicking the [**Approve**] button at the lower right. The [**Exit Print Previewer**] button takes you back to the **Content** tab without acceptance.

To ensure a good reading experience, **KDP performs extensive checks on print books** before allowing publication. The [**Approve**] button *will not* *activate* until you fix major errors. The Paperback Manual Review Checklist[41] covers common problem areas.

Figure 7-22 shows the **Quality Check** column at the left. The **Error section lists each category in separate boxes**, such as a cover size mismatch or illegible text. After the description follows a series of numbers, **clickable links to the corresponding page preview**. Like the range at the bottom, this is the absolute page number starting with the cover

KDP will fix *minor problems*, like removing **non-printable markup**, which often means hyperlinks. The **Fix** section will list each occurrence.

A **Please check** section gives **recommendations to avoid a failure of the manual review done by Amazon**, like a mismatch between information on the **Details** page and the manuscript or bleed issues.

The **Quality Check** helps get your manuscript in shape for error free printing. Take advantage of it and **fix the problems. Any book with 100 or more pages, save as a print-ready PDF**, for the sake of your thatch. KDP's handling of margins, widows, and orphans differs so much from MS Word that its **table of contents will rarely agree with the page numbers assigned by KDP**. And the latter can't generate one of its own.

Save yourself and readers the grief. **For paperbacks, follow the Zon's advice and upload the PDF or use D2D's print on demand**. Both use the same Extended Distribution option to sell to bookstores. If you want access to Amazon Advertising (see 12.5), **you can download D2D's print-ready PDF** and use it with KDP to ensure consistency between the two versions. Since both companies use different printers, the paper thickness may vary. For novels, the change in spine width means you'll need to create two separate covers.

Resources

KDP: Paperback Manual Review Checklist[42]

---

41. https://kdp.amazon.com/en_US/help/topic/GYEKAVKMSE23PFTM

KDP: Send to Kindle by Email[43]

---

42. https://kdp.amazon.com/en_US/help/topic/GYEKAVKMSE23PFTM

43. https://www.amazon.com/gp/sendtokindle/email

8. End Matter

———

Rejoice, literate, for your hirsute journey nears what matters in the end. Thanks to Draft2Digital, and a lesser extend Kindle Create, the hair-ripping process of formatting front and back matter has turned as simple as petting pileous puppies (or your preferred pet pick—Brought to You by the Letter "P").

The pages at the beginning and end of your writing can showcase the rest of your work or tell readers more about the book, the authors, and the publisher.

As the IBPA Industry Standards Checklist for a Professionally Published Book[1] and the menus in Figure 8-4 show, what this guide lumps together under end matter consists of a wide variety of pages. **Industry conventions require certain information in a prescribed format and order.** Violating these rules suggests an amateurishly self-published book to insiders like agents.

Limited formatting control in e-books and the emergence of Look Inside have soften this stance considerably, however. Sections previously in front now hide in the back to make room for more narrative. Rather than scare potential buyers with boring text, even big name publishers have reduced sections, such as the copyright notice, to almost nothing.

Breaking formatting rules in print books will still show you as inexperienced. **Most front matter has no headers. Page numbers, if present at all, use lowercase Roman numerals** to distinguish them from the body, which restarts the count at one in Arabic numerals. Nowadays, back matter continues the numbering from the body, but still suppresses the headers.

---

1. https://www.ibpa-online.org/page/standards-checklist-download

In a word processor, you had to break off end matter into multiple separate sections and fiddle with advanced page layout features. Never mind remembering the order and requirements for each page. No more (almost).

Our new tools partially automate the creation of end matter. After an introduction, the following sections show a side-by-side comparison of various pages generated by D2D and KC.

8.1. Automated Creation

BALDNESS INDUCING KDP offers no help, hence shall remain mostly nameless. Reminiscent of the Barbershop Quartet Wars, if not the Burger Wars, our two remaining stylists take vastly different approaches. D2D's "We do it all for you" checkmark simplicity earns it a coveted one-scalp rating, issues with the title and copyright page notwithstanding. KC lets you have it your way, giving you the flexibility to put (almost) any text (almost) anywhere. At a price, hence three scalps.

D2D

ADDING END MATTER WITH D2D could hardly be easier. **Checkmark the sections** you wish for (preferably under a shooting star) and **fill in a little information**—done! No need to read a long style guide.

Auto-generated end matter ignores the selected theme. The pages always look the same.

For e-books, you'll find the choices on the [**Layout**] tab next to the chapter detection.

TIP Uploading a new manuscript resets the interior file. You have to go through the [Layout] step again, even if you make no changes there, to add the End Matter.

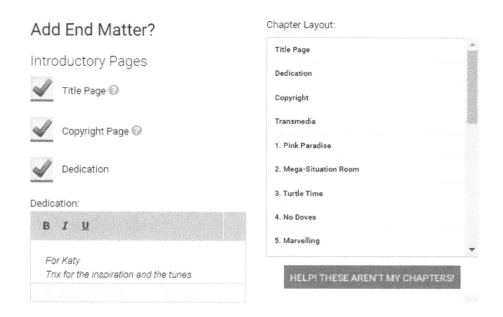

Figure 8-1: D2D E-Book Front Matter Entry

UNLIKE KC, THE INTEGRATION at D2D really shines (even without pomade or vitamin E). As you can see in Figure 8-1 and Figure 8-2, the process requires minimal data entry. **Most information comes from the Details, Contributors, and Publisher pages**.

As the examples below for each section show, though, you are also stuck with **choices that don't completely follow industry standards**. If you want a custom copyright page, you either have to accept a non-standard ordering or include your own dedication and following pages. Print books add another twist. Since D2D treats custom material as body text, they trigger the page numbering in Arabic numerals. Your first chapter hence will *not* start on page 1.

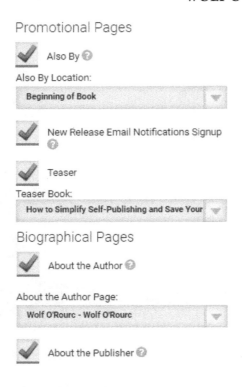

Figure 8-2: D2D E-Book Back Matter Entry

THE MARKETING SECTIONS pull **content from information you entered on tabs separate from a single book's metadata. Also By and Teaser look at all books on your D2D bookshelf under the [My Books] tab**. The two **About pages** use what you provide in [**Contributor Profiles**] and [**Publishers**] **under the [My Account] tab** in the main menu atop the website. Their [**Edit**] and [**View Profile**] buttons bring up various fields and a WYSIWYG editor to enter the text displayed with **bold**, *italics*, and underline options. A [**Browse**] button lets you **upload an image**. A separate field accepts a **URL to a contributor's website**. You can label each entry to differentiate profiles by genre for the same author.

The **lists to select books and profiles only appear when you checkmark a field**. Once picked, D2D **hides the information**. To change a selection, **uncheck then checkmark the field again**.

For print books, you'll find the choices at the bottom of the [**Details**] tab. There's no separate chapter detection.

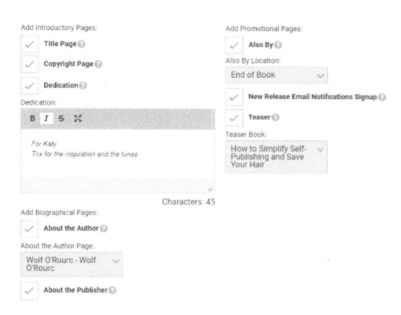

Figure 8-3: D2D Print Book End Matter Entry

AS THE EXAMPLES BELOW show, **D2D end matter doesn't have headers or page numbers**. Unless you suppress them on the chapter pages in general, custom entries in your manuscript *will* have page numbers.

To generate the end matter, click the [**Save & Continue**] button. If you use the tabs at the top to go to the previewer without saving, D2D will not create the specified pages.

TIP D2D's import attempts to detect elements like a title page or table of contents. **If you want them generated, remove the matching pages from your manuscript**.

KC

YOU HAVE CONSIDERABLY more flexibility in customizing the end matter generated by KC, but at the price of heaps of hair. Without access to KDP's **Details** pages, **you must enter the book and author information all over again.** Just to see that **effort wasted when you need to upload a revised manuscript.** Consider copying the generated pages from the editor pane to your word processor for safekeeping or create the sections there to begin with.

TIP D2D includes its generated end matter in the MOBI file, which you can upload to KDP instead of going through all the hassle with KC.

All the end matter follows the broad formatting imposed by the selected theme.

Unlike D2D's simple checkmark procedure, you have to **add end matter one by one with the [(+)] buttons** of either the **Front-** or **Backmatter** list. Each menu in Figure 8-4 offers a selection specific to the section in the commonly used order, although you can drag headings up and down to rearrange them.

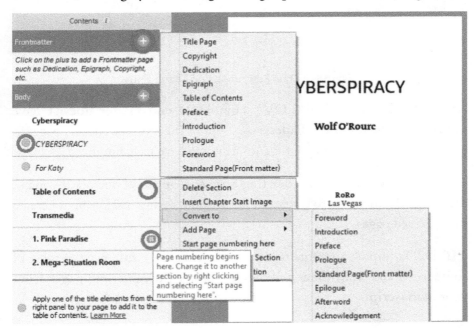

Figure 8-4: KC Front Matter Selection

THE **Contents** pane distinguishes between two major types of end matter with different behavior. [**Title Page**], [**Copyright**], [**Dedication**], **and the marketing pages require you to fill out forms.** Other than changing the theme, you have no formatting control. Some fields accepts HTML codes but the results are hit or miss. Once created, update the information by clicking the [**Edit Page**] button in the **Page Properties** pane as shown at the right of the sample in Figure 8-5 below.

All the other end matter types are freeform and fully editable. They merely differ in their page numbering convention. Their **Page Properties** pane offers the same formatting options as the body text, except for the **distinct formatting elements Page Title** and **Page Subtitle** instead of the chapter versions.

KC's chapter detection makes some effort to find end matter, but all pages end up in the **Body** list of the **Contents** pane. You can **drag headings up or down to rearrange their order**, but you can't drag them from **Body** to the **Front-** or **Backmatter** list. To **move any custom end matter sections included in your manuscript** to the correct position, **right-click the heading**, select [**Convert to**], and make an end matter choice. The same function changes from one freeform end matter type to another. **You can't convert text to a type requiring a form**, such as the [**Title Page**] or [**Copyright**].

As shown in Figure 8-4, KC **flags pages it could not properly identify with a yellow dot**. To force a new page and include the heading in the table of contents, format its beginning as [**Chapter Title**] in the editor pane.

The [**Standard Page**] choice lets you create a custom entry from a blank page. You can't move these entries between the two lists. If you change your mind, right-click the heading and [**Delete Section**], then recreate it at the other side.

As the examples below show, **KC end matter doesn't have headers**. Front matter types that commonly have page numbers, such as the [**Foreword**], use lowercase Roman numerals. Some back matter may have them in Arabic numerals.

The **hashtag icon** in Figure 8-4 **marks page 1** of the body text. If you created a [**Prologue**] in the front matter, it will use Roman numerals. To include these pages in the body's count, right-click the heading and select [**Start page numbering here**]. Since you'll lose any prologues created in KC if you need to upload a new manuscript, you might as well include those pages in the body.

Zon

KDP OFFERS NO HELP with end matter. 'Nuff said.

Resources

IBPA: Industry Standards Checklist for a Professionally Published Book[2]

D2D: Automated End-matter[3]

D2D: Creating your Ebook - Ebook Publishing Step 2: Layout (VIDEO)[4]

D2D: D2D Print - Converting Your Ebook to Print - Step 1: Details (VIDEO)[5]

D2D: D2D Print - Step 1: Details (VIDEO)[6]

Author Level Up: Optimize Your Book's Back Matter with Draft2Digital's Formatting Tools[7]

KDP: Kindle Create Help - Format the title page and other front matter[8]

2. https://www.ibpa-online.org/page/standards-checklist-download

3. https://www.draft2digital.com/account/endmatter/

4. https://www.youtube.com/watch?v=PtKydXLBeX4

5. https://www.youtube.com/watch?v=iQyfSQQqsaY

6. https://www.youtube.com/watch?v=56JkPSYaDc8

7. https://www.youtube.com/watch?v=4tZfETvsdF4

8. https://kdp.amazon.com/help?topicId=G7R2L7V5X6SJH948#front

The following sections cover specific end matter types in the order commonly found in a book. Examples generated by D2D generally appear on the left with a **blue frame**, KC ones on the right in **orange**.

8.2. Title Page

THE **title pages show the book title, subtitle, series title, author names, and publisher information**. A print book can have as many as three back to back.

D2D pulls data from the [**Details**] page and the [**Contributor Profiles**] and [**Publishers**] **under the** [**My Account**] **tab**. A detected title page in your document may suppress auto-generation.

KC requires you to fill out the form in Figure 8-5 that also allows uploading a Publisher's logo.

Figure 8-5: KC Title Entry

NEITHER PLATFORM GENERATES half title (only the book title) or series title pages. Since KC allows you to add multiple [**Title Pages**] to its **Frontmatter**, you can almost achieve that effect by entering series titles in the **Book Title** field. KC will generate a blank page after each, however. Customarily the series title is on the back (verso) of the half title. In print, the title type matches the cover's font.

If you list more than one author, D2D shows them all on one line separated by "and," shown in Figure 8-6. To add names in KC, click the [(+)] button next to **Author Name**. The resultant page has them stacked one on top of the other.

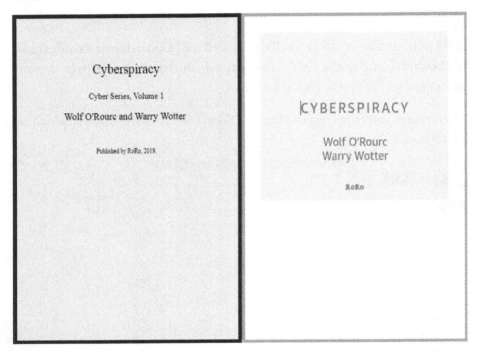

Figure 8-6: Generated D2D and KC E-Book Title Page

CUSTOMARILY FOR A PRINT book the publisher name, logo, and city appear at the bottom of this page. As shown in Figure 8-7, Draft2Digital uses the lower placement. KC doesn't.

Both platforms bunch up the information for e-books so everything still displays on one page in a horizontal view in Figure 8-6.

Neither has a field for the city. You can add it on the same line as the name, of course. D2D adds the year of publication.

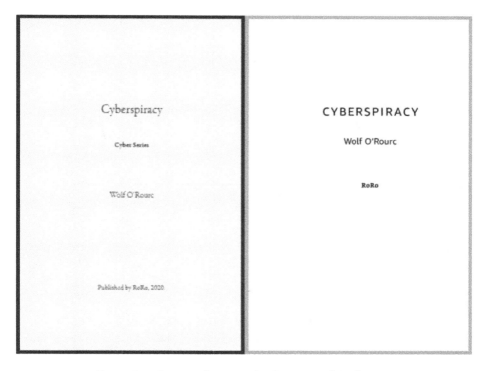

Figure 8-7: Generated D2D and KC Print Book Title Page

8.3. Copyright Page

THE **copyright page, usually the back of the title page, displays the book title, author, copyright year and holder, other legal notices, edition, publishing, and cataloging information**.

D2D pulls data from the **Details** page. KC requires you to fill out the form in Figure 8-8.

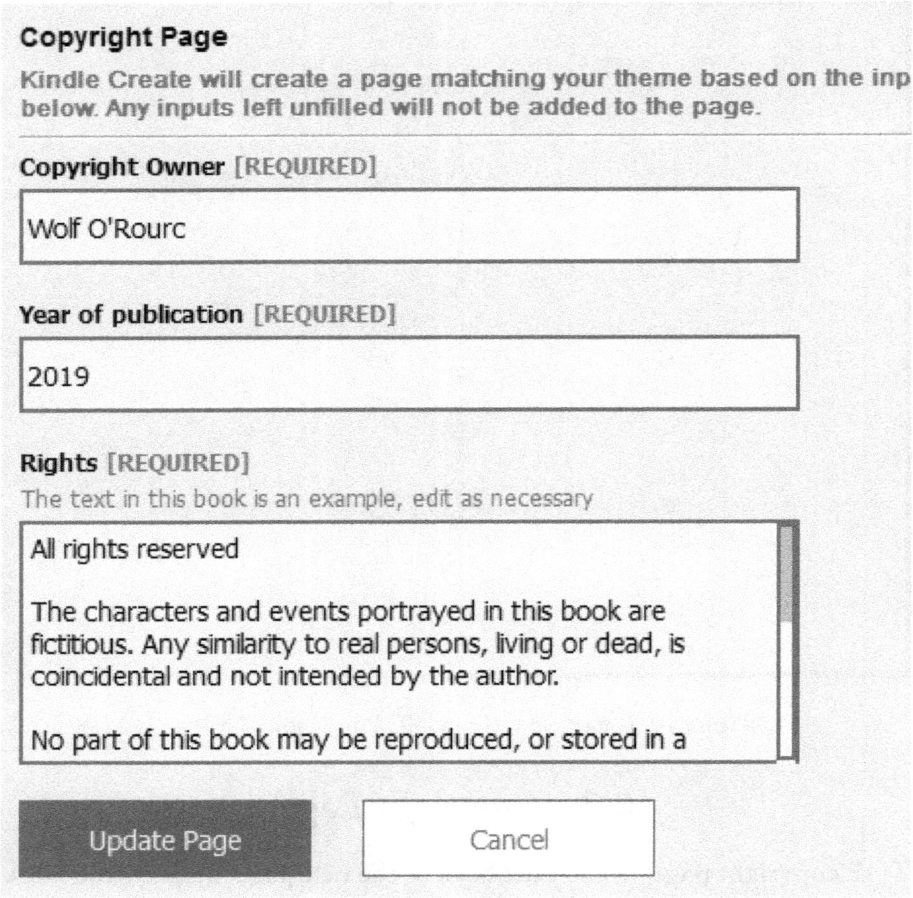
Copyright Page
Kindle Create will create a page matching your theme based on the inp
below. Any inputs left unfilled will not be added to the page.
Copyright Owner [REQUIRED]
Wolf O'Rourc
Year of publication [REQUIRED]
2019
Rights [REQUIRED]
The text in this book is an example, edit as necessary
All rights reserved
The characters and events portrayed in this book are fictitious. Any similarity to real persons, living or dead, is coincidental and not intended by the author.
No part of this book may be reproduced, or stored in a
Update Page
Cancel

Figure 8-8: KC Copyright Entry

HISTORICALLY, THE PAGE had information for **ordering and shelving a book** in a library. In the USA, that included both the ten- and thirteen-digit **ISBN**, a **Library of Congress Control Number** (LCCN), and a **Cataloging in Publication (CIP) block**. With most users now downloading such information from online sources like WorldCat.org, even large publishers have switched to a minimal page.

D2D uses such industry-standard boilerplates for the waiver and copyright, shown on the page in Figure 8-9.

While every precaution has been taken in the preparation of this book, the publisher assumes no responsibility for errors or omissions, or for damages resulting from the use of the information contained herein.

CYBERSPIRACY

First edition. August 31, 2019.

Copyright © 2019 Wolf O'Rourc.

ISBN: 978-1951187002

Written by Wolf O'Rourc.

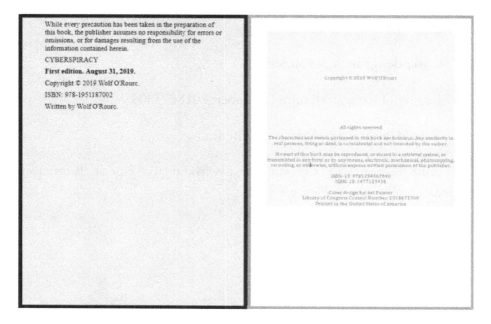

Figure 8-9: Generated D2D and KC E-Book Copyright Page

KC USES A LONGER FORMAT with a waiver and dummy copyright data. Don't forget to change the placeholders to the correct information or delete unused lines.

WOLF O'ROURC

ISBN-13: 9781234567890

ISBN-10: 1477123456

Cover design by: Art Painter

Library of Congress Control Number: 2018675309

Printed in the United States of America

The print version uses the same text without the e-book formatting limitations, as shown in Figure 8-10.

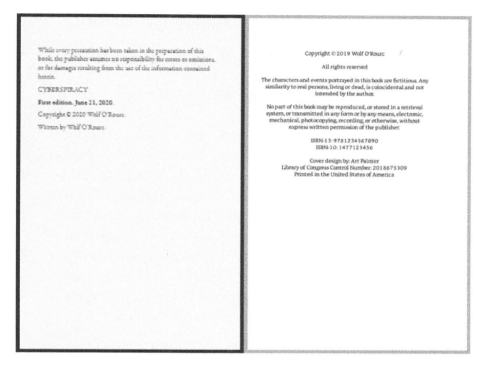

Figure 8-10: Generated D2D and KC Print Copyright Page

SOME AUTHORS INCLUDE **additional information for their readers**, often in humorous form.

Like Amazon, many publishers list **credits for cover designers and other contributors** at the bottom. For reasons having to do with the random disulfide bonds that cause hair to curl, D2D explicitly **chose to exclude Non-Author Contributors from the page**. Any information you entered in that section will not show up anywhere.

Since D2D offers no data entry field, to provide more information you currently have to create a custom copyright page, which will be out of order to any generated table of contents or dedication.

Cyberspiracy, for example, has this long one to claim rights in any galaxy in the known universe, just in case.

CYBERSPIRACY

WOLF O'ROURC

---

9. http://www.Cyberspiracy.com

ISBN-13: 978-1-951187-00-2 (ebook), 978-1-951187-01-9 (paperback), 978-1-951187-02-6 (audiobook)

Cover design by Gina Parham, Art Of Gina

Publishers Cataloging-In-Publication Data

Names: O'Rourc, Wolf, author.

Title: Cyberspiracy / Wolf O'Rourc.

Description: First edition. | Las Vegas : RoRo, 2019 | Summary: While hiding from bullying behind her macho avatar, a lonely, pink-haired hacker girl battles the high-tech henchmen of a president provoking nuclear war.

Identifiers: LCCN 2019909786 | ISBN 9781951187019 (paperback) | ISBN 9781951187002 (ebook) | ISBN 9781951187026 (audio disc)

Subjects: CYAC: Computer hackers—Fiction | Computer crimes—Fiction | Bullying—Fiction | Sexism—Fiction | Sex discrimination against women—Fiction | Women in technology—Fiction | Women computer programmers—Fiction | Presidents—United States—Election—Fiction | BISAC: YOUNG ADULT FICTION / Thrillers & Suspense | YOUNG ADULT FICTION / Computers & Digital Media | YOUNG ADULT FICTION / Social Themes / Bullying.

Resources

VERVANTE: What to put on your book copyright page[10]

Vervante: The Right Way to Copyright a Book[11]

---

10. https://vervante.com/blog/2020/06/copyrightpage

11. https://vervante.com/blog/2017/05/howtocopyright

BookBaby: What To Include On Your Book's Copyright Page[12]

The Book Designer: Getting Creative with Disclaimers[13]

New Shelves Books: What Authors And Publishers Need To Know About CIP, PCIP, MARC, LCCN, PCN[14]

Midwest Book Review: How to Get a CIP or PCIP[15]

ALLi: Copyright for Indie Authors[16]

Kindlepreneur: How to Copyright a Book in the U.S. (Written by a Lawyer)[17]

Poets & Writers: Copyright Information for Writers[18]

U.S. Copyright Office: Frequently Asked Questions about Copyright[19]

Self Publishing School: How to Copyright a Book Quickly Step-by-Step[20]

Creative Law Center: How to Copyright a Series of Books[21]

8.4. Dedication

THE **dedication explains, usually in two short lines, who you dedicate your book to and why.**

---

12. https://blog.bookbaby.com/2019/12/your-books-copyright-page

13. https://www.thebookdesigner.com/2016/03/getting-creative-with-disclaimers

14. https://newshelves.com/2016/03/16/
    what-authors-and-small-publishers-need-to-know-about-cip-pcip-marc-lccn-pcn

15. http://www.midwestbookreview.com/bookbiz/advice/cip1.htm

16. https://selfpublishingadvice.org/copyright-for-indie-authors

17. https://kindlepreneur.com/how-to-copyright-a-book

18. http://www.pw.org/content/copyright

19. http://www.copyright.gov/help/faq

20. https://self-publishingschool.com/how-to-copyright-a-book

21. https://creativelawcenter.com/copyright-book-series

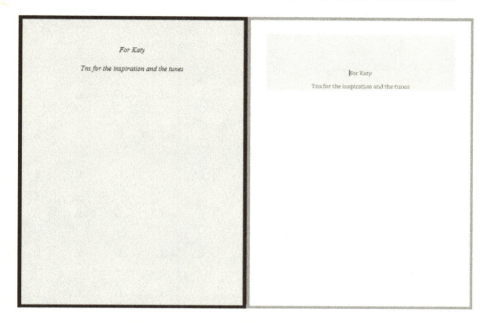

Figure 8-11: Generated D2D and KC E-Book Dedication Page

D2D PROVIDES A WYSIWYG editor for freeform entry and formatting, customarily italics, as shown in Figure 8-11 and Figure 8-12. KC requires you to fill out a form. The formatting is hence at the mercy of the theme. Three italicize the text, but not Cosmos.

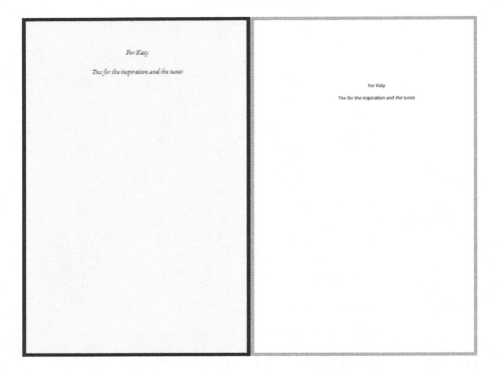

Figure 8-12: Generated D2D and KC Print Dedication Page

8.5. Epigraph

ONLY KC OFFERS THIS **fancy way of saying "a quote that complements your book's subject"** to go along with the periwig you'll need once you finished publishing with KDP.

8.6. Table of Contents

THE TABLE OF CONTENTS (ToC) **lists the major sections of the book with their starting page numbers (print) or hyperlinks to them (e-book).** KDP's sloppy conversion of Word documents, leading to disagreements between the ToC and chapter starting page numbers, murdered more author hair than all biblical plagues combined. Admittedly, not a high bar, since most ancient Egyptians shaved their heads.

Few readers may have cared about inconsistencies as long as they found the right chapter a few pages later. The e-book gave the ToC new prominence and importance. **Without page numbers, the hyperlinks provided the only means to quickly reach a specific point deep into the file**.

Regardless, D2D took care of this plague on writer's tresses despite the challenges these scribes presented it with.

Since time immemorial, or at least since the year 1 AE (After E-book), conversion software followed the same convention as MS Word that **Heading 1 style marks a chapter title**. Technically, Microsoft includes in its table of contents any paragraph with a **style at Outline level 1**, which usually includes **Title** and others. But many writers ignore styles, choosing instead to apply formatting such as **bold, centered, or larger font size**.

End matter only worsened the situation. **Copyright and Dedication pages, for instance, have no heading**. Conversely, non-fiction, like this guide, may use three or more levels of headings to finely divide the information into chunks.

Rather than force authors into conforming to one hairstyle, **D2D created a flexible detection algorithm**. It takes a best guess at commonly used sections **based on key phrases, formatting, and position in the book**. The results appear for review in the **Chapter Layout** list of the [**Layout**] tab shown at the right of Figure 8-1.

With e-books, D2D gives you considerable leeway but no choice, because of the importance of a table of contents. A Microsoft Word generated one, or even typed text with a title like "Contents" can prevent the auto-generation. If these pages don't include proper hyperlinks, the result will be useless to readers. **To avail yourself of a proper, generated ToC, remove any existing ones from your manuscript**.

Kindle Create takes a simpler approach. Both face similar challenges, however.

In fiction, **end matter included in the manuscript may throw the algorithm**. As mentioned, some sections' titles won't follow the same formatting as the body or mention the word "chapter."

Complex non-fiction, like this guide, make the detection task much harder. The platforms have diverging ways of dealing with the problem.

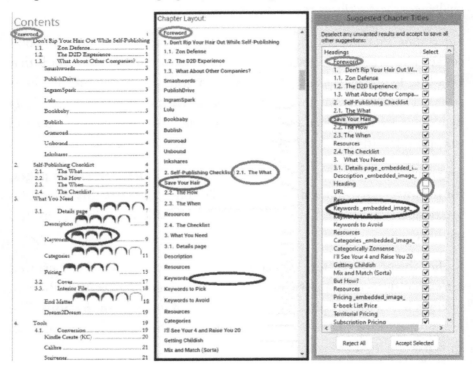

Figure 8-13: Word, D2D and KC Table of Contents

MICROSOFT WORD'S AUTOMATIC tables of contents include **Heading 1 through 3** and any other styles at the top three outline levels. The table at the left of Figure 8-13, for example, includes the Foreword because it uses the level 1 **Title** style. Word's custom option allows you to specify any level up to 9. You can give any styles an outline level to include those entries. To exclude an entry, change its style. Word doesn't look at any text formatting when building a ToC.

In contrast, **D2D looks at the top three headings and any lines that stand out due to bold, centered, or larger text**. To ensure detection, they suggest increasing the font size at least 4 points. If lines are too similar, the algorithm may combine them, as happened in the center table of Figure 8-13. The headings for 2 and 2.1 had almost the same formatting, differing only by 2 points in size, and followed each other without intervening text. The algorithm also looks for phrases commonly used in books, such as "chapter" or "Contents," at the beginning of sections. It considers any line following a page break, as you can see in the center of Figure 8-15.

Images instead of chapter titles require additional work. Give files unique names and add unique Word bookmarks to each. Then build a table of contents out of them.

A click on [**Help! These Aren't My Chapters!**] (can you imagine *that* button at the Zon?) brings up the **Improper Chapter Detection** dialogue box which presents you with various choices found in your manuscript, including multiple levels of **headings**, **bold**, **larger**, and/or **centered** text.

Improper Chapter Detection   ✕

We strive to have a system that does not require you to preformat your book to a predetermined style guide, but we're not always able to detect all styles correctly. **The best thing you can do is make sure your chapter titles are consistently formatted.** Please select the formatting option below that indicates your correct chapter headings.

Select Chapter Formatting Option

Bold, Larger Text	Header 1	Header 2	Header 3
Gumroad	How to Simplify Self-Publish...	How to Simplify Self-Publish...	How to Simplify Self-Publish...
Unbound	1. Don't Rip Your Hair Out Wh...	1.1. Zon Defense	Smashwords
Inkshares	2. Self-Publishing Checklist	1.2. The D2D Experience	PublishDrive
2. Self-Publishing Checklist l...	3. What You Need	1.3. What About Other Com...	IngramSpark
Save Your Hair	4. Tools	2.1. The What	Lulu
2.2. The How	5. Creating Your Sales Page	2.2. The How	Bookbaby

‹   ›

[BACK TO MY LAYOUT]   [SUBMIT]

Still not fixed?

We recommend checking out our formatting guidelines. You can find them here on our blog. Or you can submit a request to the layout team.

We receive a high volume of layout requests. Due to the amount of time that requests of this nature require, it takes longer than our typical customer support response times to fully address them.

Figure 8-14: D2D Improper Chapter Detection

AS SHOWN IN Figure 8-14, for this complex guide the algorithm decided to pick any lines with bolded *and* larger text. You can limit the detection to **one of the top three headings**, but not a combination. To get the multi-level list in Figure 8-13, use one of the offered combinations of bold, centered, or larger text. In this case, specifying "**Bold, Centered**" would limit the ToC to **Heading 1** and **Title** lines, since the next two levels are left aligned instead of centered.

The new criteria also excluded the "Save Your Hair" ad. Otherwise, **to remove individual entries, you'd need to change the formatting of that particular line**. That becomes an issue if your manuscript includes custom end matter, as shown in Figure 8-15.

Every section you include in the chapter detection will not only appear in the table of contents, but also **add a page break and drop or phrase caps**.

At present, you can't change the detection for print books. Leaving **Include Table of Contents** on the **Inside** tab unchecked will drop it.

KC falls in between. You **can't change the broad detection criteria**. The **Suggested Chapter Titles** dialogue box only **lets you toggle inclusion of individual entries**. Obviously, for complex works like this guide, it becomes a chore. To split off headings KC didn't detect, you have to change their formatting in the manuscript, or apply [**Chapter Title**] in the editor. Chapter Subtitle won't do.

Neither platforms offers the ideal of turning on entries individually *and* adjusting criteria. I have hair hopes that D2D may do so in the future.

Whereas Word includes the scalp graphics in its ToC in Figure 8-13, KC includes alternate text. Only D2D, with their ability to read authors' minds, cleans up the clutter.

A novel with its simpler structure causes little trouble, especially if you let the platform generate the end matter. Both D2D and KC include those sections automatically. For e-books, all entries have hyperlinks to the corresponding section, shown in Figure 8-15. Both platforms will also correctly convert links in a table of contents generated by MS Word.

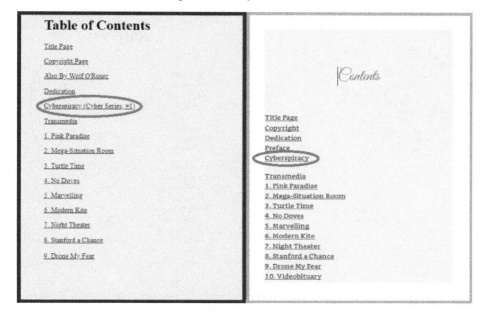

Figure 8-15: Generated D2D and KC E-Book Table of Contents Page

FOR PAPERBACKS, BOTH D2D and KC's table of contents generation solve the problem of wrong page numbers. The two differ in handling of end matter without them. As shown in Figure 8-16, D2D on the left doesn't bother including those pages. KC lists the sections with blank space to the right.

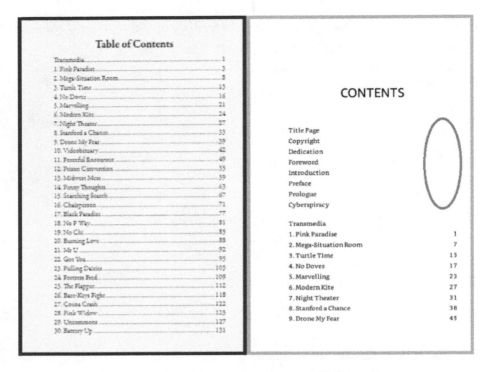

Figure 8-16: Generated D2D and KC Print Table of Contents Page

D2D STARTS EVERY CHAPTER on a new page. For paperbacks with many small sections, like this guide, the increase in size may become an issue. I chose a compromise by limiting the levels in the table of contents. **Uploading a print-ready PDF**, like I did for *Word Wizardry for Writers*, of course **gives you complete control**.

Resources

D2D: Draft2Digital's Pocket Guide to eBook Layout[22]

D2D: Style Suggestions[23]

KDP: Kindle Create Help - Build your table of contents[24]

---

22. https://www.draft2digital.com/blog/the-pocket-guide-to-ebook-layout/

23. https://www.draft2digital.com/style-suggestions/

24. https://kdp.amazon.com/help?topicId=G7R2L7V5X6SJH948#toc

8.7. Foreword/Introduction/Preface

KC'S FRONT MATTER INCLUDES almost identical freeform introductory pages, which differ mostly in purpose rather than formatting. A **foreword** is typically an introduction **written by someone other than the author**. Otherwise, **explanatory text at the beginning of a novel is called a preface. Nonfiction books usually use the term introduction**.

D2D doesn't auto-generate these pages. If you include them in your manuscript and create a print book, they will start the page count for the body in Arabic numerals.

8.8. Prologue/Epilogue

UNLIKE THE INTRODUCTIONS above, **prologues and epilogue show parts of the story that precede or follow the main timeline to set the scene or wrap up subplots.** They typically belong in your manuscript as part of the body text.

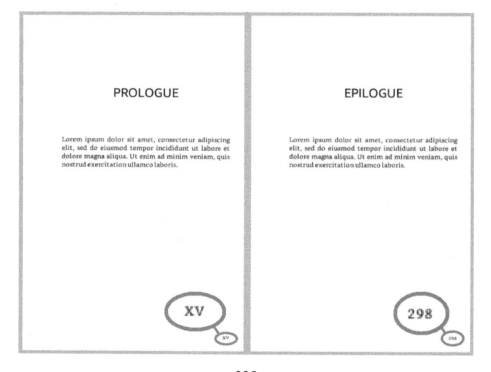

Figure 8-17: Generated KC Print Prologue and Epilogue Page

KC LETS YOU ADD THEM as separate sections with page numbers in the paperback, as Figure 8-17 shows. Following the Chicago Manual of Style, the prologue uses Roman numerals. Some consider this an artifact left over from a time when inserting pages in the front matter would otherwise trigger a cumbersome repagination. If you prefer to bind a prologue tighter to the body, right-click the heading and select [**Start page numbering here**] to trigger the page count in Arabic numerals.

Since D2D doesn't generate prologues, including them in the manuscript will automatically number them that way.

8.9. Afterword

KC'S BACK MATTER INCLUDES a freeform **afterword for closing statements or comments**, such as how the book came into being, or anything else you can think off like a glossary or a list of characters in the book. Of course, you could simply start with a blank [**Standard Page**].

D2D only generates marketing sections at the end of a book. If you include an afterword or glossary in your manuscript, it will look like another chapter in your book and display the theme's graphics. Since the page numbering of back matter follows the body, you don't have to wrack your *hairbrain* about it.

You can take advantage of readers' emotional high after a satisfying ending by using the first page of your back matter to **gently remind them to leave a review**. **Universal Book Links** can direct them to their favorite store.

8.10. Acknowledgement

KC INCLUDES A FREEFORM acknowledgement for thanking people who helped create the book, such as sources, critique partners, or sponsors.

Interestingly, D2D doesn't generates this common section. If you don't mind the theme's graphics, you can roll your own by including the pages in your manuscript, as shown in Figure 8-18.

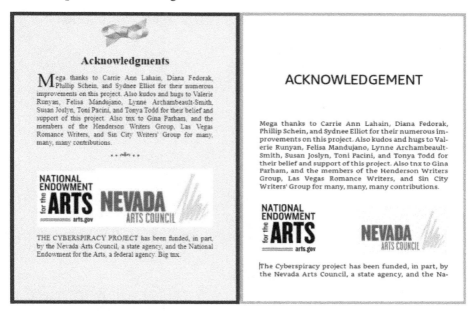

Figure 8-18: Generated D2D and KC E-Book Acknowledgement Page

FOR PAPERBACKS, D2D will add page numbers that follow the body's count, seen in Figure 8-19, unless you turn them off globally.

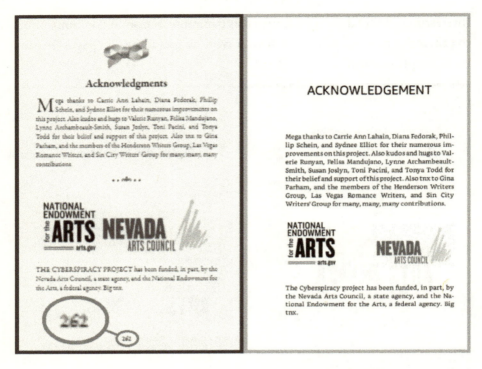

Figure 8-19: Generated D2D and KC Print Acknowledgement Page

8.11. Also By

ALSO BY is such a **powerful author-marketing tool** that D2D lets you include it in the front and back matter. For every author in the [**Details**], D2D generates a page with a **list of every book by that author on the account's bookshelf.**

In e-books, readers who enjoy your work can click the corresponding **Universal Book Link** to go directly to a book's sales page at their favorite online store. Each list ends with the **webpage address from the [Contributor Profiles] under the [My Account] tab.**

TIP Taking advantage of automatic downloads of new versions, **Draft2Digital can update the Also By pages in all of your e-books.** Whenever you release something, go to the [**Layout**] (e-book) and [**Details**]

(print) pages of items on your bookshelf and **click the [Save & Continue] buttons to generate new end matter.**

KC offers two sections in **Backmatter**, [**Books By This Author**] and [**Books In This Series**]. Since the software lacks access to your bookshelf, you have to enter titles, descriptions, and Amazon links for each book in a form like Figure 8-20.

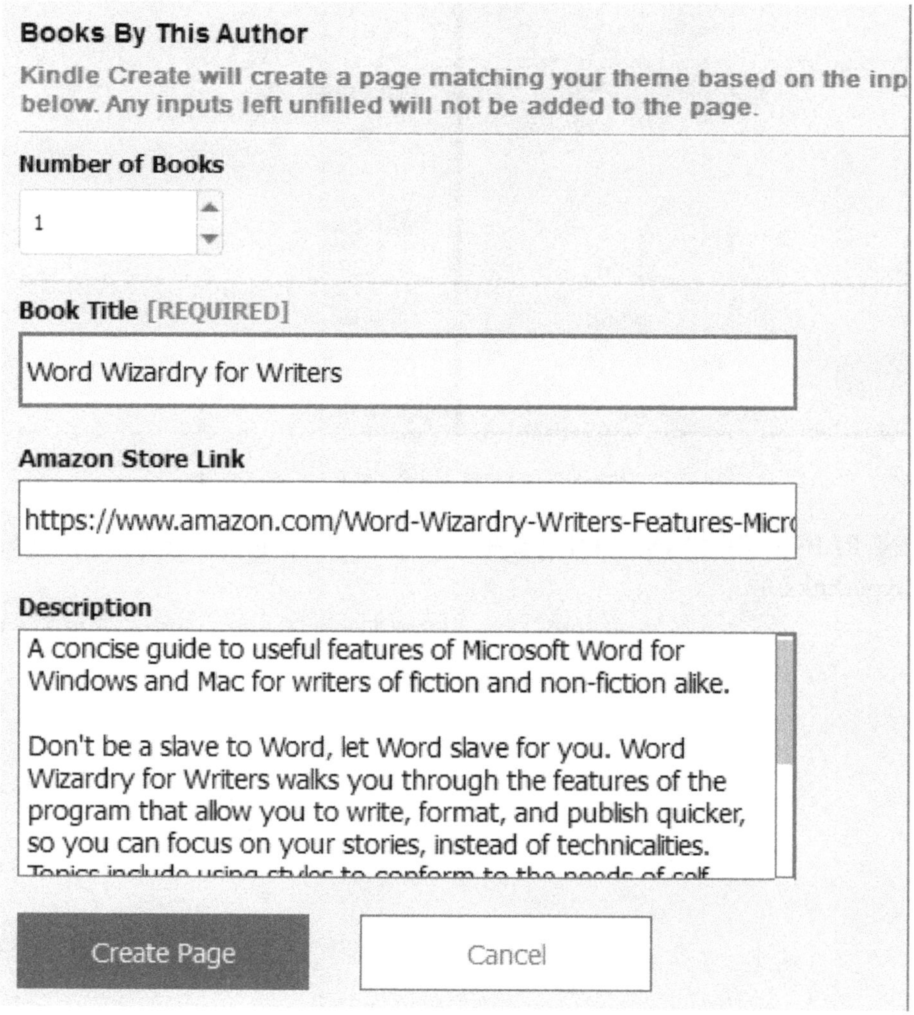

Books By This Author

Kindle Create will create a page matching your theme based on the inp below. Any inputs left unfilled will not be added to the page.

Number of Books

1

Book Title [REQUIRED]

Word Wizardry for Writers

Amazon Store Link

https://www.amazon.com/Word-Wizardry-Writers-Features-Micro

Description

A concise guide to useful features of Microsoft Word for Windows and Mac for writers of fiction and non-fiction alike.

Don't be a slave to Word, let Word slave for you. Word Wizardry for Writers walks you through the features of the program that allow you to write, format, and publish quicker, so you can focus on your stories, instead of technicalities.
~~Topics include using styles to conform to the needs of self~~

Create Page   Cancel

Figure 8-20: KC Books By This Author Entry

SINCE YOU CAN PUT ANY URL into the Link field, you can add any book you want, such as from your D2D catalogue or your website. KC applies the selected theme, as shown in Figure 8-21.

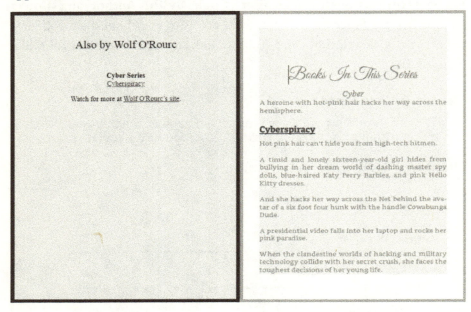

Figure 8-21: Generated D2D and KC E-Book Also By Page

IN PRINT BOOKS, THE pages in Figure 8-22 look similar but lack hyperlinks.

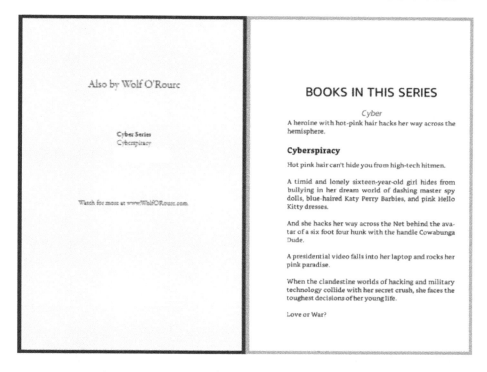

Figure 8-22: Generated D2D and KC Print Also By Page

8.12. New Release Email Notifications Signup

NEW RELEASE NOTIFICATIONS **let your readers know the minute you release new books with Universal Book Links.** Draft2Digital manages this primary marketing strategy on your behalf. No mailing list or newsletter for you to deal with to keep reader's attention.

D2D currently can't generate signups for books with more than one author.

KC has no equivalent. Like Books2Read, Amazon offers a similar service with a [**+ Follow**] button on **Sales Pages** and **Author Pages**, but not integrated into a book's end matter.

In e-books, shown in Figure 8-23, the page has a clickable **signup link at Books2Read.com**, the website for managing UBLs.

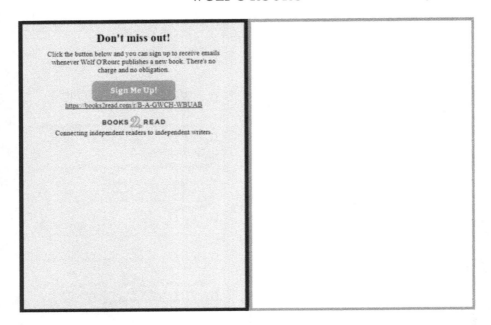

Figure 8-23: Generated D2D E-Book New Release Email Notifications Signup Page

FOR PRINT BOOKS, SHOWN in Figure 8-24, the page lists a cryptic web address. No scannable QR code (sigh, pulling on hair).

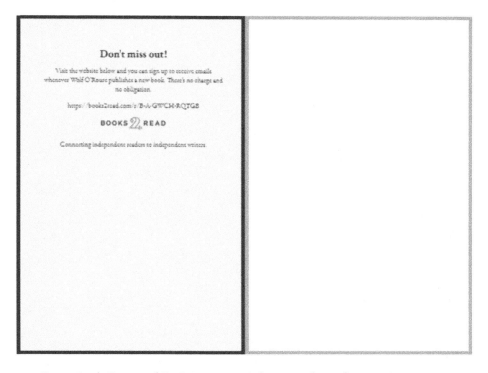

Figure 8-24: Generated D2D Print New Release Email Notifications Signup Page

8.13. Teaser

WITH A FEW CLICKS, you can add **any one of the titles on your D2D bookshelf as a teaser with a thumbnail of the cover**. This does not include a sample chapter, merely the sales description with all the formatting specified in [**Details**]. For e-books by a single author, the teaser starts with **Books2Read links** and wraps up with a call to action and the **clickable website address from the [Contributor Profiles]**.

For KC, you can roll your own with the [**Books By This Author**] section. The entry form accepts chapter length prose without formatting or images. You can add a clickable Amazon book link. Actually, any website address works, but the displayed text will be whatever you enter under Book Title. Of course, you can create any teaser to your liking with a [**Standard Page**]. Figure 8-25 shows the pages for e-books.

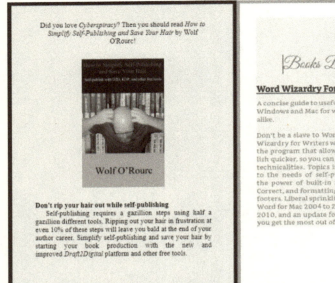

Figure 8-25: Generated D2D and KC E-Book Teaser Page

THE D2D PRINT VERSION spells out the Books2Read URLs and the author website address. KDP's doesn't, unless you type the information into the form, as shown in Figure 8-26.

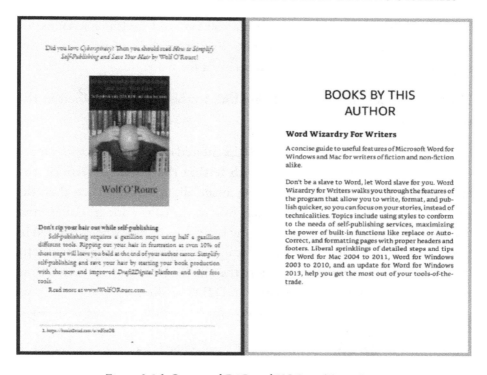

Figure 8-26: Generated D2D and KC Print Teaser Page

8.14. About the Author

CUSTOMARILY, **About the Author** shows an **image of the author with a brief, informative biography** appropriate to the genre and topic of the book. Readers love tidbits about their favorite writers.

D2D pulls the needed pieces from the [**Contributor Profiles**] **under the** [**My Account**] **tab**, same as the Author Page. See 12.3 for tips on bios and headshots. You can include social media information, but any links will only display as text.

With multiple writers, unlike Also By, you pick any *one* to include. To cover different genres, you can create additional profiles under the same contributor name.

D2D allows customary formatting and, in e-books, extended characters like emoji.

KC permits neither in its entry form. You can add multiple sections for additional authors, however. A separate [**Praise for the author**] uses a form to gather quotes with attributions in praise of the work.

In e-books, D2D includes a **clickable link to the website specified in the selected profile**.

KC's form has no such option. Any URLs entered only display as text. Figure 8-27 also **illustrates the problem with letting the theme determine the formatting**. While I could change the image alignment to match the title, the author name remains off on the left. Worse, the editor doesn't understand apostrophes and lowercased the R in my last name despite what I entered in the field. That alone deserves another scalp, but pulling on a wig of synthetic hair really hurts my fingers. Also, note the placeholder box within the name on the right page, instead of the emoji in D2D's version.

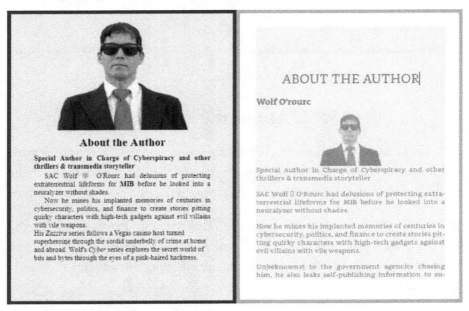

Figure 8-27: Generated D2D and KC E-Book About the Author Page

THE D2D PRINT VERSION in Figure 8-28 shows the website address.

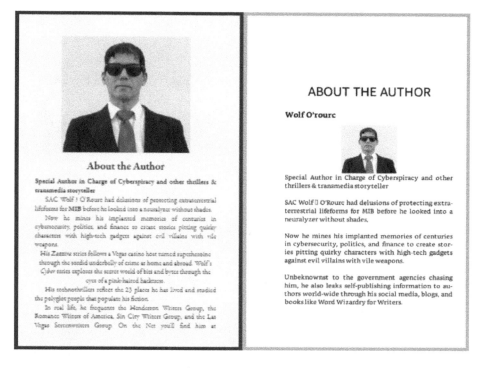

Figure 8-28: Generated D2D and KC Print About the Author Page

BOTH PLATFORMS HAVE **separate entry fields for the bio customarily found on the back cover, so it can differ from this page**.

8.15. About the Publisher

IF READERS ENJOY ONE author in a publisher's catalog, they may like others. The **About the Publisher** page **allows promotion of your publisher or imprint**.

D2D pulls the information from [**Publishers**] **under the [My Account] tab**. KC uses a freeform page. Both hence allow customary formatting and an image, such as a logo, as shown in Figure 8-29. You can also list where to find catalogs of books or social media for other authors. D2D currently does not provide a means to include clickable links. Like other KC freeform pages, you can insert a hyperlink by right-clicking selected text.

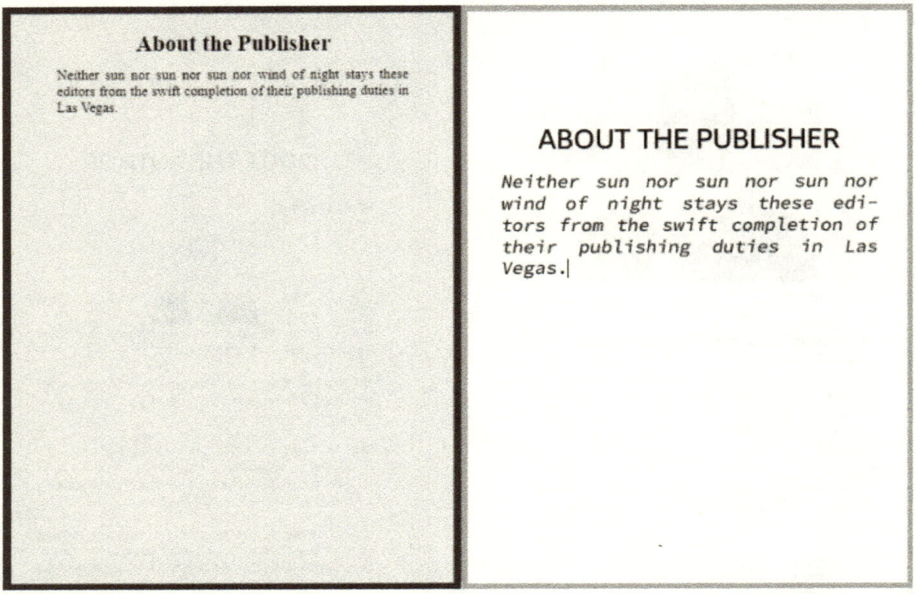

About the Publisher

Neither sun nor sun nor sun nor wind of night stays these editors from the swift completion of their publishing duties in Las Vegas.

ABOUT THE PUBLISHER

Neither sun nor sun nor sun nor wind of night stays these editors from the swift completion of their publishing duties in Las Vegas.

Figure 8-29: Generated D2D and KC E-Book About the Publisher Page

THE PRINT VERSIONS in Figure 8-30 look the same, other than KC's having a page number.

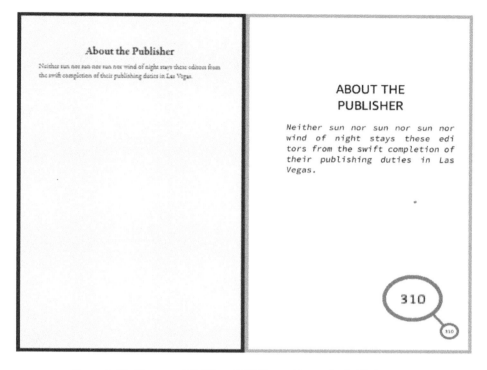

Figure 8-30: Generated D2D and KC Print About the Publisher Page

9. Cover

———

L est someone accuse this guide of discriminating against orange hair, KDP definitely has the edge in e-book cover creation. Draft2Digital does hold its own when extending a front cover to wrap around across the spine and back. Kindle Create does not deal with covers.

TIP Both D2D and KDP will add your ISBN as barcode to the bottom of the back cover. You do *not* need to buy one.

9.1. Working with Images

TO UNDERSTAND COVER requirements, we have to take a trip down Imaging Lane. Computers commonly **mix Red, Green, and Blue (RGB) light to produce a pixel on screen. Varying the intensity of each of the three primary colors** by 256 steps **results in millions of possible shades.** Three numerical values, or a string of their hexadecimal equivalent, precisely specify a digital color. Various technologies render them differently, however. For instance, Draft2Digital's blue on their website—RGB 28, 37, 89 or hex code #1C2559—uses 11% (28 divided by full intensity of 255) red, 15% green, and 35% blue. Two brands of monitors may diverge in how they reproduce this color.

The cover of this guide in print may have a third shade, despite the identical specification. Additive light produces white at full intensity of the three beams, i.e. 255, 255, 255 or #FFFFFF. In contrast, printers layer dots of cyan, magenta, yellow, and black (CMYK) that only reflect said color and absorb the rest. Complete subtractive mixing of inks reflects nothing, or black with an RGB equivalent of no light, or #000000.

Physics makes the conversion more complicated. Most printing technology can't dispense ink in 256 precise quantities. Even high-end laser printers produce fewer colors than most monitors do. The dots also spread out differently on various grades of paper. To achieve the same crisp display requires much smaller dots than pixels.

Table 9-1: Key Printer Numbers

	US	Metric
Conversion	1 inch	25.4 mm
Conversion	0.3937 in	1 cm
Typographic Point	0.01388 in	0.3528 mm
Recommended resolution	300 DPI	118 DPCM
Offset max resolution	≈300 DPI	≈118 DPCM
Inkjet max resolution	720 DPI	283 DPCM
Laser max resolution	2,400 DPI	945 DPCM

The screen resolution of Microsoft Windows defaults to 96 pixels per inch (PPI). Apple started with 72 PPI to exactly reproduce printed documents using points, the physical unit of measure in typography, where 1 point is 1/72 of an inch, as shown in Table 9-1.

A typical notebook computer with an 800 pixel vertical resolution on a 6.5 in high display (12 inch diagonal) only has 123 PPI.

Printers use dots per inch (DPI), the number of individual dots that can be placed in a 1-inch line, or the metric equivalent dots per centimeter (d/cm or DPCM). **The greater the DPI, the smoother and crisper the printed image**. Since the accuracy of an offset press maxes out around **300 DPI, that became the industry standard**. The inkjet and laser printers used in digital printing can reach much higher resolutions, shown in Table 9-1.

Many people use DPI and PPI interchangeably. But inches have no significance on the computer screen. You can zoom in to view details of an image. Its resolution only means something in dot density when you decide to reproduce the picture as a physical entity.

If a 480 pixel (px) high image fills a third of the e-book preview page on the above notebook screen, the computer scales it down to 800 / 3 = 267 PPI and it still looks fine. If that preview were for a 5.5 x 8.5 in paperback, the image would print at 480 / (8.5 / 3) = 169 DPI, half the recommended resolution. To reach offset standard, you need an image around 900 px high.

For a cover with many shades of color, such as photographs, you want higher PPI and DPI. Dithered printing, creating the illusion of new colors and shades by varying the pattern, can require four to six dots to faithfully reproduce the color of a single pixel. **The DPI often needs to be considerably higher than the PPI to produce similar-quality output.** Using the above example, D2D's recommended cover height of 2400 px (see 4.2) comes out to 847 DPI, well within the laser printer range used by POD services.

If your manuscript contains many large color images, you have to balance quality with e-book file size. For example, Cyberspiracy's relatively simple JPEG cover came in a 697 KB. The final MOBI file totaled 1.2 MB. Adding ten such images would blow up the size considerably, resulting in longer down- and upload times and additional charges from Amazon. They do compress the file for delivery, but with complex images that only goes so far. **Both platforms let you upload separate manuscripts and covers for print and e-book**, if you need to optimize them for each format.

Of course, the resolution doesn't matter if you start with blurry images. **If you purchase them, get the highest resolution possible.** You can always downsize them, but upscaling rarely works.

Don't copy and paste images into your word processor. Use the **Insert Pictures** function to embed the original into the document itself.

For best results with **e-books, center images in-line with Text.**

9.2. E-book Cover

E-BOOKS ONLY HAVE A front cover. It must display the title and author name, and any possible subtitle. D2D accepts the common bitmap formats JPG, GIF, PNG, TIF, and BMP. KDP only takes JPG and TIF. With the many advanced reading devices now available, you should **use a color cover even if your interior is only black and white.**

You can create your own using the tools in 5.3. **KDP offers an easy to use Cover Creator. You can upload the output to D2D**, which has no tool of its own. Their Partner Page[1] does have a section for cover designers. You can also try freelance sites like 99 Designs or Fiverr[2].

A good cover design follows psychological principles to attract and guide the eye. Every genre also has conventions that readers recognize, even if only subconsciously. If you create your own, check out covers of bestseller in that subgenre and emulate their practices.

For example, Cyberspiracy's poppy, fun design fits right in with Amazon's Teen & Young Adult thrillers in Figure 9-1. In contrast, it looks out of place in the darker, moodier adult genre.

Figure 9-1: YA and Adult Thrillers Covers (Source: Amazon Best Seller List)

---

1. https://www.draft2digital.com/partners

2. https://www.fiverr.com

D2D

UPLOAD YOUR FRONT COVER at the top of the **Create New Book Project** page. You can change the cover art on the **Edit Book Metadata** page.

Resources

D2D: Setting Up a New Book (VIDEO)[3]

D2D: Setting Up Your Ebook - Ebook Publishing Step 1: Details (VIDEO)[4]

Zon

AFTER YOU'VE FILLED in the **Details**, upload your front cover on the [**Kindle eBook Content**] tab. Amazon considers a **height/width ratio of 1.6:1** ideal, with a minimum of 1,000 x 625 px, and a **recommended 2,560 x 1,600 px**.

Clicking [**Launch Cover Creator**] lets you make a cover from scratch.

You can **upload your own JPG, TIF, or PNG image** that should meet the Amazon Publishing Guidelines[5] and have a minimum resolution of 300 DPI. Any text on it should be legible.

Cover Creator comes with premade elements, including an **Image Gallery** with categories from Animals to Concepts and Ideas to Technology. A search field at the top lets you enter keywords. Since "pink hair" came up empty, I selected guinea pigs for their fabulous fur and subliminal marketing of the sequel *Cyberfurry*.

TIP You may not use covers made using stock images from the gallery outside KDP. **If you want to build a cover for D2D, upload a picture to which you own the rights.**

---

3. https://www.youtube.com/watch?v=zevfgrLVq90

4. https://www.youtube.com/watch?v=v4dLDKpZjVw

5. https://kdp.amazon.com/help?topicId=A1MMZZIUU7LTIB

Once you pick an image, Cover Creator combines it with information from the **Details** tab to create ten **starting designs** shown in Figure 9-2. The help comes at the price of flexibility. The two equally-sized colored bands of this guide's cover were not possible.

Figure 9-2: KDP Front Cover Creator Designs

THE **thumbnail view shows which designs work** on sales pages like the Kindle store. With some, the long title and subtitle become impossible to read, particularly with image-based designs, and thus the cover loses a lot of value in an ad. Since many readers will only see the small version to entice them to click the Buy button, make sure it gets the critical information across.

Once you find a good starting point, [**Style & Edit**] lets you customize **most elements of the cover.**

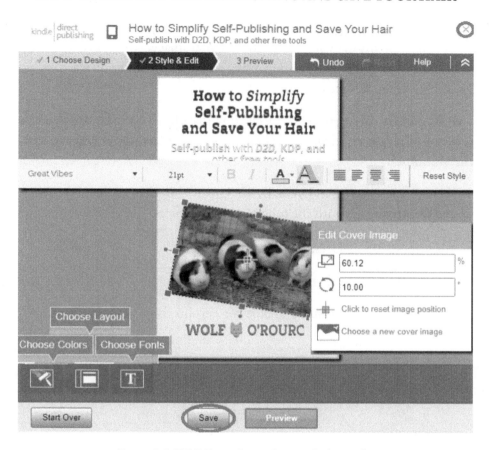

Figure 9-3: KDP Front Cover Creator Style & Edit

THE **three buttons** at the lower left of Figure 9-3 apply **quick styles**.

• Select a pre-styled **color scheme** or create your own by picking primary, secondary, and text colors,

• Choose one of eight **layouts** to reposition the existing design elements,

• Choose **typeface sets**, pre-matched combinations of **fonts**.

Once you've refined the design, you can change individual items. Clicking the photograph brings up a dialogue box with options to **resize and rotate the image**. Dragging the square handles also resizes, whereas the round handles rotates. Dragging the entire picture will **reposition** it. [**Click to reset image position**] will restore the original image, which may be larger than the design. Similarly, **Undo** may not return to the state you want. To go back to picking a design, click [**Start Over**].

TIP Regularly save your work by clicking [Save]. **If you mess up, you can return to the last saved state by clicking the [x] in the upper right to exit, then relaunch.**

To format text elements individually, clicking within their dashed box brings up the formatting bar with the following style choices.

- a good 40 typefaces,

- Autofit or one of 14 font sizes,

- **Bold** or *italics* (only available for certain fonts after selecting text),

- font color,

- drop shadow,

- alignment.

To pick a color, Cover Creator brings up a color palette. You can't specify number codes for a shade, so the blue and orange lettering has an approximation of the corporate colors used on the real cover.

TIP To apply bold and italics to a typeface that doesn't activate the buttons, pick one that does. Format the text as desired, then change to the font you want.

You **can insert or delete text.** Keep in mind, however, that **Cover Creator checks if writing on the cover matches the entries on the Details tab in KDP. Adding returns with [Enter] lets you wrap long titles or subtitles in a logical way without running afoul of this Amazon requirement.** Nothing wrong with adding a wolf emoji either, but Cover Creator, after demanding scores of times to correct the mismatch with KDP, will not show extended characters on the final cover.

Figure 9-3 shows the mismatched mess that comes from exercising as many formatting options as possible. Don't try this at home (or in a barbershop). Make sure that the design follows good layout principles and all elements work together.

Preview lets you check the design in color mode, grayscale, and as a thumbnail. You can zoom in one level to focus on details. To see the cover with different device configurations, use the KDP Online Previewer once you exited Cover Creator. Click [**Save & Submit**] to upload the cover and return to KDP.

TIP Cover Creator doesn't have a button to download the cover for use with D2D or the paperback. **Right-clicking the Preview image lets you save a high-resolution version**. Right-clicking the cover in the KDP Online Previewer saves a low-resolution image. The HTML book download includes the high-res one.

9.3. Paperback Cover

FOR A PRINT BOOK, YOU need to **extend the front cover across the spine and back**. Customarily, **the color scheme wraps around all three sides**.

You **can't finish a wraparound cover for a paperback until you have converted your interior file** and know the exact number of pages. The platforms calculate the spine width based on the following.

- paper type (white/cream),

- print type (color/black and white),

- interior page count.

TIP Don't create the final wraparound cover until you have finalized the manuscript and the paper details. Text blocks should have equal margins on all sides. Changing the cover width may require repositioning many elements.

Amazon and D2D provide tools that help with the final layout of your chosen design. Customarily, the **back contains blurbs**, information printed on the back cover to describe the book and make it attractive to buy, **such as the book description and your author bio, plus your headshot**. You should already have prepared these pieces for the [**Details**] page.

Retail channels also require an **ISBN barcode**. Amazon and D2D will provide it, but you need to block that area in the lower right corner of the back cover. The two platforms don't agree on the exact dimensions. They also use different printers. For a novel-size book, different paper may change the thickness of the spine. **If you publish separately through both, you'll need to plan for two different covers**.

Both companies offer two ways to create a wraparound cover. If you want to have complete control, **download the template for your size and page count** and lay out your design elements on it. Or, use the print cover creators to take care of dimensions and placement.

TIP To check that nothing important falls within the trim safety zone, **overlay the template** in a graphics editor that supports layers. Lower the opacity to see the design below the gridlines.

D2D

WHEN YOU REACH THE [**Cover**] tab, D2D automatically generates a wraparound one from the front cover in the paper size specified on the [**Inside**] tab. The **background color from the top extends all around**.

TIP Right-clicking the cover lets you save it as a JPEG image. Its low resolution makes it *unsuitable for printing*, but you can use it as a template to place higher-quality versions of the various elements to produce a cover for use somewhere else. Unfortunately, **you cannot download a high-res wraparound cover**. The print-ready PDF from the Print Book tab only contains the interior.

Figure 9-4: D2D Generate Wraparound Cover

THE [**Browse**] button at the top lets you upload your own wraparound cover as a print-ready PDF or PNG file with the back, spine, and front cover as one image with bleed. If you need placement guidance, download the custom template specific to your book, shown in Figure 9-5, with the [**Download Blank Template**] button. A **checkbox at the right turns on black, blue, and red guides** that delineate the three parts of the cover and the **approximate trim region**, as shown in Figure 9-4. **Text within the blue areas may become illegible** when folded or cut off.

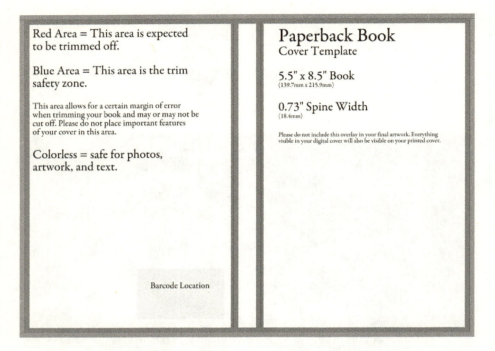

Figure 9-5: D2D Custom Wraparound Cover Template

TIP Neither D2D nor KDP accept a print cover in standard JPEG format. If you build your own, save it as PNG from the start to preserve the higher print quality.

The generated cover follows industry practices. Its **spine shows the primary author name and book title in a contrasting text color**. D2D tries to fit the entire **book description from the Details tab** on top of the back cover in the same text color. The lower half splits up into the **bio of the primary author from [My Accounts] | [Contributor Profiles]** on the left, the matching profile picture on the right, and the **automatically generated ISBN barcode** below them.

D2D's hair care shop does the restorative work for you at the price of less flexibility. All the text automatically resizes to best fit the designated area. You can't change the typeface or select a size.

The blurbs may not fit even at the smallest allowed font size. After all, a description for a sales page may go on for five paragraphs or longer. A bio written for the Author Page can cover a similar amount of real estate. A compact paperback doesn't offer that luscious luxury. You'll see a warning and text will disappear off the end. The [**Save & Continue**] button deactivates until you fix the problem.

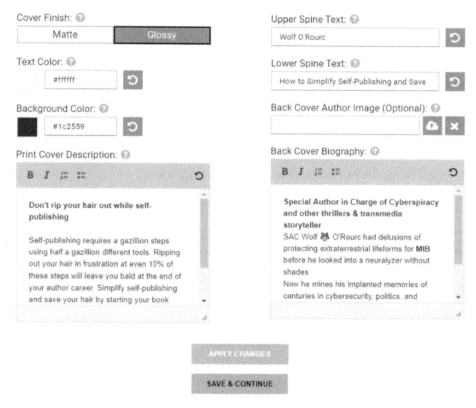

Figure 9-6: D2D Wraparound Cover Options

THE FIELDS BELOW THE cover hold **copies of the description and biography.** You can change them to fit the space available and format them as desired in the WYSIWYG editor. **Undo buttons at the right will restore one step back only.** If you've made multiple modifications and want to return to the original version, copy it from the respective sections. Anything you do on this tab doesn't affect the e-book or [**My Accounts**].

Additional fields let you override the copied text on the spine and the author picture on the back. Unlike the Zon, D2D's cover creator **does not**

rigorously enforce a match of name and title to the [Details] page. Nevertheless, have a good reason to deviate from this industry standard.

Three fields at the left control the overall appearance. Pick a more natural [**Matte**] look that hides scratches and scuffs better or a [**Glossy**] shine with richer colors. You can also **change the text and background color** by typing in hex codes. **Clicking the color field to the left brings up color pallettes** to find the perfect hue or **enter the Red, Green, and Blue values for conversion to hexadecimal**.

TIP While some genres show a preference for matte or glossy covers, in the end it is a personal decision. A particular design may look better in one or the other. If you have the time, order proofs in both versions and judge for yourself. Some authors choose to offer both finishes.

The cover preview does not reflect your work until you click [**Apply Changes**]. To save the cover and continue to the [**Publish**] tab click [**Save & Continue**].

Zon ⌒⌒⌒⌒

ON THE [**Paperback Content**] tab, KDP offers you the use of the **print Cover Creator** or **uploading a print-ready PDF** of the back, spine, and front cover as one image with bleed.

. If you have a PNG or JPG file, you must print it to PDF. Newer versions of Windows and Mac offer this option. Make sure to turn off or zero out any margins. You may have to create a custom paper size to **get rid of white borders in the PDF**. KDP may otherwise misread the dimensions and complain that the cover doesn't fit the trim size you selected. To ensure correct reproduction of text, **embed your fonts when creating the PDF**. You can <u>download **Paperback Cover Templates**</u>[6] or use the **Paperback file setup calculator**[7] to figure out dimensions.

---

6. https://kdp.amazon.com/en_US/cover-templates

7. **https://kdp.amazon.com/en_US/help/topic/G200735480#setup_calculator**

To save yourself hours of *hairache*, use the Cover Creator to build a wraparound cover.

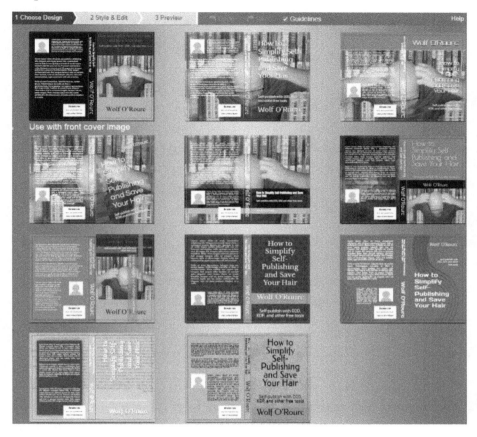

Figure 9-7: KDP Wraparound Cover Creator Designs

COVER CREATOR WILL accept an appropriately sized front cover and extend it in its first design as shown in Figure 9-7. In a sequel to the *hairripping* adventures in interior formatting, the Zon once again offers **more flexibility with less automation. You have to pick a matching back cover color yourself**, quite a challenge with the incomplete palette and no means to enter color codes. For usage of the controls, see the front cover version in 9.2.

TIP D2D print cover creator and most **graphics programs have color pickers that will determine the color code from a sample.** KDP's **Cover**

Creator does not. If you use the e-book version to create a front cover, write down the exact position of the color square you used, so you can match it when building the back cover. If you create the front cover in a graphics program but plan to build the wraparound one in KDP, create a test cover in it with your color choices and use your graphics program's color picker to match them.

Unlike D2D, the **Cover Creator doesn't blurbs from your book's Details or Author Central.** When you reach the [Style & Edit] page, warning triangles flag each of the three blocks as placeholders. **Until you replace the text, you can't Preview the cover.** Click on the placeholder text to make it disappear and type or paste in yours. You have access to the same formatting bar options as described in 9.2

The image placeholder will not stop you from proceeding, but will show as blank space. The [**Choose Layout**] button offers **two without pictures.** Incidentally, Cover Creator doesn't offer a layout that matches D2D's exactly. The closest one, selection 2, has the image at the lower left instead of right.

KDP will automatically place a 2 in (50.8 mm) by 1.2 in (30.5 mm) white box with the **ISBN barcode in the lower right corner of the back cover.** It will hide any images or text, so don't put anything important there.

Use the [**Save**] button to save your work regularly, so you can roll back to a previous point if you mess up. [**Preview**] **lets you check the design in color mode, grayscale, and as a thumbnail.** You can zoom in one level to focus on details. To see the cover with different device configurations, use the KDP Online Previewer once you exited Cover Creator. If you receive no blocks, click [**Save & Submit**] to upload the cover and return to KDP.

Resources

D2D: Creating a Print Layout using Draft2Digital[8]

---

8. https://www.youtube.com/watch?v=wJ3gzjWYSXg

D2D: D2D Print - Converting Your Ebook to Print - Step 3: Cover (VIDEO)[9]

D2D: D2D Print - Step 3: Cover (VIDEO)[10]

D2D: Partner Page[11]

KDP: Cover Creator[12]

KDP: Paperback Cover Templates[13]

KDP: Create an eBook Cover[14]

KDP: Create a Paperback Cover[15]

KDP: Paperback Cover Templates[16]

KDP: Paperback file setup calculator[17]

KDP: Creative cover solutions (VIDEO)[18]

KDP: Paperback file setup calculator[19]

KDP: Publishing Guidelines[20]

---

9. https://www.youtube.com/watch?v=ZWlXk7Tvs7c

10. https://www.youtube.com/watch?v=9xyJUkxdUCM

11. https://www.draft2digital.com/partners

12. https://kdp.amazon.com/en_US/help/topic/G201113520

13. https://kdp.amazon.com/en_US/cover-templates

14. https://kdp.amazon.com/en_US/help/topic/G200645690

15. https://kdp.amazon.com/en_US/help/topic/G201953020

16. https://kdp.amazon.com/en_US/cover-templates

17. https://kdp.amazon.com/en_US/help/topic/G200735480#setup_calculator

18. https://kdp.amazon.com/en_US/help/topic/G202193670#cover

19. https://kdp.amazon.com/en_US/help/topic/G200735480#setup_calculator

20. https://kdp.amazon.com/help?topicId=A1MMZZIUU7LTIB

10. Pricing

———

Y ou've done the hard work and earned your reward, setting the price for
your book. But the *Hairwaymen* won't rest on their locks just yet. Both
e-book platforms, for different reasons, have one more chance to rob your
ringlets. Draft2Digital asks for pricing for its many outlets. Kindle Direct
Publishing has to deal with Amazon's countless stores and royalty plans. The
simplicity of print pricing seems quaint by comparison, with the wrinkle that
proof or author copy ordering also appears on those pages.

Wildly varying tax schemes make figuring your earnings harder still.
In the USA and Canada, **retailers add sales tax** when the customer pays.
Nothing for you to worry about unless you sell direct. On the other hand, the
list price you set includes **value-added tax** (**VAT**) in territories that have one.
Even within the Euro block of the European Union, rates vary considerably.

During a sale, the **companies deduct the tax before calculating your
royalties**. They don't factor in the reduction when converting a US or
Canadian dollar price into other currencies. Unless you change territorial
prices individually, you may receive lower royalty rates in these countries. The
often small tax charged on books, however, may not justify the extra work.

10.1. E-book Pricing

PART OF THE COMPLEXITY of e-book pricing comes from its
flexibility. Without physical production and transportation costs to worry
about, you can offer them free the world over. Of course, the platforms still
have to pay for their digital stores and have different ways to encourage you
to charge enough. Both require a minimum of $0.99, but you can drop below
that for temporary promotions.

Table 10-1: E-book Pricing and Royalty Rate Comparison

	Allowed	Recommended	Royalty Rate	Territories
D2D	$0.99 - $39.99	$2.99 - $9.99	59.5 / 29.7%	15
KDP	$0.99 - $200	$2.99 - $9.99	70 / 35%	13

Both companies agree on an optimal pricing range based on sales data. It's difficult to sustain a business with books selling below $2.99. Unless you have an established brand, buyers shy away from paying more than $9.99. When considering the low end in Table 10-1, keep in mind that according to the Authors Guild, publishers customarily pay 25% of net in e-book royalties.

D2D

D2D HAS TO WORK WITHIN the guidelines of many different vendors. The **Projected Royalties** and **Special Considerations** columns on the [**Publish**] tab shown in Figure 10-1 gives a hint of the complexity.

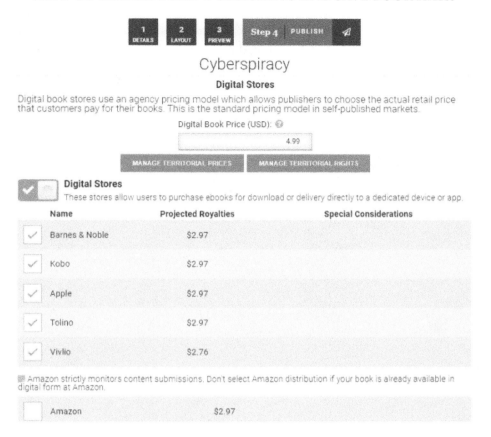

Figure 10-1: D2D Digital Stores Pricing

YOU CAN TAKE THE EASY way out and enter the **Digital Book Price** in US dollars at the top. D2D will try their best to fit your target price to the various vendor requirements and project the royalties from each. Many of them change your rate depending on the list price you set. **For best results, D2D recommends one between $2.99 and $9.99**. If you don't care about maximizing your earnings, **you can pick any price from $0.99 to $39.99**.

Because **Amazon strictly monitor for e-books already available in their Kindle stores**, D2D has the company separately below everybody else without a checkmark by default, as shown in Figure 10-1. Only enable sales to Amazon, if you haven't published the exact same title and edition through KDP. When you check the box, the dialogue box in Figure 10-2 asks you to certify that your book meets the Zon's requirements. Minimum prices depending on file size apply, as detailed in the Zon section below.

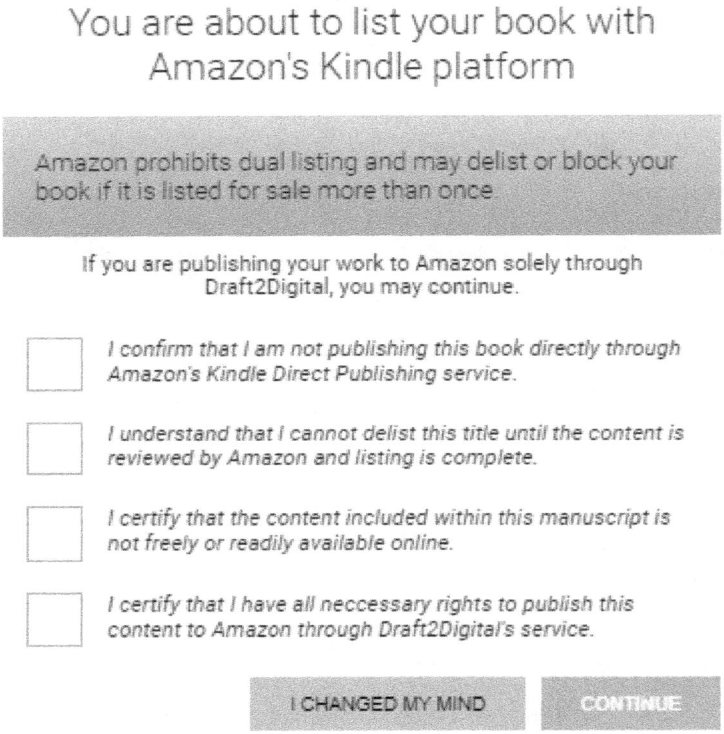

You are about to list your book with Amazon's Kindle platform

Amazon prohibits dual listing and may delist or block your book if it is listed for sale more than once

If you are publishing your work to Amazon solely through Draft2Digital, you may continue.

☐ I confirm that I am not publishing this book directly through Amazon's Kindle Direct Publishing service.

☐ I understand that I cannot delist this title until the content is reviewed by Amazon and listing is complete.

☐ I certify that the content included within this manuscript is not freely or readily available online.

☐ I certify that I have all neccessary rights to publish this content to Amazon through Draft2Digital's service.

[I CHANGED MY MIND]   [CONTINUE]

Figure 10-2: Kindle Publishing Requirements

TIP D2D currently doesn't support pre-orders through Amazon.

For vendors with operations **outside the USA**, D2D converts your USD price into other currencies. Where appropriate, they make them look pretty by ending in ".99" or ".00." Clicking [**Manage Territorial Prices**] (see Figure 10-1) displays the list shown in Figure 10-3. When you check the box to the left of an amount, you can override it. Unchecking the box restores the automatically calculated value.

TIP D2D assumes that you have worldwide rights to publish a book. To exclude territories, check [**Enable Territorial Rights Management**] under the [**My Account**] | [**Advanced User Options**] menu choice. A [**Manage Territorial Rights**] button will appear on the [**Publish**] tab as shown in Figure 10-1.

Territorial Pricing

Automatic territorial price conversions are listed below. If you would like to customize a territorial price, check the box next to the field you would like to change and then type the price you want into the field. If you change your mind, simply un-check the box next to the price to return the amount to Draft2digital's automatically generated price conversion.

Your price selections will affect **Digital Stores** (including **Subscription Services**) and **Wholesale** ebook distribution.

	4.99	**$** USD US DOLLAR	

☐	7.99	**$** AUD AUSTRALIAN DOLLAR	☐	27.90	**R$** BRL BRAZILIAN REAL
☐	6.99	**$** CAD CANADIAN DOLLAR	☐	5.0	**CHF** CHF SWISS FRANC
☐	35.00	**kr** DKK DANISH KRONE	☐	4.49	**€** EUR EURO
☐	3.99	**£** GBP BRITISH POUND	☐	38.99	**$** HKD HONG KONG DOLLAR
☐	374	**₹** INR INDIAN RUPEE	☐	550	**¥** JPY JAPANESE YEN
☐	119.00	**$** MXN MEXICAN PESO	☐	49.00	**kr** NOK NORWEGIAN KRONE
☐	7.99	**$** NZD NEW ZEALAND DOLLAR	☐	49.00	**kr** SEK SWEDISH KRONA

Territories will not be saved until you click "Apply Changes" on the Publish Page.

APPLY TERRITORIES   CANCEL

Figure 10-3: D2D Manage Territorial Prices

THE CONVERTED **target price** *includes* **value-added tax (VAT)** in territories that have one. **D2D does not adjust for it when converting from US dollars.** The prettified prices may make up for the often small tax charged on books.

TIP D2D sends you a notice each day after your book goes live at a channel. Click the [**Published**] links in the email to check out a store's sales page. The [**this book**] link takes you to D2D's version of the Books2Read sales page. The [**View My Books**] button jumps to the D2D bookshelf.

Amazon's Kindle Unlimited[1] **subscription service helps voracious readers discover many new books**, but requires exclusivity. You can't join once your e-book goes wide at D2D, but they **can enroll your book in the alternatives** shown in Figure 10-4.

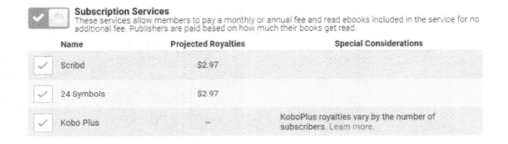

Figure 10-4: D2D Subscription Services Pricing

FINALLY, A FEW CLICKS **make your e-book available to various library distributors**, a feat much harder to achieve with Kindle. **Pricing defaults to double of retail**, so Cyberspiracy's $4.99 in Figure 10-1 turned into $9.99 in Figure 10-5. If your local library uses one of the services, their acquisition department can order copies for lending. Royalties vary by the model a buyer selects.

TIP Give some thought to the list price so you don't have to change it later. Hoopla won't allow it once submitted.

---

1. https://kdp.amazon.com/en_US/help/topic/G201537300

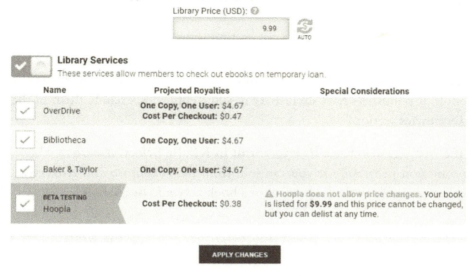

Figure 10-5: D2D Library Services Pricing

ONCE YOU'RE SATISFIED with all selections, click [**Apply Changes**] in Figure 10-5 and celebrate. You have published your e-book and made it available for preorder ☺. Changes may take a week to appear on all the vendor's websites.

TIP D2D no longer distributes to **Google Play**. You can add a book yourself using your own ISBN or a Google book ID.

Resources

D2D: Get your ebook into stores online! - Step 4: Publish (VIDEO)[2]

D2D: Exploring the Ebook Tab on the View Book Details Page (VIDEO)[3]

WritePublishSell: How to Add a Book to Google Play (VIDEO)[4]

---

2. https://www.youtube.com/watch?v=bTRwDcOHLPw

3. https://www.youtube.com/watch?v=BL06yohC8Kc

4. https://www.youtube.com/watch?v=K57Lz2CDE5E

Reedsy: How to Publish on Google Play Books in 2020[5]

Zon

AT KDP, YOU HAVE TO read and understand the guidelines yourself. Right from the top in Figure 10-6, the [**Pricing**] tab asks you for a legal certification. By default, Amazon assumes you have worldwide rights to your book. If publishers have exclusivity in some countries, exclude them in the **Territories** section.

The webpage also has a **link to enroll in Kindle Select**, Amazon's e-book promotion program. Or you can join from the [**Promote and Advertise**] choice available in the [**...**] menu for a book on your [**Bookshelf**].

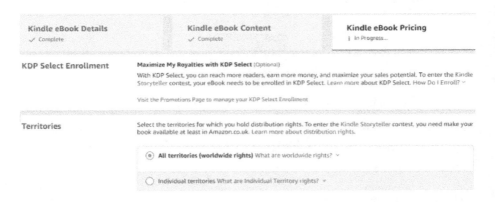

Figure 10-6: KDP Distribution Rights Certification

AMAZON OFFERS TWO ROYALTY rates as shown in Figure 10-7. **Any book from $0.99 to $200 can use the 35% plan.** The minimum price you can set rises when the file size reaches 3 MB and again at 10 MB. These thresholds also apply to books submitted through Draft2Digital.

Picking the 70% royalty rate shrinks the allowed range to $2.99 to $9.99, the same as the recommended one at D2D. The Zon also **deducts a delivery charge based on the compressed file size** shown above the **List Price**. This option only applies to books sold **in countries on the Digital Pricing Page[6]**.

---

5. https://blog.reedsy.com/how-to-publish-a-book-on-google-play

For other sales, Amazon automatically uses the lower rate without delivery charges. Finally, they require you to price the e-book at least 20% below the paperback or audiobook. You'd be forgiven, if by now you suspect a conspiracy to sell more hair-growth products.

TIP The higher rate stays in effect during Kindle Countdown Deals, even if you drop the price below $2.99. On the other hand, If Amazon lowers a price below the threshold, you will only receive 35%. You can appeal the price match through the **Contact Us** form.

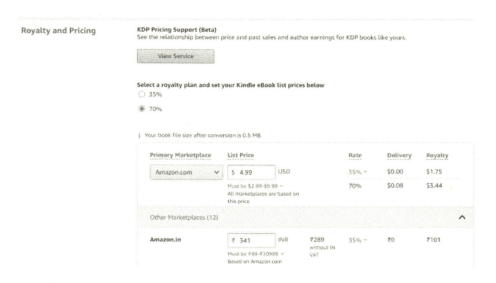

Figure 10-7: KDP Digital Stores Pricing

THE PRIMARY MARKETPLACE defaults to your account's location. Change it if you prefer a base price in a different currency. Amazon automatically converts your entry into other currencies but does not attempt to make the prices look pretty, unlike D2D. Click [**Other Marketplaces**] in Figure 10-7 to adjust them.

The **List Price** *includes* **value-added tax (VAT)** in territories that have one. Like D2D, **Amazon does not adjust for it when converting from US dollars.** You can see the net prices used to calculate the royalties next to

---

6. https://kdp.amazon.com/en_US/help/topic/G200634500

the entry fields. Unless you up these territorial prices individually, you will effectively receive a lower royalty rate.

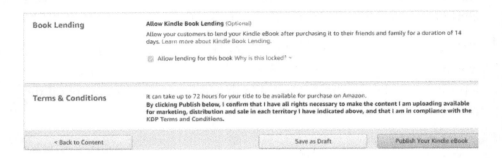

Figure 10-8: KDP Book Lending and Terms

IF YOU CHOSE THE 70% rate plan, you must participate in **Kindle Book Lending**, shown in Figure 10-8 below the pricing section. The program allows buyers to lend their purchases to friends and family for 14 days.

Once you're satisfied with all selections, click [**Publish Your Kindle eBook**] at the bottom of Figure 10-8 and celebrate. You have published your e-book and made it available for preorder ☺. Changes may take 72 hours to appear on all Amazon websites.

Resources

KDP: Digital Pricing Page[7]

KDP: Lending for Kindle[8]

KDP: Enter Pricing Information[9]

---

7. https://kdp.amazon.com/en_US/help/topic/G200634500

8. https://kdp.amazon.com/en_US/help/topic/G200652240

9. https://kdp.amazon.com/en_US/help/topic/G200641280

10.2. Paperback Pricing

THE **cost of production sets a floor for print pricing**. Neither company will let you sell books at a loss. The complex logistics of print distribution mean that both platforms have similar offerings, as shown in Table 10-2.

Table 10-2: Paperback Pricing and Royalty Rate Comparison

	Max Price	Royalty Rate	Territories	Expanded	Returns	Copies
D2D	None	45%	1	Ingram	X	√
KDP	$250	40-60%	8	Ingram	X	√

Royalty calculations differ depending on who sells the book.

1. **Author Copies**: Both companies will sell you paperbacks at cost, which includes printing, shipping, and a handling fee for small runs. You keep whatever profit you can make on selling them yourself.

2. **Expanded/Extended Distribution**: Both companies can distribute to stores and libraries who can order from the Ingram catalogue. This option is not available outside the USA. **The minimum sales price factors in the customary 50%+ discount expected by stores.** The list price hence has to be more than double your author copies price. Your royalties calculate as follows.

(List Price - Minimum Sales Price) * Royalty Rate

At the minimum price, you earn nothing.

3. **Amazon Stores**: For KDP print books sold through its own websites, Amazon uses a different formula and rate. Your royalties calculate as follows.

List Price * Royalty Rate - Minimum Sales Price

Because Amazon only takes 40%, the minimum sales price is considerably less, if you do not opt for **Expanded Distribution**.

Most stores can't afford the risk of a book not selling. Unlike publishers, **neither Amazon nor D2D have a facility for accepting returns of unsold inventory**. You probably have to negotiate with individual stores to get them to take a chance on yours. Libraries usually don't bother with returns. If their acquisition departments has access to the Ingram catalogue, **Expanded/ Extended Distribution** makes it easier for them to order your book.

D2D

D2D'S PRINT PRICING stands out for its simplicity. Easy, since it only **uses Ingram's standard distribution system in North America** to supply bookstores and libraries large and small. No other territories or currencies to worry about. On the [**Publish**] tab, enter one price in US dollars to see the projected royalties in Figure 10-9. That's it.

Amazon & Extended Distribution

PROJECTED ROYALTIES

$0.60

Print Book Price (USD):

10.99

● I have reviewed this book and approve it for release to print on demand.

○ I want to order a copy of my book before I approve distribution.

Figure 10-9: D2D Paperback Pricing

ANOTHER D2D HIDDEN treasure stares you in the face (or enviously at your remaining hair). Figure 10-9 shows off a **computer-generated three-dimensional montage of your books**. Right-click and save the high-resolution image. You can easily remove the neutral white background with a magic wand tool to get a clean picture for marketing without the need for a photographer, lights, or staging. Highlight your new release in website or social media banners as shown in Figure 10-10. Pink hair optional.

Figure 10-10: 3-D Book Image in Action

TWITTER SHRINKS THE banner to fit a phone display. Facebook instead narrows the view, so to get the front cover to display on the right side, you may have to separate it from the rest.

You can go through one last check and opt to **order printed proofs** before publishing the paperback. A good idea, particularly if you care about **balanced margins, a mark of a well-designed front cover**. Due to tolerances in the machines, the computer-generated pictures may differ from the printed product. Regardless of which radio button you select, clicking

271

[**Submit**] brings up a dialogue box for you to confirm the rights you hold. Clicking [**Publish My Book**] does *not* **make it available for distribution unless you approved it** through the radio button. The final dialogue lets you check the books details or start an e-book or audiobook project.

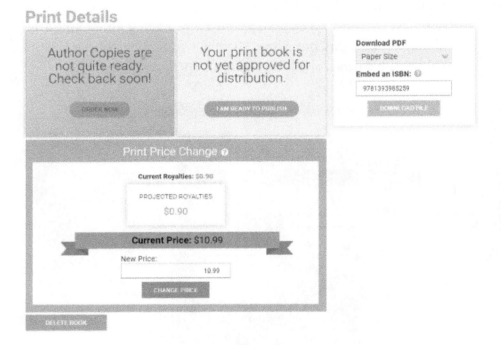

Figure 10-11: D2D View Book Print Book Details

TO ACTUALLY ORDER PROOFS, on **View Book**'s [**Print Book**] tab, click the [**Order Now**] button under **Print Details**, shown in Figure 10-11. Unlike Amazon, D2D doesn't distinguish between pre- and post-publication author copies. Once you're satisfied with the proofs, you can return to the [**Publish**] tab to submit and celebrate ☺ by clicking [**I Am Ready to Publish**]. The **Print Price Change** section lets you update pricing without going through the certification again. Finally, the [**Delete Book**] button lets you remove both the e-book and paperback after a confirmation.

Resources

D2D: D2D Print - Converting Your Ebook to Print - Step 4: Publish (VIDEO)[10]

D2D: D2D Print - Step 4: Publish (VIDEO)[11]

D2D: Exploring the Print Tab and Ordering Author Copies (VIDEO)[12]

Zon

KDP'S [**Paperback Rights & Pricing**] tab in Figure 10-12 starts with the same legal certification of distribution rights as for the e-book.

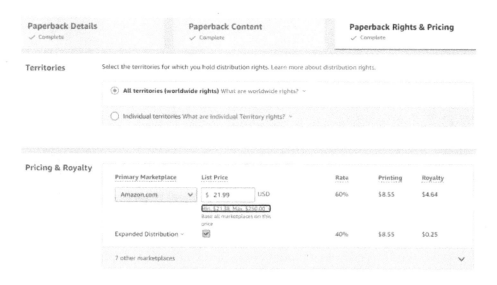

Figure 10-12: KDP Papberback Pricing

ALTHOUGH MORE COMPLEX than D2D, the print pricing is downright simple compared to e-books. Once you pick a **Primary Marketplace**, enter a **List Price between the distribution cost and $250.**

---

10. https://www.youtube.com/watch?v=fmT6I8Zi9oM

11. https://www.youtube.com/watch?v=7VQttorFLUA

12. https://www.youtube.com/watch?v=as5gmTK8uUs

KDP displays your 60% **Royalty** minus the **Printing** cost and **value-added tax (VAT)** where applicable. That's it for most territories outside the USA.

On Amazon.com, you can opt for Expanded Distribution, which makes your paperback available to **bookstores and libraries**. Because of the customary store discount, your **royalty rate drops to 40% of the net price after costs and VAT**.

Clicking [**Base all marketplaces on this price**] will link and update the territorial prices with your primary figure. You can view them by clicking [**other marketplaces**]. **In those with VAT, the list prices include it**.

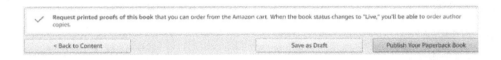

Figure 10-13: KDP Printed Proofs

YOU CAN [**Request printed proofs of this book**], as shown in Figure 10-13, and review them before publishing. Amazon marks these with a gray "Not for Resale" band across the cover. Once the book goes "Live," you can [**Order author copies**] from the [**...**] menu for a book on your [**Bookshelf**].

TIP Amazon places your author copies into your regular shopping card. You have all regular features available including clicking [**This is a gift**] and **entering any recipient address**. In other words, you can use their fulfilment service to send paperbacks at your cost to family, friends, or reviewers.

If you are satisfied, click [**Publish Your Paperback Book**] and celebrate ☺.

11. Audiobook

———

Without going into too much detail, I can't fail to mention the availability of a fast growing third format at both companies, the audiobook. As shown in Table 11-1, Amazon sticks with its narrow distribution, while D2D partners with a company that goes extra wide.

Table 11-1: Audiobook Comparison

	Distribution	Stores	Giveaway Codes
Amazon	ACX	3	√
D2D	Findaway Voices	43	√

D2D

D2D MAKES THE FORMAT available through a partnership with Findaway Voices. If you start the process from the [**Audiobook**] tab of [**My Books**], **D2D will send the details to Findaway**, and they'll waive their casting fee. You can also add the audiobook sales page URLs to the **Universal Book Link**.

Findaway Voices distributes to 43 channels, including Audible.com, Amazon.com, iTunes, Google, Hoopla, and Walmart. You can market your audiobook through **BookBub's Chirp platform**.

Zon

KDP DOESN'T HAVE THE same tight production integration with Amazon's ACX subsidiary. The company does offers cross-format marketing programs. **Whispersync for Voice-ready** offers buyers of the Kindle version the audiobook at a discount and synchronizes the reading experience between both. You can also promote the audiobook through **Amazon Advertising** (see 12.5).

ACX distributes to three channels, Audible.com, Amazon.com, and iTunes. To get a **higher royalty rate requires an exclusive seven-year contract.**

Resources

D2D: Options for After Publishing Your Ebook on Draft2Digital (VIDEO)[1]

D2D: How to create an audiobook from your ebook (VIDEO)[2]

KDP: Audiobooks Through ACX[3]

ALLi: The Trials and Tribulations of DIY Audiobooks[4]

---

1. https://www.youtube.com/watch?v=duXe3Uisw9Y

2. https://www.draft2digital.com/blog/
how-to-create-an-audiobook-from-your-ebook-with-d2d-and-findaway-voices-d2d-answers

3. https://kdp.amazon.com/en_US/help/topic/G201014330

4. https://selfpublishingadvice.org/opinion-the-trials-and-tribulations-of-diy-audiobooks

12. Sales & Marketing

<hr>

Post publication both platforms have more tools to offer that help you with sales and marketing. Draft2Digital builds key elements like the book sales and author pages around its Universal Book Links (UBL), a useful feature not offered by the Zon. We once again see the latter part its hair in confusing ways, with different pieces of book marketing strewn among different programs and websites.

12.1. Universal Book Link

D2D'S UBL SOLVES A fundamental problem for authors going wide in the digital age—**how to direct readers to a book's sales pages at their preferred vendors in their preferred location?** Amazon can rely on the users selecting the website for their country. If you want to give them multiple choices, you'd have to compile a list of Uniform Resource Locators (URL), i.e. web addresses for all the sites selling your book in a particular area. And keep it up to date.

Enter **Books2Read.com**. This site, run by D2D, instead offers you a simple UBL, "one link for every reader everywhere." When you point it to one of your sales pages, you get a URL of the form "https://Books2Read.com/u/<string>," ending in a six-character string that uniquely identifies the book. A program then scours vendor sites for matches and associates them with the UBL.

Figure 12-1: Books2Read Universal Link Page

AS SHOWN IN Figure 12-1, you can [**Rescan**] for matches or manually add and remove e-book and audiobook links.

TIP Books2Read doesn't automatically update the information it displays when you edit sales pages. If you change the cover, for instance, [**Rescan**] to update the UBL, sales, and author pages.

Clicking [**Show all supported stores**] at the bottom gives you access to the 49 companies on the Supported Stores[1] list. **Books2Read only automatically scans nine fully supported stores**. Clicking a logo adds a line for entering the link of a partially supported store.

TIP Regularly open [**Show all supported stores**] and click any logo with a green square and arrow icon. This will kick off a search of the title at that website, and if successful, add the URL to the UBL list with little effort on your part.

UBLs don't support print books directly. They will show up on the sales pages of any vendor that allows linking them to the e-book version.

For ease of use, **you can assign a custom name to the URL**, such as a short title or abbreviation. For example, the top of·Figure 12-1 shows the link ending in "Cyberspiracy."

TIP The **<string> for generated UBLs** *is* **case-sensitive**. Domain names and what you pick as **custom names are** *not* **case-sensitive**. The links Books2Read.com/Cyberspiracy[2], books2read.com/cyberspiracy[3], and BOOKS2READ.COM/CYBERSPIRACY[4] all work the same.

Two icons below the URL create text to post the UBL to Twitter or Facebook. The message includes a picture of the cover and the link, as shown in Figure 12-2.

---

1. https://books2read.com/guide/supported-stores

2. https://Books2Read.com/Cyberspiracy

3. https://books2read.com/cyberspiracy

4. https://BOOKS2READ.COM/CYBERSPIRACY

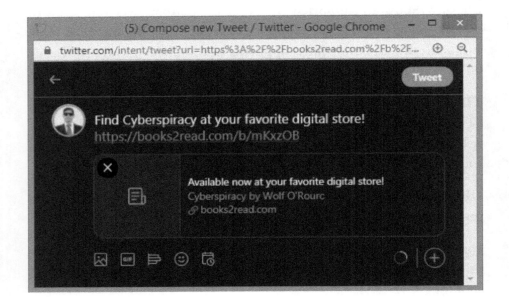

Figure 12-2: Books2Read Twitter Share Text

TO CREATE A COLLECTION of UBLs that you can manage together, create a free account at Books2Read.com. D2D automatically does that if you publish a book through them.

TIP To make it easy to manage UBLs tied to your D2D published books, use the same email address to log into both websites.

Use the UBL instead of a vendor-specific link on your website, social media, in email, or anywhere else you showcase your work.

TIP If you include a UBL on the end matter page of your e-book where you ask for reviews, you make it easy for the reader to post to multiple vendor sites.

When a reader clicks the link, Books2Read builds a page with logos and links for all the stores associated with the UBL as shown in Figure 12-3. Buttons at the top limit the logos shown to only stores offering the selected format.

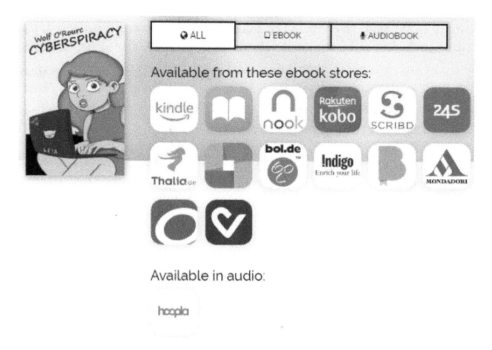

Figure 12-3: Books2Read Universal Book Link Page

THE FIRST TIME A USER clicks a logo in a UBL, **a dialogue box asks to save their choice as preferred store**. A link in the page footer allows deleting the saved setting.

For Amazon, automatic geolocation uses the connection's Internet address to **pick the site appropriate for the country**.

Every UBL comes with a Sales Page (called **Book Tab**) and an Author Page that D2D has integrated into their publishing process. They also use this link for collecting emails for New Release Notifications.

TIP If you plan to publish a book through D2D, do *not* create a UBL for it ahead of time. During the publishing process, D2D creates one linked to your book. You can see this UBL on the [**Ebook**] tab. Clicking [**Edit This UBL**] on the [**Promotion**] tab will take you to the Books2Read page to manage the link.

Even a book exclusively in KDP Select[5] can benefit from using a UBL instead of an Amazon link. If you go wide, you can add other vendors without any changes to promotional material. If international visitors click the link, geolocation will direct them to the store for their country. Even Amazon Associates links won't do that. Finally, UBLs aggregate reporting of page views and click-throughs for all vendor sites.

If you enter a book in KDP Select (see 12.4) later, you can make a store-specific link that redirects to Amazon stores by adding "?store=amazon" to the end. The same trick works for promotions with other vendors by substituting the appropriate case-sensitive store code, "apple," "bn," "kobo," "google", "scribd", "smashwords," etc. Your UBL Dashboard, shown in Figure 12-4, has a column with pre-built Store-Specific Links. Custom links follow the same rule, for example "https://books2read.com/Cyberspiracy?store=google" sends the reader directly to the Google Play store.

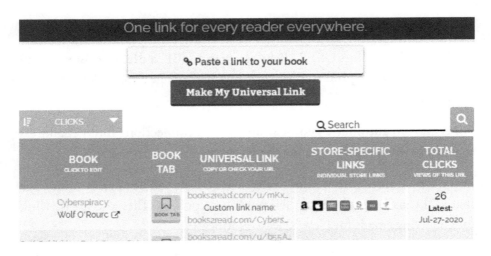

Figure 12-4: Books2Read Universal Book Link Dashboard

A BUYER CAN FIND RETAIL stores through UBLs. They do not support wholesalers like Baker & Taylor, even though D2D distributes to them.

---

5. https://kdp.amazon.com/en_US/help/topic/G200798990#eligibility

Resources

BOOKS2READ: Universal Book Links User Guide[6]

Books2Read: Frequently Asked Questions For Authors[7]

Books2Read: Supported Stores[8]

Aaron Pogue: A Quick Guide to Books2Read[9]

12.2. Sales Page

THE BOOK DETAIL PAGE lies at the heart of online sales efforts. Vendors provide one for each book Draft2Digital distributes to them. The company separately offers a store-independent version based on Universal Book Links. Amazon has localized sales pages for each country's stores.

Table 12-1: Sales Page Comparison

	Buy Link	Author Link	Share Link	Social Link	Print Link	Audio Link	Sample	Review	Custom Layout
Amazon	√	√	2	X	√	√	√	√	X
D2D	√	√	4	√	X	√	X	X	√

Of course, both platforms include the cover, description, and links to allow viewers to buy the book. They also hyperlink the author names, although their targets differ somewhat. From there, design and content diverge, as shown in Table 12-1.

D2D

D2D, THROUGH THEIR **Books2Read.com** brand, **offers a combined sales and author page that you can use as a stand-alone landing page or website for book sales.** The unusual design in Figure 12-5 shows the cover,

---

6. https://books2read.com/guide/ubl

7. https://books2read.com/faq/author

8. https://books2read.com/guide/supported-stores

9. https://books2read.com/u/bQ6VP0

title, and buy link above the fold, what you see when the page loads. Scrolling up reveals the description hidden under the author information.

Figure 12-5: Books2Read Sales Page

THE TWO SOCIAL MEDIA icons at the top create text to post the **Universal Book Link** to Twitter or Facebook (see 12.1).

Clicking the author name takes the reader to the **Author Pages**, essentially the same information presented in a different design. If you like it better, use it instead as sales page.

The format buttons restrict the view of the **Universal Book Link** page to e- or audiobooks. Like the underlying UBL, the paperback version doesn't appear. Vendor sites that sell both print and e-book usually display them on the same sales page, though.

Clicking the [**Get It Now**] shopping cart button takes readers to the UBL page, which may immediately redirect to their preferred store, as discussed in 12.1.

Although D2D produces a preview sample of the e-book, it doesn't include it on the sales page. You can roll your own by pasting a chapter or two below the description. Not quite the same as Amazon's **Look Inside**, however. Fancy formatting, including bold and drop caps, vanishes. The editor also can't convert paragraph marks to blank lines, leading to blocks of text that you have to split by hand or ahead of time.

Unlike Amazon, **D2D doesn't bother with boring technical details** like publication date, ISBN, or even page count. Include anything you want to show in the description.

The **Author Page** chapter covers the information below the fold, including the [**Follow the Author**] button to sign up for New Release Notifications and the social media links.

Author View

THE AUTHOR VIEW HAS buttons and links at the top for managing the pages, if you log in with the Books2Read account associated with it.

Clicking the [**See Reader View**] button **switches to the look of the public webpage**. Only the **links visible** at the top change. The rest of the content stays the same. Social media share buttons show up at the top left. The group at the top right includes [**Find More Books**] to sign up for the Books2Read's mailing list—not specific to the author—and links to log in or out of the **UBL Dashboard**. The company encourages readers to create and share lists of UBLs.

[**Back to Dashboard**] brings up your **UBL Dashboard** (see 12.1).

If you don't want the Books2Read sales page visible, you can [**Deactivate**] the UBL on its page, or hide just the **Book Tab** with the [**Deactivate This Book**] button at the top. Neither will remove the vendor sales pages, of course.

Edit Mode

D2D CREATES THE UBL at the same time as the sales page and links the two. They don't update it with changes to book **Details**, unlike the vendor sites. Do the hairs standing up on the back of your neck tell you what's coming? Yes, save yourself extra work and have everything ready before you start data entry.

If you do need to update what D2D calls the book tab, click the [**Visit This Book Tab**] button on the [**Promotion**] tab or the appropriate [**Book Tab**] button in your [**UBL Dashboard**] shown in Figure 12-6.

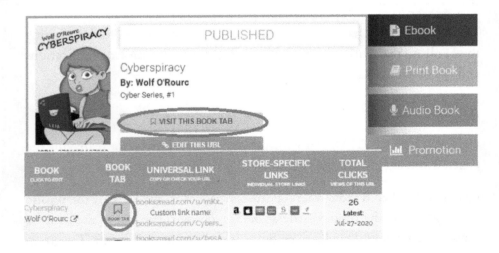

Figure 12-6: Books2Read Universal Book Link Book Tab Button

CLICK THE [**Enter Edit Mode**] button. If you then click the description, you can make changes in a WYSIWYG editor.

Click the Promo Tag (**First in Series** in Figure 12-5) to change it.

You can't alter the page design other than hiding the carousel of other books by the author.

[**Save Changes**] before navigating to another page.

Zon

THE SALES PAGES FORM the public face of Amazon's business, and their complexity has grown with the company. **Above the fold** in Figure 12-7, visible when the webpage loads, you see the **cover, title, format and buy buttons, and the first few lines of the description**. Much older than the flashy Books2Read design, the Zon uses a simple [**Read more**] link to show the rest of the text.

Figure 12-7: Amazon Sales Page

WHEREAS **KDP delivers the information for the sales page**, the author page falls under Author Central (see 12.3). Those without an account at the latter may not have their name hyperlinked at all, or clicking it shows the search results for all books by them. For newer pages, Amazon offers the reader a choice of the **Author Pages** or the search results. When a logged-in user clicks the [**+ Follow**] button, Amazon adds the associated email address to the author's **New Release Notifications** list.

Four icons create text for sharing the sales page URL in email and on Pinterest, in addition to Twitter and Facebook.

The format buttons switch to the respective product page. Amazon includes every version the author linked together in their bookshelf, including paperback, hardcover, audiobook and audio CD. Clicking [**Buy Now**] or [**Add to Cart**] puts the currently selected format into your shopping cart.

Clicking a cover with a **Look Inside** banner loads a preview of the e-book or scanned print book, usually 15% of the pages.

In keeping with the conventions in its giant hypermarket, Amazon does display a book's technical details, but banishes them deep down below **Frequently bought together**, **Books you may like**, **Sponsored products related to this item**, **Special offers and product promotions**, **From the Publisher**, and **Editorial Reviews**. Of interest to author, given the Zon's notoriously lacking sales reporting, the **Best Sellers Rank** gives a better indication of relative standing compared to other writers. The trend chart in Author Central (see 12.3) has made checking the sales page unnecessary, though.

Similar to D2D, the author information follows, if available, and usually only a one-paragraph excerpt from the **Author Pages**.

You can't update the sales page directly. Any changes have to come through KDP or AC, including [**Unpublishing**] books from their [...] menu on the [**Bookshelf**]. Publishers have limited ability to change the layout. Indie authors have none.

TIP The **data entry for a number of sections of the Amazon sales pages takes place at the much easier to use AC**. These include the **Author Page** and related items like **About the Author** or upcoming events, the back cover blurb, and the **editorial reviews**.

Like the stores, print and e-books have distinct sales pages requiring separate data entry. If you complete one before starting the other, the [+ **Create Kindle eBook**] and [+**Create Paperback**] buttons in a book's [**Bookshelf**] **Your Books** record will prefill the data entry screens and link the pages together across stores. Separate [**Link existing Kindle eBook**] or [**Link existing paperback**] buttons allow you to search for the other format in the stores and link them together. If Amazon matched the books by title, the

[**Link Books**] choices in the [**...**] menu will connect them. [**Unlink Books**] lets you break the link, if you no longer want the different formats appearing on the other sales pages.

TIP Unlike D2D, **KDP doesn't copy the uploaded e-book interior or cover files when you click** [**+Create Paperback**].

Resources

AC: Editorial Reviews[10]

12.3. Author Page

THE AUTHOR PAGE **ties together the marketing for multiple books**. It contains a **photograph**, a **biography**, and usually a carousel of the writer's **bibliography**, horizontally arranged. Users can scroll left and right through book-cover thumbnails that appear to go round and round like a carousel.

Fans want to know all about their favorite authors. Engage with readers on a very personal and very human level with your bio. Include fun trivia, insights into your background, or your path to writing. If the page does not point them to your social media (yes, the Zon), include your handles.

Both platforms offer their own version of the core features. As Table 12-2 shows, they differ on some optional sections. Since both have **clickable links to buy books**, the author page gives you a **free way to get a sales website up quickly**, either vendor neutral at D2D or limited to Amazon stores.

Table 12-2: Author Page Comparison

	Buy Link	Carousel	Social Link	Print Link	Audio Link	Follow
Amazon	√	√	X	√	√	√
D2D	√	√	√	X	√	√

Resources

TARA KACHATUROFF: Top Ten Tips for Writing a Professional Overview or Biography[11]

Chris Robley: How to write a great author bio that will connect with readers[12]

Marisa Murgatroyd: How to Introduce Yourself Powerfully in a Facebook Group or Online Community[13]

Marisa Murgatroyd: How to Create a Showstopper Tagline that Instantly Tells Your Clients You're the One They've Been Looking For[14]

Michelle Knight: How to Write a Magnetic Brand Bio for Your Online Business[15]

Chris Well: Writing Your Author Bios | Ultimate Guide to Creating an Author Media Kit [16]

Chris Well: Taking Your Own Author Photo | Ultimate Guide to Creating an Author Media Kit [17]

ALLi: How to Build a Power Author Brand and Increase Book Sales (VIDEO)[18]

---

11. http://www.improvehomelife.com/
   Top_Ten_Tips_for_Writing_a_Professional_Overview_or_Biography-20179.htm

12. https://blog.bookbaby.com/2014/03/how-to-write-a-great-author-bio

13. https://www.liveyourmessage.com/
   how-to-introduce-yourself-in-a-facebook-group-or-online-community

14. https://www.liveyourmessage.com/how-to-create-a-showstopper-tagline

15. https://www.brandmerry.com/theblog1/write-magnetic-brand-bio

16. http://buildyourbrandacademy.com/blog/573637/
   author-bios-ultimate-guide-to-creating-an-author-media-kit-2-of-10

17. https://buildyourbrandacademy.com/blog/1294920/
   taking-your-author-photo-ultimate-guide-to-creating-an-author-media-kit-7-of-10

18. https://www.youtube.com/watch?v=LLaX1h_BjEU

D2D: Using Custom Carousels (VIDEO)[19]

D2D

DRAFT2DIGITAL TIGHTLY couples Books2Read author and book pages to the point that they contain the same information in different formats. Both function the same, except you can only edit the biography from a page that has the photograph at the top left like Figure 12-8. All Books2Read **Sales Pages**, also known as **Book Tab** (see 12.2), share the same author page. From a reader's point of view, either format works as landing page or sales website.

Also by Wolf O'Rourc...

Cyber Series

Other books by Wolf O'Rourc

ABOUT THE AUTHOR

Wolf O'Rourc

Special Author in Charge of Cyberspiracy and other thrillers
Transmedia storyteller

SAC Wolf ❀ O'Rourc had delusions of protecting extraterrestrial lifeforms for **MIB** before he looked into a neuralyzer without shades. Now he mines his implanted memories of centuries in cybersecurity, politics, and finance to create stories pitting quirky characters with high-tech gadgets against evil villains with vile weapons. His *Zazztra* series follows a Vegas casino host turned superheroine through the sordid underbelly of crime at home and abroad.

Wolf's *Cyber* series explores the secret world of bits and bytes through the eyes of a pink-haired hacktress. His technothrillers reflect the 23 places he has lived and studied the polyglot people that populate his fiction. In real life, he frequents the Henderson Writers Group, the Romance Writers of America, Sin City Writers Group, and the Las Vegas Screenwriters Group. On the Net you'll find him at www.WolfORourc.com or WolfORourc at the fashionable social media channels.

Figure 12-8: Books2Read Author Page

SOCIAL MEDIA LINKS and a [Follow the Author] button also appear at the top left. Clicking the latter brings up a sign up for New Release Notifications similar to Figure 12-23.

The same featured book's cover and blurb show at the top right regardless of which Sales Page led to the author page. Clicking the thumbnail or [Get It Now] jumps to the book's Universal Book Link page or directly to the preferred store depending on the user's configuration (see 12.1).

If the account's UBL list contains one or more series, Books2Read presents them in separate configurable carousels below. An Other books by carousel holds the remaining ones with the same author name. Clicking any of these thumbnails jumps to that book's Sales Page.

The same bio appears at the bottom of Author and Sales Pages.

Author View

THE AUTHOR SHOWS BUTTONS and links at the top for managing the page, if you log in with the Books2Read account associated with it.

Clicking the [See Reader View] button switches to the look of the public webpage. Only the links visible at the top change. The rest of the content stays the same. Social media share buttons show up at the top left. The group at the top right includes [Find More Books] to sign up for the Books2Read's mailing list—not specific to the author—and links to log in or out of the UBL Dashboard. D2D encourages readers to create and share their own lists of favorite UBLs.

[Back to Dashboard] brings up your UBL Dashboard. (see 12.1)

The misleadingly labeled [Deactivate This Author] button at the top merely hides the author page from readers. The About The Author section with all its buttons will still appear at the bottom of every Book Tab. Only the link on the name at the top deactivates. If you are logged into Books2Read as the author, i.e. you can edit the page, the change will not be visible even if you click [See Reader View].

Edit Mode

LIKE THE PRINT BOOK's **Back Cover Biography**, once created, **the author page bio and photograph don't update with the [Contributor Profiles] in [My Accounts]**. Yes, if you want to make changes after you submitted a book for publishing, you have to apply them to all three sections separately.

To update the author page, click the **author name link** in the **Book** column of your [**UBL Dashboard**] (see Figure 12-4) or at the top of a book's **Sales Page** (see Figure 12-5). Click the [**Enter Edit Mode**] button shown in Figure 12-9. You can then click most elements on the page to modify them.

Figure 12-9: Books2Read Author Page Edit Mode Toolbar

OTHER THAN THE AUTHOR name, which jumps to the biography, clicking anything in the upper left lets you update it. You can also **drag a file onto the photograph** with the green circle in Figure 12-10.

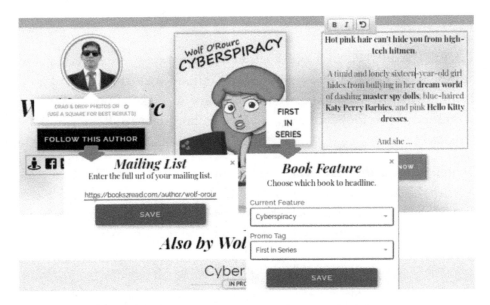

Figure 12-10: Books2Read Author Page Edit Mode Top

BY CLICKING [**Follow the Author**], you can **change the mailing list sign up link to a custom webpage**. This, however, **does *not* alter the short Books2Read link** for **New Release Notifications** in e-books, which redirects to a different webpage.

TIP Write down the original mailing list link in [**Follow the Author**] before changing it. Depending on when you created your account, the **URL may differ from the one listed under [My Reports] | [My Mailing Lists]**.

Click the top cover thumbnail to change the featured book or its Promo Tag (**First in Series** in Figure 12-8). Clicking covers in carousels does nothing.

The blurb to the right only contains an **excerpt from the beginning of the book description**. Click the text to change it without affecting the full description on the **Sales Page**.

Clicking the **social-media section** brings up the dialogue box shown in Figure 12-11. You can enter your website URL and those for seven popular social networks.

Figure 12-11: Books2Read Website and Social Media Entry

YOU CAN'T ALTER THE page design other than adding or hiding carousels. Each series starts out with its own.

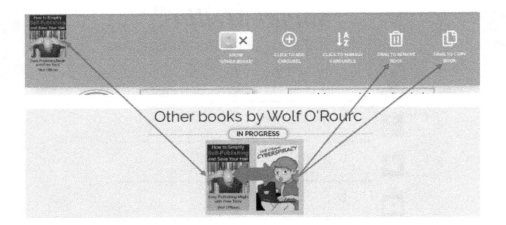

Figure 12-12: Books2Read Author Page Edit Mode Carousel

ON THE GREEN TOOLBAR in Figure 12-12, [**Show Other Books**] toggles the display of the default **Other books by** carousel with all uncategorized book covers by the author in the [**UBL Dashboard**].

TIP If you turn off **Other books by**, its cover thumbnails will move to the toolbar. You can drag books from it like any carousel.

To add more books, you must create UBLs for them (see 12.1). One of the hyperlinked authors on the sales pages you submit to kick off the process must exactly match the name already in the UBL Dashboard, since you cannot edit the ones retrieved by Books2Read. Unlike Amazon's Author Central below, you cannot send a request to have customer service verify spelling variations or check the book blurb or interior for a match. Inconsistencies across different sales pages will prevent the program from grouping books together. Keep these limitations in mind, if you do not have access to some publishing accounts or write under various pen names. For example, despite adding one of the anthologies verified by AC in Figure 12-13 to my [**UBL Dashboard**], the title doesn't show up on my carousels.

Since UBLs don't support print books, **only e- and audiobooks appear**.

[**Click To Add Carousel**] creates a custom one to **organize books by any criteria you wish**, such as Nonfiction or Holiday Promotion. Place books by dragging a cover from another carousel and dropping it on the green area of the new one.

[Click To Manage Carousels] brings up a list of buttons that you can rearrange to change the order of the carousels on the page. Clicking the [x] next to a name will remove that section. You can also drag all covers somewhere else to make it disappear from view when you [Save Changes].

To **rearrange the order of books in a carousel**, drag and drop them within its green outline.

Dragging a thumbnail on the [Drag To Copy Book] button in the toolbar **duplicates a cover for use in two sections**.

TIP If you have a hard time dropping a thumbnail on the correct button in the vertical toolbar, **shrink the width of the browser window until the toolbar appears horizontally at the top**.

Dropping a cover onto the [Drag To Remove Book] button deletes it. If you do so with the last copy of a book, a dialogue box asks if you want to deactivate its **Book Tab**. Doing so is equivalent to removing the book from all carousels of any book in your Dashboard. [Save Changes] automatically removes any duplicates in the same carousel.

TIP If you accidentally remove a cover completely from the page, **deactivate and re-activate its UBL** to place it back into **Other books by**.

Clicking the ovals under a carousel name toggles its status from blank to **In Progress** to **Complete**. This lets readers know if the complete series is already available.

Finally, if you click the biography, you can make changes in a WYSIWYG editor. It limits formatting to **Bold** and *italics* and removes all other HTML codes available in D2D's editor.

TIP Unlike D2D, **Books2Read does not support multiple author profiles**. If you write in unrelated genres, such as YA Thrillers and

Nonfiction, you'll have to get creative in the one biography that links to every book, or use different pen names to have separate author pages.

[**Save Changes**] before navigating to another page.

Resources

D2D: Author Pages - Feature Walk-Thru (VIDEO)[20]

D2D: Using Custom Carousels (VIDEO)[21]

Zon

AMAZON'S **Author Central** (AC) website, as the name implies, manages a writer's information including biography and a book carousel. Filling out the profile information on the [**Author Page**] will create something similar to the one shown in Figure 12-13.

TIP Unlike D2D, you *cannot* deactivate an AC author page. If, for whatever reason, you don't want one, do *not* create an author profile.

---

20. https://www.youtube.com/watch?v=oW1cE_ETJWg

21. https://www.youtube.com/watch?v=ddHE1OlVsC4

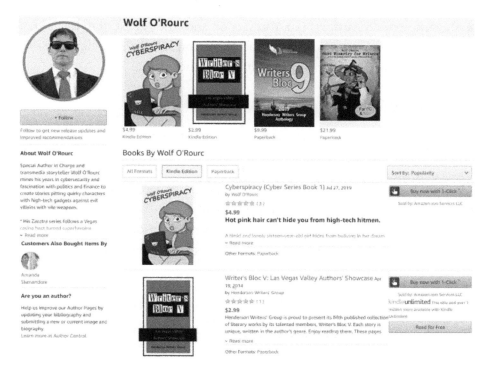

Figure 12-13: Amazon Author Page

THE LEFT COLUMN CONTAINS all the author information starting with a photograph.

When a logged-in user clicks the [+ **Follow**] button, Amazon adds the associated email address to the author's **New Release Notifications** list.

The beginning of the biography follows. [**Read more**] expands it to the full length.

Customers Also Bought Items By shows photos and links to authors whose books Amazon determined also appeal to your readers.

Learn more at Author Central at the bottom left jumps to AC.

On the right, the **book carousel on top and the same titles as search results below** take up most of the page. Buttons allow readers to limit the list by format and sort it by various criteria.

A **Recommended Authors For You** section ends the page. Off to its right, a [**Manage your follows**] link jumps to a **Who you follow** list, where you can make changes without needing to visit each author page.

Editing the Page

LIKE THE **Sales Page**, Amazon provides no edit link on its author pages. You must navigate to the appropriate tab at AC.

[**Author Page**], shown in Figure 12-14, lets you update most of the author information. Under **Biography**, add at least 100 characters of **plain text**. The editor supports none of the customary formatting options or HTML code. You can add photos and videos with the links at the lower right.

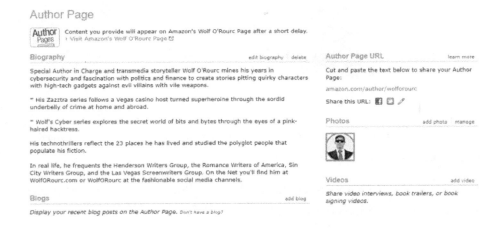

Figure 12-14: AC Author Page

TO MAKE YOUR PAGE LOOK more like your own sales website, **Author Page URL** lets you create a custom address such as "amazon.com/author/ wolforourc." Nevertheless, visitors see the full Amazon branding at the top. Also, as you can tell from the domain name, the link doesn't localize to an international visitor's country store. In contrast, clicking the author name on a sales page will display pricing in the appropriate currency. Until Amazon adds the magic translation module, biography and descriptions will appear in the language entered at AC or KDP, of course.

Clicking the **Share this URL** icons creates text to share the link to Facebook or Twitter.

TIP Once created, **only AC customer service can change a custom URL**.

Consistent with the Zon's desire to keep users in its world, it doesn't give you a means to add social media links or your own website's URL. Surprisingly, you can **add one Really Simple Syndication (RSS) feed to a blog**. The beginning of each post, which links to your blog website, appears in a section titled **Author Updates** between the book carousel and the search results list.

A **Visit Amazon's** link at the top lets you open the author page to check what visitors will see. Impatient writers may commit *hairakiri* with it, however, when encountering the usual processing delays that come with much of the Zon's online data entry. New accounts may wait even longer until verification completes[22].

[**Books**], shown in Figure 12-14, lets you add book information to Author and Sales Pages.

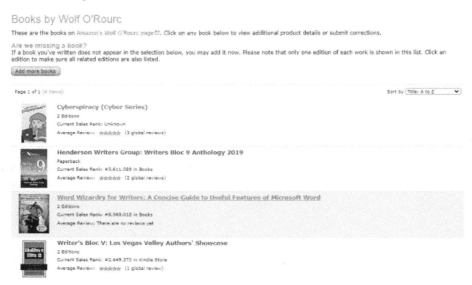

CLICKING [**Add more books**] brings up a **Search** field. Enter a book title, ISBN, or author name and click [**This is my book**] below an entry on the

22. https://authorcentral.amazon.com/gp/help?ie=UTF8&topicID=200620850

results list. If Amazon finds an exact name match among the hyperlinked authors, it adds the book. Otherwise, it gives you a link to **contact customer service**. They will **check the sales page and the book's end matter, if necessary, for references to you or your pen names**. The process can take days, so heed the hairakiri warning above.

You can't alter the page design other than adding sections by filling in the required information. Unlike Books2Read, **you can't add additional carousels or reorder books** within the one available. The most popular books appear first based on rules designed to provide the best customer experience. By example in Figure 12-13, *Writer's Bloc 9* follows *Writer's Bloc V*, which had four more years to accumulate sales.

Resources

AC: Setting Up Your Author Central Account[23]

AC: Managing Your Profile[24]

AC: Managing Your Biography[25]

AC: Managing Blog Feeds[26]

AC: Adding a Book[27]

12.4. Price Promotion

BOTH PLATFORMS OFFER ways to **promote your books by lowering the price temporarily**. As usual, the Zon has a hairbrained mess of restrictive programs.

---

23. https://authorcentral.amazon.com/gp/help?ie=UTF8&topicID=200620850

24. https://authorcentral.amazon.com/gp/help?ie=UTF8&topicID=200649520

25. https://authorcentral.amazon.com/gp/help?ie=UTF8&topicID=200649530

26. https://authorcentral.amazon.com/gp/help?ie=UTF8&topicID=200649550

27. https://authorcentral.amazon.com/gp/help?ie=UTF8&topicID=200777990

D2D

EACH **View Book** page has a [**Promotion**] tab similar to Figure 12-15.

Figure 12-15: D2D Promotion Tab

UNDER **Promotion Details**, the heart of this page lets you **schedule a promotional price, either universally or for specific territories**. For the entered US dollar price, D2D shows the expected royalties and the amount for the full price for comparison. Setting different prices for individual countries lets you test pricing strategies in different markets.

You can name a promotion as a reminder to yourself. That information is not passed on to vendors.

TIP Promotional pricing doesn't affect your library prices.

To **edit a promotion, click its pencil button** in the list on the right. **Clicking the trashcan button deletes the promo.**

Pick a start date at least a week out to give all the vendors time to update their sales pages. Obviously, the further out you go, the more time you have to advertise the promotion.

You normally *cannot* **set a promotional price or offer a book free at Amazon outside of the KDP Select[28] program** as explained below. If you make a title free, D2D will submit it to Amazon for $0.99.

Its stores will **usually match a lower price**, including free, with a couple days delay, though. To accelerate the process, you can let KDP know once one of your vendor sites updated its price. Use the [**Contact Us**] button under [**Help**] to bring up the KDP contact form[29]. Select **Pricing | Price matching**. Send an email request in the form

Add Price Match

1. [ASIN] | [Kindle Store: .COM, UK, DE, etc.] | [Competitor link] | [Current competitor price]

You can add multiple numbered lines to change prices in difference stores with one email. Once the promo has ended, send another request titled **"Remove Price Match."**

TIP If you selected Amazon's 70% royalty plan and a price match takes it below $2.99, you will only receive 35%.

---

28. https://kdp.amazon.com/en_US/help/topic/G200798990#eligibility

29. https://kdp.amazon.com/en_US/contact-us

Zon

THE [**Promote and Advertise**] choice of a book's [...] menu brings you to the **Promote your book on Amazon** page shown in Figure 12-16. You can run two types of price promotions **provided you've enrolled said book in exclusive KDP Select**[30]. If you want to run a promo for a book sold wide through D2D, use the price-matching trick discussed above.

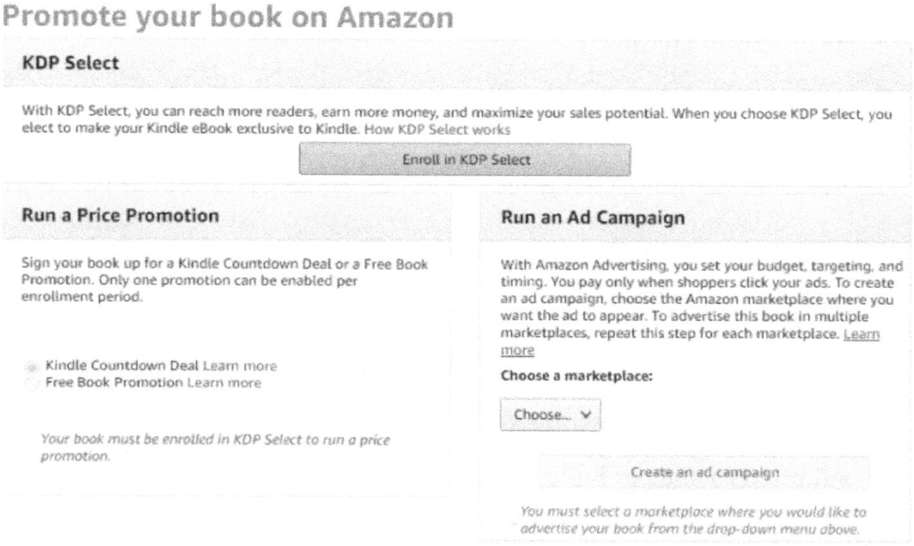

Figure 12-16: Amazon Promotion Page

DURING **Kindle Countdown Deals (KCD),** the book's detail page displays the crossed-out list price and one of up to five lower prices as scheduled. A countdown clock shows the time left until the end of the promo. Amazon also advertises all deals grouped by genre on the Featured Kindle Countdown Deals[31] webpage.

KCD might as well mean Kindle Curls Deduction for its complexity. **To participate, you must meet *all* the following requirements**.

---

30. https://kdp.amazon.com/en_US/help/topic/G200798990#eligibility

31. https://www.amazon.com/Kindle-eBooks/b?ie=UTF8&node=7078878011

- **title enrolled in KDP Select[32] exclusivity program for at least 30 days, i.e. e-book not available anywhere else**

- e-book list price in the range $2.99 - $24.99 on **Amazon.com** or £1.99 – £15.99 including VAT on **Amazon.co.uk** (KCD is not available in other Amazon stores)

- e-book list price unchanged for 30 days before or 14 days after its promotional runs

- minimum discount of $1.00 USD or £1.00 respectively

- maximum 5 price changes

- promo duration from minimum 1 hour to a maximum 7 days without interruptions

- ends at least 14 days before your 90-day KDP Select term ends (unless you renew)

- limited to one per KDP Select term

- no free promotion during the same KDP Select term (as you can see from Figure 12-16, the radio buttons lock in one program)

- scheduled at least 24 hours before your start date

TIP Your selected royalty rate stays in effect during Kindle Countdown Deals, even if you drop the price below $2.99.

In comparison, **Free Book Promotions** are a breeze in your fluttering hair. In all Kindle stores for which your title is enrolled in **KDP Select**, you can offer the e-book free (below Amazon's minimum price) for up to 5 days during each 90-day term. You can schedule multiple promotions of at least 1 day until you've used up your allotment. Make the request at least the day before your start date. The last period must end before the KDP Select

---

32. https://kdp.amazon.com/en_US/help/topic/G200798990#eligibility

term. Amazon excludes the title from the Kindle Owners' Lending Library during promotional periods. Of course, you receive 0 royalties during the promotions.

Resources

KDP: Kindle Countdown Deals[33]

Amazon: Featured Kindle Countdown Deals[34]

KDP: Free Book Promotions[35]

KDP: Merchandising Tips: Ten ways to market your books[36]

12.5. Other Marketing Tools

D2D

AS DISCUSSED, A BOOK's [**Promotion**] tab, shown in Figure 12-17, has links to manage its **Universal Book Link** (see 12.1) and its **Sales Page**, also known as **Book Tab** (see 12.2).

---

33. https://kdp.amazon.com/en_US/help/topic/G201293780

34. https://www.amazon.com/Kindle-eBooks/b?ie=UTF8&node=7078878011

35. https://kdp.amazon.com/en_US/help/topic/G201298240

36. https://kdp.amazon.com/en_US/help/topic/G200673650

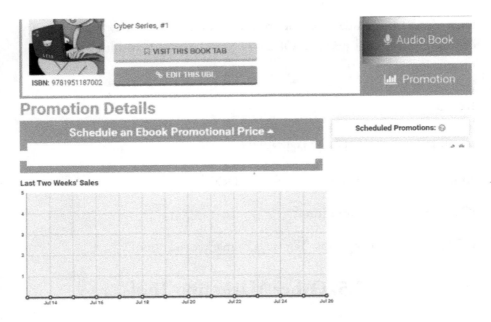

Figure 12-17: D2D Promotion Tab Marketing Features

At the bottom, you see a graph of the last two weeks' sales reported to D2D by all vendors.

The [**My Reports**] menu choice gives you access to the sales dashboard shown in Figure 12-18, various sales reports and charts, and downloads of your statements, tax forms, and raw sales data.

Figure 12-18: D2D Sales Dashboard

TIP Draft2Digital pays monthly by electronic funds transfer (EFT) to your bank or PayPal with only a $10.00 minimum.

A column in the [UBL Dashboard] shows the total number of clicks for each book's link (see Figure 12-4). Each **Universal Link** page gives you the breakdown for the **top 3 stores** (see Figure 12-1).

D2D currently does not give you access to Amazon Advertising for books published through them. They do pass on to their mailing list special advertising opportunities from vendors.

Another aggregator, **PublishDrive, has a marketing program where you *can* run Amazon ads** to a book not published with them by creating it as a draft.

Conversely, **selling wide increases your chance of winning a BookBub Featured Deal**[37], which they send to highly targeted mailing lists of voracious readers. You can leverage a similar advantage on independent book marketing sites like Freebooksy[38], Bargain Booksy[39], or Book Hub[40]. Particularly outside the USA, where other companies have large market shares, running ads beyond the Amazon system lets you reach readers who don't use its stores. Considerably more people in other countries read English than the entire population of the United States.

Some paid platforms like StoryOrigin[41] also offer free promotion features.

Finally, you can **get free exposure by asking local stores, community centers, or libraries** to display print books or flyers. Many authors had success **promoting in the locations featured in their stories**. Many websites also list books free, such as DigitalBookToday.com[42],

Draft2Digital introduced a program to automatically post new releases to catalog sites like BookBub[43] or Amazon-owned Goodreads[44]. So far, technical issues between the various systems have delayed implementation. Checking the [**Submit books to Catalog Sites**] option under [**My Account**] | [**Advanced User Options**] will prepare your account for this program.

Resources

PUBLISHDRIVE: Amazon Advertising: PublishDrive's built-in marketing feature[45]

---

37. https://www.bookbub.com/partners/pricing

38. https://www.freebooksy.com/freebooksy-feature-pricing/

39. https://www.bargainbooksy.com/sell-more-books-2-2/

40. https://bookhub.online/authors-news/monthly-book-promotions

41. https://storyoriginapp.com

42. https://digitalbooktoday.com/join-our-team/

43. https://www.BookBub.com

44. http://www.Goodreads.com

BookBub: Featured Deals Pricing and Statistics[46]

BookBub: 9 Reasons a Book Was Rejected for a BookBub Featured Deal[47]

BookBub: A Beginner's Guide to the BookBub Ads Auction Model[48]

BookBub: 10 Successful Advertisers' Tips for Targeting Readers with BookBub Ads[49]

BookBub: Ads Bidding for Authors: Strategy Guide + Bid Calculator[50]

BookBub: 9 Book Advertising Tactics I've Tried... And Which Ones Worked![51]

BookBub: Biggest BookBub Ads Mistakes Authors & Marketers are Making[52]

Freebooksy; Sell more books with a Freebooksy Feature[53]

Bargain Booksy: Sell more books with a Bargain Booksy Feature[54]

Book Hub: Monthly Book Promotions[55]

StoryOrigin: All features FREE while in open-beta[56]

---

45. https://publishdrive.zendesk.com/hc/en-us/articles/
   360016162914-Amazon-Advertising-PublishDrive-s-built-in-marketing-feature

46. https://www.bookbub.com/partners/pricing

47. https://insights.bookbub.com/reasons-book-rejected-bookbub-featured-deal

48. https://insights.bookbub.com/a-beginners-guide-to-the-bookbub-ads-auction-model

49. https://insights.bookbub.com/successful-advertisers-tips-targeting-readers-bookbub-ads

50. https://insights.bookbub.com/ads-bidding-for-authors-strategy-guide-bid-calculator

51. https://insights.bookbub.com/book-advertising-tactics-tried

52. https://insights.bookbub.com/biggest-bookbub-ads-mistakes

53. https://www.freebooksy.com/freebooksy-feature-pricing/

54. https://www.bargainbooksy.com/sell-more-books-2-2/

55. https://bookhub.online/authors-news/monthly-book-promotions

56. https://storyoriginapp.com/pricing

The Creative Penn: Sell More Books And Reach More Readers. How To Market Your Book[57],

DigitalBookToday.com: Author Advertising – Paid and Free[58]

BookMarketingBuzzBlog: Advertising Books With Small Budgets[59]

Carolyn Howard-Johnson: The Frugal Book Promoter[60]

Apple Books: How to Use Promo Codes to Build Buzz[61]

Goodreads: Five Tips for Getting the Most Out of Your Goodreads Giveaways[62]

BookBaby: The #1 mistake of self-published authors for worldwide book sales[63]

Molly Greene: Writer: 5 Tips To Make Direct-Sale Events A Rousing Success[64]

ALLi: Get Out of the Writing Cave: Turning Readers into Fans[65]

ALLi: Book Marketing Begins at Home[66]

ALLi: 50 Ways To Reach Your Readers: Book Promotion Ideas From ALLi Members[67]

---

57. https://www.thecreativepenn.com/marketing

58. https://digitalbooktoday.com/join-our-team/

59. http://bookmarketingbuzzblog.blogspot.com/2014/10/advertising-books-with-small-budgets.html

60. https://books2read.com/FrugalBookPromoter

61. https://authors.apple.com/market-your-book/499-how-to-use-promo-codes-to-build-buzz

62. https://www.goodreads.com/blog/show/
    1148-five-tips-for-getting-the-most-out-of-your-goodreads-giveaways

63. http://blog.bookbaby.com/2017/01/mistake-self-published-authors-make-worldwide-book-sales

64. http://molly-greene.com/5-tips-for-direct-sale-event-success

65. https://selfpublishingadvice.org/get-out-of-the-writing-cave-turning-readers-into-fans-natalie-wright

66. https://selfpublishingadvice.org/book-marketing-begins-at-home

67. https://selfpublishingadvice.org/50-ways-to-reach-your-readers

Marisa Murgatroyd: How Much Sales & Marketing Do You *Really* Need to Do In Your Business?[68]

Your First 10,000 Readers: How To Find Your First 10,000 Readers[69]

Vervante: Tips and strategies for retail book sales success[70]

ALLi: International Insights for Indie Authors: Africa[71]

ALLi: International Insights for Indie Authors: Asian Markets[72]

ALLi: International Insights: Europe[73]

ALLi: International Insights: Middle East, North Africa and Arab Markets[74]

Zon

LIKE OTHER FEATURES, Amazon scatters its sales reporting across different sites. You can access the notoriously incomplete KDP [**Reports**] next to [**Bookshelf**] on its main menu. See Figure 12-19 for available information. A new <u>KDP Reports</u> site tries to **unify reporting of store sales and Amazon's subscription service Kindle Unlimited[75] reads.**

68. https://www.liveyourmessage.com/
   how-much-sales-marketing-do-you-really-need-to-do-in-your-business-the-answer-may-surprise-you

69. http://yourfirst10kreaders.com

70. https://vervante.com/blog/2018/04/retailbooksales

71. https://selfpublishingadvice.org/international-insights-for-indie-authors-africa

72. https://selfpublishingadvice.org/international-insights-for-indie-authors-asian-markets

73. https://selfpublishingadvice.org/international-insights-europe

74. https://selfpublishingadvice.org/middle-east-north-africa-arab-markets

75. https://kdp.amazon.com/en_US/help/topic/G201537300

Figure 12-19: KDP Sales Dashboard

AMAZON NO LONGER DETERMINES its **recommendations on sales pages** solely by its own algorithms, instead **forcing authors now to bid for keywords and categories**. Some writers with large backlists have resorted to bidding on their own titles to ensure other books don't show up next to theirs. That said, Amazon only charges for clicks on the ad, thus considerably lowering the cost of simply showing your book. Because you can target titles in Amazon bookstores, you can narrow the audience to people interested in books to begin with.

Clicking on the [**Create an ad campaign**] button on the **Amazon Promotion Page** will take you to the **Amazon Advertising** website for a selected territory. When you log in, you can create ads and campaigns from the dashboard shown in Figure 12-20.

Figure 12-20: Amazon Advertising Dashboard

YOU HAVE LIMITED CREATIVE ability. **Amazon ads look like the Books you may like section**, a **cover thumbnail, some text, review count, and price**. A tag or title will identify them as **sponsored**.

TIP Amazon Advertising's **default bid often considerably exceeds the suggested bid for a keyword. Cut it in half or lower to test ads** and only raise it on those that actually convert clicks to sales. Otherwise, you may be paying to attract the wrong audience.

Finally, the [**Marketing**] choice on KDP's main menu takes you to the **Marketing Resources** page shown in Figure 12-21. You can access the same features as from the Promote page, plus Author Central (see 12.3). Links buried at the bottom jump to the help pages for [**Kindle Pre-Order**], [**Gifting for Kindle**], and [**Kindle Instant Book Previews**] (A **Look Inside** sample you can embed on your website).

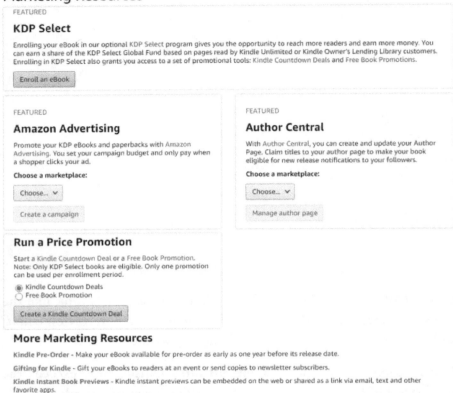

Figure 12-21: KDP Marketing Resources

Resources

KDP: KDP Reports Dashboard[76]

Amazon Advertising: What are Sponsored Products for Books? (VIDEO)[77]

Amazon Advertising: Create a Sponsored Products campaign[78]

KDP: Kindle Pre-Order[79]

---

76. https://kdpreports.amazon.com/dashboard

77. https://www.youtube.com/watch?v=8BsRt-8tEUA

78. https://advertising.amazon.com/help?entityId=ENTITY3LTM3XWE7WZJZ

79. https://kdp.amazon.com/help/topic/G201499380

KDP: Gifting for Kindle[80]

KDP: Kindle Instant Book Previews[81]

Reedsy: Amazon Ads for Authors (COURSE)[82]

Self Publishing Formula: Learn Amazon Ads: Use AMS to Find More Readers and Sell More Books[83]

12.6. New Release Notifications

WE COVERED ALERTS ABOUT new releases in **New Release Email Notifications Signup** in the end matter and the **Sales Pages** and **Author Pages**. The service lets your readers opt-in to notifications every time you release a new book. When you submit a title for pre-order or publishing at D2D or KDP, people on their respective lists receive an email with ordering information.

D2D

LIKE WITH MOST OF D2D's marketing materials, **Books2Read provides the New Release Notifications**. Subscribers receive an email with a cover thumbnail and the book description similar to Figure 12-22.

---

80. https://kdp.amazon.com/help/topic/G200652260

81. https://www.amazon.com/b?ie=UTF8&node=13489836011

82. https://blog.reedsy.com/learning/courses/marketing/amazon-ads-authors/

83. https://books2read.com/AmazonAds

Figure 12-22: Books2Read New Release Notifications

READERS CAN SIGN UP from the link in the auto-generated **end matter** (see 8.12) of your books or the **Sales Pages** and **Author Pages** (see 12.2 and 12.3). All these options pop up a page similar to Figure 12-23. It asks for name, email address, and confirmation. Books2Read manages the list for you.

Like Wolf O'Rourc?

Don't miss out on a single new release!

Sign up and we'll make sure you hear about every new book Wolf O'Rourc publishes as soon as it hits the stores.

If you'd like suggestions on books like those Wolf O'Rourc writes, check the box below and we'll send those recommendations straight to your inbox.

Name:
_____

Email address:
_____

I find books to read at...

| Other | ⌄ |

☐ Yes! Send me suggestions for more books like this.

Sign Me Up

Figure 12-23: Books2Read New Release Notifications Sign Up

TO TURN OFF SENDING of all notifications, uncheck [**I would like for Books2Read.com to send New Release Notifications on my behalf**] under D2D's [**My Account**] | [**Advanced User Options**] menu choice. The [**My Reports**] | [**My Mailing Lists**] option shows the number of signups to an author's list and provides a signup link that jumps to a page like Figure 12-23 for use with your websites or social media.

Resources

D2D: Feature Highlight - New Release Notifications[84]

Zon

AMAZON FOLLOW IS A storewide brand-follow system lacking integration with KDP or Author Central. Besides new releases, it can send out personal updates, if Amazon invites an author to do so. In addition to email notifications, readers can see an archive of their **Follow Updates** shown in Figure 12-24.

Your Follow updates

Manage your follows   Discover more to follow

Melodee Meyer **released** The Game Changer (vol. 3):
2 years ago

The Game Changer (vol. 3): Inspira
by Iman Aghay (Author), Denise T

Figure 12-24: Amazon Follow Updates

VIEWING THE ARCHIVE or managing one's follows requires clicking a series of links starting with the well-hidden [**Manage your follows**] at the

---

84. https://www.draft2digital.com/blog/feature-highlight-new-release-notifications

bottom of any **Author Pages** (see 12.3) or clicking an author name in [**Your Profile**[85]]'s **Who you follow** section shown in Figure 12-25.

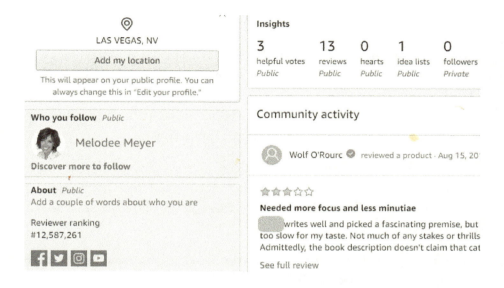

Figure 12-25: Amazon Follow in Your Profile

READERS CAN SIGN UP with the [**+ Follow**] button on the **Sales Page** or **Author Page** (see 12.2 and 12.3) or [**Discover more to follow**] in [**Your Amazon profile**].

I have yet to find any way for authors to get at the data about their followers or manage the process in any way.

Resources

AMAZON: Amazon Follow[86]

Amazon: Sharing Your Release with Followers Through Amazon Follow[87]

Amazon: Edit Your Profile[88]

---

85. https://www.amazon.com/gp/pdp/profile/

86. https://www.amazon.com/gp/help/customer/display.html?nodeId=GNUPK6RZMQDSL52X

87. https://www.amazon.com/gp/help/customer/display.html?nodeId=GUL66754C4CSHWU3

12.7. Publisher

D2D

AS MENTIONED IN 6.1, **Draft2Digital lets you create multiple publishers or imprints**, basically brands for releasing different types of books. This feature, together with multiple [**Contributor Profiles**] under [**My Account**], makes it easy for a group of authors to collaborate or act like a small press. These writers can also share books in carousels without needing to recreate unconnected UBLs in separate D2D accounts.

The [**My Account**] | [**Publishers**] menu choice leads to the **Account Publishers** page. You can add a name, description, and logo. D2D provides no field to enter a website address. **Any URLs you type into the description are *not* clickable**.

If you specify a publisher, **the data shows up on the generated End Matter** pages **Title** and **About the Publisher**. D2D does *not* list the publisher on the copyright page, however.

If you don't specify a separate brand, D2D defaults to the primary author's name, and creates an entry on the **Account Publishers** page without copying the description or photo. If you do not add that information before enabling **About the Publisher** in the End Matter, the page will only show a name.

You can see a list of all books linked to a publisher by clicking their [**View Books**] button on **Account Publishers**. Since the bookshelf's URL requires a login to access, you currently **cannot use the page as a public catalogue for a brand**.

Other than appearing on various pages and having its own bookshelf, Draft2Digital grants the Publisher no other privileges. To receive payment under that name, you would have to create a business entity and specify it under [**My Account**] | [**Payment Options**].

---

88. https://www.amazon.com/gp/help/customer/display.html/?nodeId=GF49TDCLY9PVQB8R

To treat the account like a publisher for yourself, **you can create pen names** to write in different genres under [**Contributor Profiles**]. Each name has its own **Author Page**. According to Draft2Digital, they never release who's behind a pen name.

D2D plans to roll out its **Shared Universes platform** in 2020 to allow **sharing of royalties among collaborating authors**.

Zon

IN CONTRAST, **Amazon doesn't have pages for separate brands**. The **account that submits a book has all the privileges of the publisher**, regardless of what you specify in the optional **Publisher** field. The entered imprint shows up on the sales page, and auto-generated End Matter, if you enter the same name in KC.

The **KDP account determines what shows up together on a bookshelf** and in search results. Marketing and advertising fall under the control of that account. Amazon treats it like a publisher account where you can **type in different authors or pen names** for the books on the shelf. Consequently, if you distribute to Amazon through Draft2Digital, they become the publisher, and you lose direct access to KDP Select (see 12.4) and Amazon Advertising (see 12.5).

Like D2D, KDP does not allow public viewing of a bookshelf. Neither do they offer a catalogue page of all books sharing the same **Publisher** name.

The Zon shut down its **Kindle Worlds collaboration program** in 2018.

Resources

D2D: How do I update my About the Publisher pages?[89]

The Creative Penn: Using Author Pseudonyms[90],

---

89. https://www.draft2digital.com/knowledge-base/#how-do-i-update-my-about-the-publisher-pages

90. https://www.thecreativepenn.com/using-author-pseudonyms

ALLi: Book Marketing: How to Create a Book Catalog of Your Self-published Books & Why[91],

91. https://selfpublishingadvice.org/self-published-book-catalog

If you made it this far, ▦ congratulations ❀, you now have the tools to self-publish your books and save your hair like magic ✂.

IF YOU ENJOYED THE book, please do leave reviews. They mean a lot to writers and help us find new readers more than almost anything else. The following links take you directly to the book's review pages. I read everyone once I find out about it. Mega tnx.

Online Bookstores[1]

Bookbub Review[2]

Goodreads Review[3]

GET MORE SELF-PUBLISHING tips at www.WolfORourc.com/writes/selfpub[4] or follow @WolfORourc at fashionable social media sites across the universe.

---

1. https://books2read.com/Cyberspiracy

2. https://www.bookbub.com/books/cyberspiracy-cyber-series-book-1-by-wolf-o-rourc

3. https://www.goodreads.com/book/show/45323605-cyberspiracy

4. http://www.wolforourc.com/writes/selfpub

Don't miss out!

Visit the website below and you can sign up to receive emails whenever Wolf O'Rourc publishes a new book. There's no charge and no obligation.

https://books2read.com/r/B-A-GWCH-BFPBB

Did you love *How to Simplify Self-Publishing and Save Your Hair*? Then you should read *Cyberspiracy*[5] by Wolf O'Rourc!

[6]

Hot pink hair can't hide you from high-tech hitmen.A timid and lonely sixteen-year-old girl hides from bullying in her dream world of dashing **master spy dolls**, blue-haired **Katy Perry Barbies**, and pink **Hello Kitty dresses.**And she hacks her way across the Net behind the avatar of a six foot four hunk with the **handle Cowabunga Dude.**A presidential video falls into her laptop and rocks her pink paradise.When the clandestine worlds of hacking and military technology collide with her secret crush, she faces the toughest decisions of her young life.**Love or War?**Enjoy this first thrilling 300-page adventure in the *Cyber Series* where a hacker girl sings and dances past discrimination, prejudice, and fear to save her country and herself.**Get the exciting technothriller *Cyberspiracy* now.**"*Cyberspiracy* is stellar. *I see the movie in my mind when I think about his story line and unforgettable characters*. I cannot recommend this author more highly.This man can write."

5. https://books2read.com/u/mKxzOB

6. https://books2read.com/u/mKxzOB

— Toni K Pacini, Author ~ Poet ~ Storyteller~ Speaker"I absolutely love that the protagonist is a young woman who kicks ass in the world of computer coding and has a hand in saving the free world by making sure that democracy stays intact while falling in love, These stories are an important and empowering voice that *deserve to be added to the landscape of the Young Adult canvas.*" — Valerie J Runyan, Author, Quandaries of Love

Read more at www.WolfORourc.com.

Also by Wolf O'Rourc

Cyber Series
Cyberspiracy

Standalone
How to Simplify Self-Publishing and Save Your Hair

Watch for more at www.WolfORourc.com.

About the Author

Wolf O'Rourc (aka **Warry Wotter, Word Wizard Wextraordinaire**) brings his passion for writing and publishing to parallel universes full of categories, copies, and covers.

Drawing on his unique skills, he conjures a powerful blend of ancient magic and modern technology into practical advice on **storytelling and self-publishing**. What else can you expect from a support specialist for word processors in a previous life reborn as a graduate of the **Wogwarts School of Writing and Wizardry**?

Read more at www.WolfORourc.com/writes/selfpub.

About the Publisher

Neither sun nor sun nor sun nor wind of night stays these editors from the swift completion of their publishing duties in Las Vegas.

www.wolforourc.com